A. W. Fox

Reports of the Royal Commission on Labour

Part IV

A. W. Fox

Reports of the Royal Commission on Labour
Part IV

ISBN/EAN: 9783742801319

Manufactured in Europe, USA, Canada, Australia, Japa

Cover: Foto ©ninafisch / pixelio.de

Manufactured and distributed by brebook publishing software
(www.brebook.com)

A. W. Fox

Reports of the Royal Commission on Labour

ROYAL COMMISSION ON LABOUR.

THE AGRICULTURAL LABOURER.

VOL. IV.

IRELAND.

PART IV.

REPORTS

BY

MR. ARTHUR WILSON FOX
(ASSISTANT COMMISSIONER),

UPON CERTAIN

SELECTED DISTRICTS

IN THE

COUNTIES OF

CORK, MAYO, ROSCOMMON AND WESTMEATH;

WITH

SUMMARY REPORT

PREFIXED.

Presented to both Houses of Parliament by Command of Her Majesty.
February 1893.

LONDON:
PRINTED FOR HER MAJESTY'S STATIONERY OFFICE,
BY EYRE AND SPOTTISWOODE,
PRINTERS TO THE QUEEN'S MOST EXCELLENT MAJESTY.

And to be purchased, either directly or through any Bookseller, from
EYRE AND SPOTTISWOODE, EAST HARDING STREET, FLEET STREET, E.C., and
32, ABINGDON STREET, WESTMINSTER, S.W.; or
JOHN MENZIES & Co., 12, HANOVER STREET, EDINBURGH, and
90, WEST NILE STREET, GLASGOW; or
HODGES, FIGGIS, & Co., LIMITED, 104, GRAFTON STREET, DUBLIN.

1893.

TABLE OF CONTENTS.

ROYAL COMMISSION ON LABOUR.

THE AGRICULTURAL LABOURER.

IRELAND.

A.—SUMMARY REPORT

BY

MR. ARTHUR WILSON FOX
(ASSISTANT COMMISSIONER).

TABLE OF CONTENTS.

THE AGRICULTURAL LABOURER.

A.—SUMMARY REPORT.

To Geoffrey Drage, Esq., Secretary,
Royal Commission on Labour.

I.—Introductory.

6, Crown Office Row, Temple, London,
July 25, 1893.

Sir,

1. I have the honour to present to you a short survey of the reports I have already written and submitted to you, on the four Unions you allotted to me for inquiry, namely, two Unions in Connaught, one being the Westport Union in Co. Mayo, and the other the Castlereagh Union, which is partly in Co. Mayo, but chiefly in Co. Roscommon; one Union in Munster, the Skibbereen Union, Co. Cork, and one Union in Leinster, the Delvin Union, Co. Westmeath.*

2. In all the four Unions, agriculture is practically the only industry,† with the exception of the Skibbereen Union, Co. Cork, where the people near the coast are engaged in the mackerel fishing from the beginning of April to the beginning of July, and again from the beginning of September to the end of October.

However, those who take part in the fishing are frequently small farmers, or their sons, or else labourers, who, when the mackerel season is over, live by agricultural employment.

3. As the four Unions I had the honour to report upon are situated in widely different districts, I had opportunities of making comparisons between the circumstances of those living under dissimilar conditions. These appeared to me to exist not so much on account of racial distinctions, but rather through differences in the physical conformation of the country, and the circumstances of their surroundings, such as the existence of large estates controlled by wise, generous, and sympathetic landlords, or the reverse, and the administrative policy pursued by the Board of Guardians.

4. Comparing the position of the people in the four Unions, generally speaking, those in the Westport Union are the worst off and those in the Delvin Union the best off. Those in the Castlereagh and Skibbereen Unions are better off than the people in the Westport Union and worse off than those in the Delvin Union.

In Summary, Appendix A. 4, I have given certain figures which show that this is the case.

The Poor Law valuation per head of the population in 1891 in the Westport Union was 1*l*. 3*s*. 8*d*., in the Castlereagh Union 1*l*. 16*s*., in the Skibbereen Union 1*l*. 18*s*. 2*d*., and in the Delvin Union 5*l*. 13*s*. 3*d*.

The valuation per acre in the Westport Union is 2*s*. 6*d*., in the Castlereagh Union 8*s*. 10*d*., in the Skibbereen Union 8*s*. 2*d*. and in the Delvin Union 14*s*. 4*d*.

The number of congested districts in the Westport Union are 21, in the Castlereagh Union 2, in the Skibbereen Union 6, and in the Delvin Union none.

The money advanced under the Seed Supply Act to the Westport Union was 8,100*l*., to the Castlereagh Union 4,000*l*., to the Skibbereen Union 7,333*l*., and to the Delvin Union none.

The cost of wages on the relief works in 1891 was, in the Westport Union, 17,365*l*., in the Castlereagh Union 174*l*. 2*s*. 8*d*., in the Skibbereen Union 3,260*l*., and in the Delvin Union there were no relief works.

* Westport Union	148,303 acres.
Castlereagh Union	162,566 "
Skibbereen Union	115,025 "
Delvin	74,889 "

† Number of horses of two years old and upwards, employed for traffic and manufactories :—

Westport Union	94
Skibbereen Union	40
Castlereagh Union	97
Delvin Union	89

THE AGRICULTURAL LABOURER.

Description of the Westport Union.

5. Of the four Unions the Westport Union is by far the largest, and most certainly the poorest district. Its area is 348,295 acres, and it contains 31 electoral divisions, 23 of which are scheduled as congested districts. Much of this large Union is without railway communication, and many of the people live in wild and remote spots, and have to travel 20 or 30 miles over rough roads to get to a market town to sell their produce.

With the exception of the tradesmen living in Westport, Newport, Louisburgh, and other smaller towns and villages, and a few larger tenant farmers, the population consists of small holders on about 12 acres (Irish*), some having in addition the right to turn cattle out on to rough mountain land or bog.† Many of these holdings are situated at the bases, or on the sides of hills or mountains, or in the bog districts, and thus contain soil which is frequently almost worthless for agricultural purposes, and which is not always made as productive as it might be, partly through lack of knowledge and partly through want of capital.‡

An acre and a half to two acres are generally given up to potatoes, which form the chief food of the family, while a few cabbages and roots and a small crop of oats, are grown on the remainder. A cow or two, the most cherished possessions of the small holder, a pig or two, a donkey, frequently a goat, always some poultry, and perhaps ducks and geese are kept. The houses are built by the people themselves at the expense of about 16l. apiece.

They are made of stone, which is plentiful in the neighbourhood, with roofs of wooden beams with sods of peat wedged between them, and covered with a thin thatch of straw grown on their holdings. They usually contain two rooms on the ground floor, with clay floors. One is the living room, in which some members of the family usually sleep, in company with the cows, pigs, and poultry, and another is a room opening out of it, which is used exclusively as a bedroom.

On such holdings as these large families are often reared in the deepest poverty, with little or no hope of bettering their position, while their enforced idleness engenders those habits of which both English and Irish employers complain, namely, a want of application, and a tendency to work by fits and starts

To eke out an existence on these holdings, the greater number of which are obviously incapable of supporting large families, external aid has to be sought, by one or more of the members going to work on English and Scotch farms for a certain portion of the year, or by emigrating to America, in order to remit money home to the others.

Those who remain on the holding often supplement their means of livelihood by occasionally working for a farmer; by weaving, knitting, sewing, selling turf, or perhaps illicit whiskey, and, if they live near the coast, by fishing, selling seaweed for manure and making kelp.

This large district, with all these disadvantages, has no resident landlords, who either employ labour, build cottages, or spend money in the locality, neither have the Labourers' Acts been put into operation by the Board of Guardians.

Apart from any other consideration it is difficult to see how the rates in this Union could bear the expense which would be thrown upon them if cottage building was undertaken by the guardians.

Description of the Castlereagh Union.

6. The Castlereagh Union, which is partly in the eastern side of the county of Mayo, but chiefly in the county of Roscommon, comprises some poor districts, which are chiefly situated in the county of Mayo, or in those parts of Roscommon which are abutting on it.

Its area is 163,566 acres, and it contains 19 electoral divisions, 11 of which are congested districts.

Although there are a great number of small holdings in the Union on which the tenants cannot make a livelihood, and in consequence have to be assisted by those who emigrate to America, and migrate for certain periods of the year to England or Scotland, the condition of the people is certainly superior to those in the Westport Union. This is because the soil, particularly in Roscommon, is better, and in some districts is productive for tillage and grazing purposes, and also because there is more demand for agricultural labour.

* The Irish acre is 7,840 square yards = 1·62 statute acres approximately.

† 3,0[illegible]4, or 19·9 per cent. of the holdings, have a valuation of 1l. or under.

‡ The Annual Report of the Congested Districts Boards (1892) says: "We believe we are not exaggerating "the fact in saying that throughout the congested districts as a rule the produce of the farms might be "increased from one third to one half."

The Agricultural Labourer.

The Union has also the advantage of a main line of railway passing through it, and of an accessible market town at Castlerea[g]h. There are also several resident landlords who employ labour, and who have built some good cottages, such as are unknown in the Westport Union, though, nevertheless, there are some very bad ones. No cottages have been built by the guardians.

Description of the Skibbereen Union.

7. The Skibbereen Union situated on the south coast of the county of Cork, contains 111,028 acres, and has a population of 28,460 persons. There are 20 electoral divisions, of which six are congested districts.

This Union is purely an agricultural one, with the exception of the mackerel fishing on the coast, in which many of the small farmers and their sons are engaged between April and July and again between September and November.

The development of the fishing industry has proved a great boon to this district, as it has had the effect of driving up agricultural wages in the spring, summer, and autumn, of checking emigration in the immediate vicinity of the fishing operations, and possibly of rendering migration to English and Scotch farms unnecessary.

When the fishing season is over, many of those who take part in it work on the land as labourers, if they can get employment, and consequently the supply of labour at that time of the year is too plentiful.

In some parts of the Union the land is very poor and unproductive. The proportion of barren mountain land is returned at 14·3 per cent.

There are several resident landlords who employ labour, and give regular work. Few cottages have been built by them, but it frequently happens that the labourers that they employ are the sons of their tenants who live with their parents.

The Guardians have built 153 cottages, and 53 are now in course of erection.

A railway now runs through the Union from Baltimore to Cork, and thus gives easy access to a large market for the sale of fish, butter, and other produce. There is, besides, Skibbereen, the market town of the Union.

The emigration from this Union is very considerable, and there is no doubt that a great deal of money is received by the people from their relatives in America.

Description of the Delvin Union.

8. The Delvin Union of Westmeath is a purely rural district, situated about 50 miles from Dublin, it is accessible by a main line of railway, and contains 74,329 acres, and a population of 9,665 persons.

There are 19 electoral divisions, none of which are congested districts.

This district contains 63·9 per cent. of pasture land, so consequently a great many cattle and sheep are kept.

Notwithstanding the fact that there is but little tillage, there are a considerable number of persons employed as agricultural labourers, which is due in a great measure to there being several resident landlords, who farm somewhat extensively, and give regular employment.

Generally speaking, the labourers in this Union are better off than in any of the other three I visited. This is not because the wages are, as a rule higher, but because employment is more regular, and perquisites are more frequently given. The cottages also are, as a general rule, superior* as the Guardians have built 154, and certain landlords have provided excellent ones on their properties. Further, the soil throughout this Union is richer than in the other three, which benefits the labourers who have gardens, cow pastures, or con-acres, and also the small holders, who are thus not trying to live on land which is incapable of supporting them, as is so often the case in Mayo, on Cork, and parts of Roscommon. The Union and the neighbourhood is well supplied with markets.

No doubt a good deal of money is remitted from America to help those at home, but the emigration is not nearly so excessive from the county of Westmeath as from the counties of Mayo, Roscommon, and Cork, and of late years has been steadily decreasing.

Further, there is no migration to Scotch and English farms which shows that, apart from the money that may be received from America, those who live in this Union can make their livelihood in it.

Cultivation of the four Unions. Summary App. 12, 13, 14, 15.

9. The Westport Union contains much more waste land than any of the other three Unions.

It has 28·6 per cent. of barren mountain land, and 7·8 per cent. of marsh, while the Unions of Castlereagh, Skibbereen, and Delvin have respectively 1·3, 14·3, and ·3 per cent. of barren mountain, and 3·4, 2·7, and 1·2 of marsh.

* No cattle or pigs are kept in any of the cottages in this Union.

As regards cultivation, Westport has but 6·0 per cent. of crops, including meadow and clover, and 39·5 of grass, while of the former Castlereagh, Skibbereen, and Delvin have 21·2, 19·2, and 25·6 per cent. respectively, and of the latter 51·6, 54·5, and 63·9 respectively.

10. Of the holdings not exceeding 15 acres the Union of Castlereagh has by far the largest number, namely, 3,080, the Westport Union has 2,116, and the Unions of Skibbereen and Delvin, 554 and 350 respectively.*

Of the holdings not exceeding 30 acres, the Castlereagh Union again has the most, namely 1,714, the Westport Union has 1,337, and the Unions of Skibbereen and Delvin 864 and 358 respectively.

The Skibbereen Union contains more holdings between 30 and 100 acres than the other three Unions, but of the holdings under 200 acres it has fewer than the Unions of Castlereagh and Westport, and of the holdings of between 200 and 500 acres it has only 20, while Westport, Castlereagh and Delvin have respectively 77, 66, and 54.

Of holdings over 500 acres the Union of Westport has 101, and the Union of Castlereagh 7, of Delvin 11, and of Skibbereen none.

11. The population of the four Unions in 1891 was in Westport 37,381, in Castlereagh 37,474, in Skibbereen 22,450, and in Delvin 9,365.

Thus the number of persons to each 100 acres was in Westport 10·7, in Castlereagh 22·9, in Skibbereen 24·7, and in Delvin 15·5.

These figures without explanation would appear to show that the Westport Union, which is more than twice the size of the Castlereagh Union, is half as thickly populated, but it must be borne in mind that barren mountain and marsh absorb over 37 per cent. of the Westport Union, and only 5 per cent. of the Castlereagh Union. If, therefore, the proportion of barren mountains and marsh is deducted from each Union, Westport has 17·3 persons to every 100 acres, and Castlereagh 24·1.

Again, the Castlereagh Union and the Skibbereen Union (the former is the larger by 46,000 acres) have respectively 22·9 and 24·7 persons to every 100 acres. But if the proportion of barren mountain land and marsh is deducted, Skibbereen is still the more thickly populated, for then Castlereagh has 24·1 persons, and Skibbereen 28·7 persons to every 100 acres. The cultivation of these two Unions is very similar, there being in Castlereagh 21·2 per cent. of crops, including meadow and clover, and 51·6 of grass, and in Skibbereen 19·2 per cent. of the former, and 54·6 per cent. of the latter.

The number of persons to every 100 acres in the part of the Castlereagh Union situated in Mayo is 22, and in that part situated in Roscommon is 21.

The Delvin Union which has a population of 12·5 persons to every 100 acres, contains 63·9 per cent. of grass, a larger proportion by 10 per cent. than in any of the other Unions.

The population in the Westport Union increased ·26 per cent. between 1871 and 1881 and decreased 9·8 per cent. between 1881 and 1891, notwithstanding an excess of 4,383 births over deaths during this latter period.

The decrease per cent. in the Castlereagh Union between 1871 and 1881 was 2·8, and between 1881 and 1891, 13·7, notwithstanding an excess of 3,983 births over deaths during this latter period.

The population in the Skibbereen Union increased 2·86 per cent. between 1871 and 1881, but between 1881 and 1891 it decreased 11·80 per cent. notwithstanding an excess of 2,458 of births over deaths during this latter period.

The decrease per cent. in the Delvin Union between 1871 and 1881 was 8·8, and between 1881 and 1891 12·8, notwithstanding an excess of 280 births over deaths during this latter period.

12. The amount spent per head on indoor and outdoor relief in 1892 in the four Unions was as follows:—

Westport, 8½d.	Castlereagh, 1s. 4½d.
Skibbereen, 2s. 5d.	Delvin, 8s. 5d.

The rates in the pound in the Westport Union vary in the different electoral divisions from 6d. to 6s., in the Castlereagh Union from 1d. to 1s. 6d., in the Skibbereen Union from 1s. 4d. to 4s., and in the Delvin Union from 1s. to 2s. 9d.

13. In the spring of 1891, consequent on the partial failure of the potato crop, the Westport Union spent under the Potato Seed Supply Act, 1890, 8,100*l*., the Castlereagh Union 4,000*l*., and the Skibbereen Union 789*l*. 9s. 8d.

* The number of holdings at and under a 4*l*. valuation is—

In the Westport Union	[illegible] or 49·9 per cent.
In the Castlereagh Union	4,030 or 69·5 „
In the Skibbereen Union	319 or 10·1 „
In the Delvin Union	407 or 31·8 „

The Agricultural Labourer.

Migration to English and Scotch farms, statistics of.

In the same year extensive relief works were opened in the Westport and Skibbereen Unions, involving an expenditure on wages of 17,365*l*. and 3,260*l*. respectively.

14. There is no migration of labourers to English and Scotch farms from the Skibbereen and Delvin Unions, but from the Westport and Castlereagh Unions it is very extensive.

About six-sevenths of all the migratory labourers from Ireland come from the province of Connaught,* and of these almost two-thirds come from the county of Mayo.

The proportion of migratory labourers to the population of the county of Mayo is 39·1 per 1,000, and of the males over 20 years of age 16·4 per cent. The proportion of the migratory labourers from the Westport Union to its population is 82·7 per 1,000.†

The proportion of migratory labourers to the population of the county of Roscommon is 12·2 per 1,000, and of the males over 20 years of age 4·6 per cent. The proportion of the migratory labourers from the Castlereagh Union (Roscommon and Mayo), is 40·1 per 1,000.

In the report and tables relating to migratory agricultural labourers in 1892, the Registrar-General alludes to the large discrepancy between the total number (38,838) of migratory labourers from Ireland for 1892, given in the railway and port statistics, and that of 14,783 shown in the tables compiled from the returns made by the enumerators of agricultural statistics. The Registrar-General proceeds to say :—" On " inquiry at the Midland Great Western Railway I have been informed that about " 2,000 go twice each year, and that a large number remain in the counties near " Dublin, but the migration returns contain no information on this point. Again, " there are doubtless many persons who at the time of the collection of the information " by the enumerators of agricultural statistics did not intend to migrate, but whom " circumstances subsequently led to do so, and it is equally probable that the emigra- " tion returns include many persons who are town labourers, not agricultural labourers. " When due allowance is made for these facts, it will be found that the numbers " returned by the enumerators of agricultural statistics represent those who habitually " pursue the avocation of migratory agricultural labourers."

This difficulty became apparent to me when dealing with the migration for the county of Mayo, for the total number for 1892 is returned by the enumerators as 8,554, whereas the total number, from the returns kindly made for me by the manager of the Midland Great Western Railway Company, by Mr. O'Malley, Westport Quay, and by Messrs. Alexander Laird and Co. of Glasgow, come to the enormous figure of 18,827, or 4,044 more than the number returned by the enumerators for the whole of Ireland in that year, and 12·7 per cent. of the persons of 15 years of age and upwards in Mayo.

Apart from the reasons given by the Registrar-General for the discrepancy in the figures between the enumerators' returns and the railway and port returns, there is no doubt that some of those included in the total I have given who started from Mayo stations or ports lived in Galway,‡ but, nevertheless, the figure is a very large one.

The manager of the Midland Great Western Railway further informs me that in addition to the 17,607 harvest tickets issued from their stations in Mayo in 1892, they issued 9,443 tickets on their system that year. By far the greater number of these must have come from Galway, Sligo, and Roscommon. Thus if the number of tickets issued by the Midland Great Western Railway in 1892 is added to the passengers booked by steamer from Westport Quay and Ballina, the number amounts to 28,270.

I have also received from the Midland Great Western Railway Company the number of harvestmen they booked during the season of 1893, which shows a diminution of 3,516 when compared with the season of 1892, though the number from Mayo stations has increased by 966 (Westport, App. A. 5).

It is worthy of note that, by the 6th of September 1893, 3,346 harvestmen had returned to Ireland, whereas only 345 had returned by that date in 1892. This, it is stated, is due to the lack of employment in England this year, owing to the lightness of the crop and the increased use of the self-binder (*see* para. 17).

---

* The proportion per 1,000 to the population of Connaught is 17·6
" " " Ulster " 1·1
" " " Munster " 0·2
" " " Leinster " 0·1
" " " Ireland " 8·1

† The proportion per 1,000 to the population in the Swineford Union is 80·6.

‡ The official returns for 1892 show that 1,541 migratory labourers went from Galway.

THE AGRICULTURAL LABOURER.

Again, the official returns for the county of Roscommon in 1892 give the number of migratory labourers as 1,398 and the number for that part of the Castlereagh Union situated in Roscommon as 11·44 per cent. The returns for the whole Castlereagh Union (Roscommon and Mayo) are 1,501, hence about 300 must have come from the two electoral divisions in the county of Mayo.

The manager of the Midland Great Western Railway Station sends me a return showing that they booked 1,174 harvesters to England in 1892 from their Roscommon stations, and thus in this case the railway returns are less than those of the enumerators, but probably some of the Roscommon emigrants living near other counties started from stations in them.

According to the official returns, 32·5 per cent. of the migratory labourers from Mayo are landholders, and of these 10·1 per cent. occupy holdings under five acres, while 20·8 per cent. occupy holdings of between 5 and 25 acres. Of the Roscommon migratory labourers, 35·6 per cent. are landholders, and of these 12·4 per cent. occupy holdings under five acres, while 82·7 per cent. occupy holdings of between five and 25 acres.

83·7 per cent. of the migratory labourers from Ireland seek work in England, 13·9 per cent. in Scotland, and 2·4 per cent. in Ireland.

Possibly the existence of the mackerel fishing in the Skibbereen Union, which during the summer and autumn gives employment to many small holders and their sons, is a reason why migration has ceased in this Union, but from the county of Cork few men go now, and in 1892 the total was only 95.*

In the Dulvin Union both agricultural labourers and the sons of small holders are always able to obtain work in the spring, summer, and autumn, so there is no necessity for them to migrate, neither is there any migration among the small holders, the reason being that the land there is so much more productive than that in Mayo or parts of Roscommon.

Information as to employment of migratory labourers in England and Scotland.

15. The men from the Westport Union chiefly go to Lancashire and Cheshire, though some go to Warwickshire and Yorkshire, and a few get as far as Northumberland and Scotland, while the men from the Castlereagh Union go to Cheshire, Warwickshire, and Lancashire.

Westport, par. 18, App. A. 8, A. 9, and B. 4.

Many start as early as March for the purpose of putting down potatoes, weeding, and taking part in the ordinary work of the farm, and do not return until after potato lifting is over at the end of November or as late as Christmas. Hence to speak of the migratory labourers as "harvesters," a term which is not unfrequently applied to them, is a misnomer.

A number of married men migrate, leaving their wives and daughters to look after the holding and get in the harvest. Probably the great majority of landowners who go are married men with families.

Westport, App. C.

A number of women from the northern part of the Westport Union go to work in Scotland. In 1892 about 600 booked from Westport Quay to Glasgow (fare 5s.). They begin to go in March, but the majority go in May and June and return in September, October, or November. They are there employed in putting down potatoes, thinning turnips, weeding, harvesting, and potato lifting. (*See* evidence, Bridget Gallagher and Mary O'Donnell, Westport Report, Appendix C.)

It is frequently the custom for merchants in Scotland to buy the potatoes when in the ground, and to undertake the lifting and carting. For this purpose they communicate with a man in Ireland called "a gaffer," who collects a number of young women and takes them over to do the digging and lifting. The gaffer accompanies them from farm to farm, wherever the potatoes have been bought, and makes all the necessary arrangements as to travelling, &c.

Westport, par. 18, App. B. 4. Castlereagh, par. 37.

Some men doubtless have to undergo hardships if they cannot get work on landing. In September 1892 I saw the streets in Kelso full of labourers, and many had been there a week, as the weather was very stormy and wet and quite unfit for harvest operations. As many of them arrive with scarcely any money in their pockets they experience great difficulty in obtaining the necessaries of life under such circumstances.‡

* In 1880 877 persons migrated to work on English, Scotch or Irish farms, but since that year the numbers have steadily decreased.

† The Irishmen I met in the Glendale Union of Northumberland, when reporting there for the Royal Commission on Labour in September 1892, chiefly came from Donegal.

‡ A Warwickshire farmer (3,000 acres) says, "The men usually want to borrow money as soon as they "arrive, and this is always lent them, and it is a very rare thing for them to go away without repaying it."

In North Northumberland it is the custom for the Irishmen to go into certain of the towns on Sundays and stand in the market place after chapel to be hired by the farm bailiffs, or stewards, who go there for the purpose. When the harvest is at its height wages rise as high as 25s. a week. They nearly always remain with the same employer during harvest, though nominally they only engage themselves by the week. *The Agricultural Labourer.*

The Registrar-General for Ireland, as well as employers in the North of England, inform me that it used to be a common practice for farmers in England to write to Ireland for the men they required, but that this has now nearly died out. I did, however, meet with a few farmers, both in Northumberland and Lancashire,* who continue to do so, and there are still a number who employ the same men from year to year, though no definite arrangements are made beforehand.

In my report on the Westport Union I have alluded to the difficulty which many of the men experience in finding sufficient money to pay for their fares to England.† This is the case particularly in the spring, as they are always the worst off just when the winter is over, and before the fairs have taken place at which they sell their cattle and sheep. Sir Thomas Brady has greatly interested himself in this matter, and has started a fund for the purpose of advancing sums to those who have not sufficient to pay their fares. Sir Thomas, referring to the operation of his fund in Mayo, says:—"In this district I have frequently lent 100*l.* to 100 persons, the loans being "repayable in six months, and these have often been repaid long before the time they "were due, and in nearly all cases punctually repaid." *Westport, par. 48, App. B. 7.*

16. The number of migratory labourers has been steadily decreasing for a number of years, which is due to the decrease of tillage in England and Scotland, and to the use of machinery. In Cumberland the adoption of machinery has entirely done away with the employment of Irishmen at harvest. And for the same reasons the earnings of the migratory labourers are less than they used to be.‡ *Westport, par. 16, App. B. 1. Earnings of migratory labourers in England and Scotland.*

I asked a great number of men both in Mayo and Roscommon how much they would clear by five or six months work in England, and they mentioned sums varying from 9*l.* to 15*l.* If a man is away for nine months he probably clears over 20*l.*, but his total earnings depend to some extent on what food his employer gives, if any, and whether he gets lodging free, which is usually the case in North Northumberland, Lancashire, and, I understand, Cheshire. Men who find their own food say it costs them 7s. or 8s. a week.

In the Glendale Union of Northumberland, where Irishmen are extensively employed just for the harvest, I had the opportunity of talking to many of the Donegal men in the autumn of 1892, and they told me they usually clear 4*l.* or 5*l.* during the harvest there. Many of these men go on to a later district or go further south for potato lifting. *Earnings in Northumberland.*

The harvest wages vary from 20s. to 25s. a week, and the men are given sleeping accommodation and food, which in this district usually consists of porridge, milk, bread, potatoes, and beer.

I give, in the Westport Report, App. A. 10, the individual earnings of six men in the autumn of 1892 on a farm near Wooler, North Northumberland. They varied from 2*l.* 19s. 5d. to 11*l.* 8s. 9½d. Before harvest they were paid 2s. to 2s. 2d. a day, given skim milk, and provided with a lodging, and during harvest 3s. 9d. a day, and given all food, as well as a lodging. Most of these men went on from this farm to a later district.

In the Garstang Union of Lancashire Irishmen's harvest wages are about 24s. a week, and for ordinary farm work they are paid 15s. to 24s. a week, and when potato lifting at piece-work they earn up to 35s. a week. They usually get sleeping accommodation. Some farmers give them all food during harvest, while others give them a certain amount, and the men have to find the rest. *Earnings in Lancashire.*

* Mr. Wilkinson and Mr. Pearson, Garstang, Lancashire, have both employed two Irishmen for harvesting, &c. for 23 and 18 years respectively. Mr. Hindmarsh, Glendale, Northumberland, has written to the same man in Donegal for 15 years to bring over the number of men he requires for harvest, and also sends the money for the men's journey.

† Fare from Westport Co. Mayo, to Chester, or Liverpool (return) is 23s.

‡ The Registrar-General stated in his evidence before the Royal Commission on the Land Acts (Ireland), 1886:—"In 1841 this migration was common almost all over Ireland, but it is now confined almost to "Connaught and Donegal. In 1841 the migratory labourers were 58,000; in 1884, 11,000; in 1885, 13,000; in 1886, 18,000, of these 10,000 were from Connaught, 7,000 from Mayo alone; the diminution is said to be owing to the decrease of tillage in England and the increased use of machinery; the average earnings of these migratory labourers used to be about 18*l.*, and now it is about 10*l.*

THE AGRICULTURAL LABOURER.

Westport, App. A. 10.

In the autumn of 1892 two Irishmen employed on Mr. Pearson's farm at St. Michael's-on-Wyre, Garstang Union, Lancashire, each earned 20*l*. 10*s*. from June 15th to October 25th. They had free quarters in a corn granery. Up to the end of September they were given a good Lancashire pie twice a day, and after that only tea and coffee. Assuming that these men spent 6*s*. a week each on food, and also deducting their railway fare (50*s*. return), they each cleared 12*l*. 8*s*.*

John Coney, of Ballycroy, who has worked for farmers I met in the Garstang Union, put his net earnings there between May 1st and November 30th at 10*l*., which is obviously too low an estimate. His own figures, which agree with the current rates paid on farms in that neighbourhood, show a net profit of about 17*l*.

Earnings in Warwickshire.

Colonel Raikes, agent to the Marquis of Hertford, supplied me with particulars of the earnings of nine Irishmen on a farm of 3,000 acres in Warwickshire, in 1892. These men were not all working on the farm for the same period, but between May 11th and October 31st, a period of 21 weeks, they averaged 18*s*. a week, with lodging and fuel free. Their day wages at ordinary farm work were 2*s*. 2*d*., and at harvest 4*s*., but they did a good deal of the harvest work, and also hoeing and potato lifting by piece-work.

Earnings in Yorkshire

In the neighbourhood of York Irishmen get 25*s*. a week at hay time and harvest, and 1*l*. a week for potato lifting, the farmer providing lodging.

Earnings in Cheshire.

In the neighbourhood of Chester Irishmen arrive between March and hay harvest, and return to Ireland in October, November, and sometimes as late as Christmas. First class men are paid 15*s*. per week at ordinary farm work, and 10*s*. extra for hay harvest, and 20*s*. extra for corn harvest. Second class men only get 15*s*. a week. They are given free lodging and milk night and morning, and on Sunday they get bread and cheese and a pint of beer each at night.

Earnings in Scotland.

I am informed that in Stirlingshire the Irishmen get 5*s*. a day during harvest, or about 4*l*. for the month with food and lodging provided, and that at ordinary farm work in various districts they get between 18*s*. and 1*l*. a week, with sometimes a certain amount of food. In Paisley they spend 2*s*. 6*d*. a week on lodging, and 8*s*. a week on food.

Westport, App. C. III. (6).

The Irish girls in Scotland get paid as follows:—In the neighbourhood of Paisley 2*s*. a day for weeding or hoeing potatoes. They usually sleep in Paisley. One girl told me her lodging there cost 1*s*. a week, and her food 5*s*., and another that her lodging cost 4*d*. a night and her food 1*s*. a day.

One of these girls stated that north of Paisley, in which county she was unable to say, but in a district away from a town, farmers provide wooden beds with mattresses and blankets for the girls in an out-house. They also give as much milk and potatoes as are required, and the girls buy tea, bread, and oatmeal, extra, at the cost of 6*d*. to 7*d*. a day.

In Ayrshire, at potato digging, the girls get 13*s*. 6*d*. a week, sleeping accommodation in a barn, and the following food free:—

Breakfast: Tea, white bread, butter, and eggs.
At 11 a.m.: A piece of bread.
Dinner (3 p.m.): Fish or meat.

In Stirlingshire the women get about 3*l*. a month for harvest and their food and lodging.

Bridget Gallagher, of Achill, told me that between June and the end of September she made 9*l*. or 10*l*. clear in Scotland, 3*l*. of which she spent in clothes. It seems a common practice for the Mayo women to buy most of their clothes in Scotland, and they frequently get some for their friends at home. The fare from Westport to Glasgow by sea is 5*s*.

It will be seen that in cases where two grown-up sons go from one holding, or perhaps the father, and a son and daughter, they can make a sum which to them is a considerable one.

Some of the men complained of the sleeping accommodation provided for them by farmers in England, and a good many said that owing to sleeping sometimes in wet clothes, having no change with them, they got bad chills and rheumatism, which sometimes permanently injured their health. Of course it is obvious that farmers can only provide barns and outhouses for them, as they have no other accommodation. In cases

* Probably 6*s*. a week is not too low an estimate of what the men spend on food, as they live on very low diet. Mr Wilkinson, farmer and bailiff to the late Lord Winmarleigh, Garstang, Lancashire, says that the two Irishmen he employs pay for their food, and have milk and butter from him at less than market price, and that they chiefly live on tea, bread, and milk.

THE AGRICULTURAL LABOURER. Emigration statistics. Summary, App. 6, 7.

where they can take lodgings they nearly always prefer sleeping in a barn free of charge."*

17. The emigration from the counties of Mayo, Roscommon, and Cork is extensive, the proportion to every 1,000 of the population for 1892 being 17·0, 16·6, and 17·3 respectively. In the county of Westmeath the proportion per 1,000 was only 8·7.

Nearly all the emigrants go to America, though a few go to Australia, New Zealand, or Canada.

Thus in 1892 from Mayo 3,630 out of 3,726 emigrants went to America, from Roscommon 1,878 out of 1,896, from Cork 6,743 out of 6,920, and from Westmeath 500 out of 559.

Of the 50,867 natives of Ireland who emigrated in 1892, 91·6 per cent. went to America, 5·8 per cent. to Great Britain, and the remainder to the Colonies or foreign countries.

Of the 25,371 males who emigrated in 1892, 19,588, or 76·6 per cent., were returned as "labourers."

Among the residue were 802 farmers, 396 shopkeepers and assistants, 373 clerks and accountants, 322 carpenters and joiners, 311 bakers and confectioners, 184 tailors, 118 mechanics, and 244 servants, painters, plumbers, and masons. 3,829 males were returned unspecified, which included 1,732 children under 10 years of age.

Among the 25,429 females who emigrated in 1892, 18,944 were returned as servants, 1,769 as housekeepers, 576 as dressmakers or milliners, 50 as seamstresses, and 108 as mill workers. There were 3,829 females unspecified, including wives and children. The number returned as mill workers appears to be very small, for in Mayo I constantly heard of families who had relatives working in mills. Possibly some of those

---

* Since I wrote this report I ascertained from the manager of the Midland Great Western Railway Company that 5,516 more harvest tickets were issued on their system in 1892 than in 1893 and that by September 1893, 2,801 more harvesters had returned than by the corresponding date in 1892.

I have endeavoured to discover the reasons both for the decrease in the number of tickets issued, and for the earlier return of so many as compared with last year, and I have received the following information:—

Sir Thomas Brady, Inspector of Irish Fisheries, writes:—

"Naturally you ask what is the cause of the considerable reduction in the number of harvestmen going to England this year as compared with last year. My idea is that it has been caused by the poverty of the people. I have had a far greater number of applications for small loans to enable them to go to the harvest than I ever had, and much in excess of the funds at my disposal for such a purpose, and I had to refuse hundreds of cases for want of money.

"You will say, Why this poverty more this year than any other? I think that this was caused by the ruinous fall in the prices of cattle. The people who migrate in spring and harvest to England and Scotland for work have, almost to a man, some cattle, be they more or less. They could not, as I am aware in many cases, sell them at any price at the fairs or markets, and they were no security for loans from even the Gombeen men.

"Employment in England was short lived this year, owing to the short harvest. They have, therefore, returned in greater numbers much earlier than formerly, and many, I believe, with very little profit for their labour, so that although they will have plenty of food during the winter they will have little means of paying their debts to the shopkeepers or perhaps their rents, unless the value of cattle improves, and I am glad to say there is an improvement, both in price and demand, and the fishing, which is at hand, is also successful."

Note.—Since I wrote this Report, I have again visited the Garstang District as Assistant Commissioner to the Royal Commission on Agriculture. In the last week of September, I spoke to several hundred Irish labourers in the streets of Garstang, who were all Mayo men, and some of whom I had actually met in Ireland. They were all returning three weeks earlier than in 1892, and all spoke of decreased earnings, with the exception of some who had been harvesting in Yorkshire, and who had come on to Lancashire for potato lifting. Two of these men stated they had cleared 10*l.* in twelve weeks.—A. W. F.

St. Michaels-on-Wyre.

Mr. James Pearson, a farmer, writing from St. Michaels-on-Wyre, Lancashire, September 19th, 1893, says:—

"Our hay and corn harvests have not required more than half the labour of last year, owing to the light crops, especially hay, and the remarkable weather we have had.

"It has been the worst season that Irish labourers have ever experienced, as there was almost no waiting between the hay and corn harvest, which caused an immense number to be out of work, and so they went home.

"I myself have not employed a single Irish labourer this year, owing to our home labour being more plentiful, and I should say that on the whole the Irish labourers have not earned more than two-thirds of their usual earnings at the very outside. I speak from seeing the same men (good men) being week after week out of work."

Mr. Hindmarsh, farmer, Ilderton, Northumberland, writes:—

"The three reasons for the lessened demand for Irish harvesters in this county this year are:—

"1. The early harvest, a week's cutting having been done before the Irishmen arrived.

"2. The lightness of the crops, whereby the lifting and binding of the sheaves were able to be performed by fewer hands, enabling the farmer to secure his harvest with his own people.

"3. The increased and increasing use of the self binder in the North of England, and South of Scotland, by which probably 25 per cent. of the corn in these districts has been bound, this season being remarkably adapted for its use (light standing crops, dry grain and well ripened). Therefore the Irishmen who did arrive only found employment for about 14 or 15 days, instead of about 30, but they are coming in lessened numbers every year, this season there were fewer than I have ever known.

who go out intending to pursue some other vocation drift into them. A young woman who had just returned from America told me that girls could always find situations, either in service or in factories without difficulty. Also Lord John Browne's steward at Westport says, "You cannot now get a woman to work at any price, they all go to "the American mills. It kills them quickly, but there is always a demand for more."* (*See also* Westport, App. B. 1.)

18. The amount of money annually remitted from America to Ireland must be very large, and should be remembered when considering the ways and means of the people, especially in the poorer districts.

It is a common expression to hear used in Mayo, Roscommon, and Cork, "We could "not live without the American money."

In the three Unions in these counties nearly every family I visited appeared to have relatives or friends there. Instances of the devotion displayed by those who have emigrated towards those who remain, are of the most frequent occurrence and often pathetic in their details.

Both in the Skibbereen and Castlereagh Unions I found instances where husbands had been away for years from their families, working in mills or foundries, and regularly remitting month by month by far the greater share of their earnings. One was in America and the other in California.

In Mayo and Roscommon, I found cases of mere children who had gone out and were sending home half their earnings to help pay the rent, and to reduce the shop debts. From among these I quote the evidence of John Faherty, on Inishturk Island who has 4 acres of tillage, and also keeps a small boat for fishing. He says, "I have two girls "in America, one 13 and the other 11 years old. They have already sent me back 7*l*."

There is but little doubt that more would emigrate if they had the means, but here again the generosity of those who have already emigrated is displayed, and the tickets for the passage are frequently sent back by them to enable others to come out.

It is not uncommon to find that the necessity for emigration is looked upon as a grievance, partly on the grounds of sentiment, and partly because it is said the county is being drained of the best young men and women; but I venture to think there are few who visit the small holdings in Mayo and see lads and girls leading aimless lives, uneducated, ill-clad, and ill-fed, and who have had the opportunity of conversing with those who have returned to their homes from America for a short holiday and seen the remarkable effect of a civilised life on their manners and intellects could regret for their sakes that they had had the courage to embark on a career of industry.†

I was informed by those who had either returned from America, or who had friends there, that girls can earn from five, to seven and a half dollars a week in mills at day work, and up to 10 dollars a week at piece work. As cooks, girls of 17 or 18 years of age can earn 16*s*. or 18*s*. a week, with board and lodging, and as general servants three dollars a week, with board and lodging.†

Coachmen can earn 50 dollars a month, and men in foundries 2*l*. 2*s*. a week.

A woman told me that her husband was making 21*l*. a month in a foundry in California, but his living cost him 7*l*. a month.

19. The Westport Union has 28 electoral divisions out of 31 scheduled as congested districts‡; Castlereagh has 11 out of 19, and the Skibbereen Union has 6 out of 28. The Delvin Union has no congested districts.

If the test that constitutes a congested district, prescribed by Section 36 of 54 and 55 Vict. c. 48, is applied to the Union as a whole (*see* note) the following results are obtained: In Westport the proportion of the valuation to each person is about 1*l*. 2*s*., in Castlereagh about 1*l*. 11*s*., in the Skibbereen Union about 1*l*. 7*s*. 6*d*., in the Delvin Union about 5*l*. 6*s*.

* Owen Campbell, speaking of the emigration from Murrisk, says, "I believe about 70 per cent. of the girls emigrate to American factories."

† Owen Coneeny, a labourer working for Mr. Burke, a farmer about six miles from Westport, stated that his daughter, aged 21, was in service in the neighbourhood earning 5*l*. a year and her board and lodging, which compares very unfavourably with the wages paid to young domestic servants in America.

‡ A congested district is thus defined by section 36 of 54 and 55 Vict. cap. 48:—

"Where at the commencement of this Act more than 20 per cent. of the population of a county, or in the case of the county Cork, of either riding thereof, live in electoral divisions of which the total rateable value when divided by the number of the population gives a sum of less than 1*l*. 10*s*. for each individual, those divisions shall for the purposes of this Act be separated from the county in which they are geographically situate and form a separate county (in this Act referred to as a congested districts county")."

But as 8 electoral divisions in both the Westport Union and Castlereagh Unions and 17 in the Skibbereen Union are not scheduled as congested, it will be seen that in some of the electoral divisions where the valuation is divided by the population the sum per head is very small.* The Agricultural Labourer.

In my report on the Westport Union I have referred at some length to the practical operations now being carried on by the Congested Districts Board for permanently benefiting the condition of the people by instructing them in the best cultivation of their holdings, improving the breeds of their cattle,† horses, sheep, pigs, and poultry, stimulating industries by undertaking works and making roads, building piers and bridges, and by developing the fishing industry both with regard to the fresh and cured fish trade. Westport, par. 14. Skibbereen, par. 14.

20. In the Westport Union there are scarcely any men living exclusively as agricultural labourers. To quote the words of Lord John Browne, "They do not exist as a "class. Their place is taken, with great advantage to themselves and everybody, by "the sons of the small tenant farmers. There is no continuous employment for "agricultural labourers, as there are no tillage farms except those of a very small size, "which are cultivated entirely by the tenant occupiers and their families." Classes of labourers employed. Summary App. 9.

Herds are employed on the grazing farms to look after cattle and sheep, and there are some hired men who live and board in the farmhouses.

In the Castlereagh Union a good many sons of small holders work as labourers, but there are, unlike in the Westport Union, a class of men who live entirely as agricultural labourers. There are also twice as many herds as there are in the Westport Union, but about 100 fewer hired servants.

In the Skibbereen Union there are about 400 more agricultural labourers (cottagers) than in the Westport Union, which is more than double the size, and about 250 more than in the Castlereagh Union, which is about 45,000 acres larger. It is also the custom, as in the Westport and Castlereagh Unions, for the sons of small holders to work as labourers. There are about half as many hired men as in the Castlereagh Union, but no herds or shepherds are employed at all as there are no large grazing farms, there being only 20 farms between 200 and 500 acres.

In the Delvin Union some of the sons of small holders work as labourers, but there are a considerable number of men living entirely as labourers. Although the Union is only about 74,000 acres, there are 607 agricultural labourers (cottagers), as compared with 328 in Westport, which is nearly five times as large; 482 in Castlereagh, which is more than twice as large; and 744 in Skibbereen, which is not quite twice as large.

There are about 166 hired men as compared with 633 in Westport, 533 in Castlereagh, and 274 in Skibbereen, and there are also 43 herds.

The wealthier position of this small Union can be seen by the larger number of farms and estates that can afford to keep stewards. In Delvin there are 19; in Westport, 4; in Castlereagh, 10; and in Skibbereen, 6.

In none of the four Unions can ploughmen be said to exist as a class, as there are few farms or estates which have a sufficient amount of tillage land to give such men regular work. Usually on the farms one of the ordinary labourers, or the farmer himself, does the ploughing.

Also, except on a few estates, no cattlemen or carters are employed. On the larger farms herds look after all the animals, and on the smaller ones this work frequently falls to the lot of the hired men, or if there are no hired men, to one or more of the ordinary labourers.

It is perhaps a matter worthy of notice that the stewards are usually either Englishmen or Scotchmen. A well-known land agent in Ireland writes to me on this subject as follows:—"I have rarely met a good Irish steward outside Ulster. In the "first place, they do not get themselves educated for the business, and, strange to "say, as a rule, they do not get on well with the men under them. In Ulster you can "get really good men."

THE AGRICULTURAL LABOURER.

The stewards are usually a very superior class of men, who have frequently had an excellent education and undergone a sound training for their business.*

II.—THE SUPPLY OF LABOUR.

The supply of labour. Westport, par. 21.

21. The supply of labour in the Westport Union greatly exceeds the demand both summer and winter, notwithstanding the emigration and migration, to which I have alluded in paragraphs 14 and 16. In the late autumn, winter, and early spring, when the migratory labourers are at home, the district is full of men who would work if they could get employment. It must, however, be borne in mind that there are no agricultural labourers in the ordinary sense of the word, and that a very large number of small holders and their sons, throughout the Union, are ready at any time to do a day's work for wages if they can get it.

Castlereagh, par 16.

In the Castlereagh Union the supply of labour is rather scarce in the summer, particularly at hay-time and harvest. This is partly due to emigration, partly to migration, and partly to the small farmers, who also work for wages, being engaged on their own land. During the winter the supply is quite sufficient and wages are then lower in consequence.

Skibbereen, par 14.

In the Skibbereen Union the mackerel fishing in the spring, summer, and autumn makes labour very scarce in the neighbourhood of the coast, and in consequence drives up the agricultural wages. Of late the construction of the railway from Baltimore to Skibbereen has been an additional means of making labour scarce. In the districts away from the coast the supply of labour seems to be just sufficient in summer and more than sufficient in winter.

Delvin, par. 16.

In the Delvin Union labour is rather scarce in summer, chiefly owing to there being a great demand for men during hay harvest, which lasts a considerable time in this grass country. During the winter there is a lack of employment, which is particularly felt by the odd men who live in the villages.

Increase or decrease in supply of labour during past 10 years. Castlereagh, par. 13.

22. During the past 10 years there has been a decrease in the population in all the unions; but how far this has affected the supply of agricultural labour is difficult to say. As less labour is employed than formerly, owing to the conversion of arable land into grass, and in some degree to hard times, and as the rate of wages has been gradually rising, it would seem that labour has been getting scarcer.

I have already pointed out that the supply of labour is everywhere plentiful in winter, and that the scarcity in summer, apart from the question of increase or decrease through emigration, is due to migration, to the necessity for small holders to work on their own land, particularly at hay-time and harvest, and to special local circumstances, such as the fishing industry in the Skibbereen Union of County Cork.

Young labourers prefer a town life. Westport, par 22, App. B 1. Castlereagh, par. 12, App B 5. Skibbereen, App. B 1. Delvin, App B 1.

23. In Ireland as in England there seems to be a growing tendency among the young men to prefer a town life to a country one. A more educated generation are learning that manual labour in the fields is not only a badly paid profession but that it is socially considered inferior, that it is monotonous in the present and promises no reward in the future.

I interviewed a great many young men who were desirous of emigrating, or who were about to do so,† and they all intended to get employment in towns, in stores, in shops, on railways, or as coachmen.

In connection with this subject a very intelligent young man on a holding of 4½ acres (Irish), near Castlereagh, said as follows: "We (the family) all want to clear "out to America. I don't like the work on the land. It is very laborious, and does "not lead to anything. I have seen men who have worked on it all their lives as badly

* Mr. Cochrane, agent to the Earl of Longford, writing with reference to the steward on the Pakenham Hall Estate, says:—"He is a Scotchman, and his people were farmers, but he made up his mind to learn the "business of farm steward and general estate manager. Having worked first as an ordinary workman and "having become a foreman and then an under steward, he went to a nursery and forestry in Scotland as an "ordinary labourer, and afterwards went in much the same capacity, I think, to either Kew or Hampton "Court. Though he had many offers to go as steward he refused them, and remained on labourer's pay until "he was 25. I daresay his pay is higher than that of any steward in Westmeath; but I never came across a "man so efficient and who knows so much agriculturally. He is really an authority on the Polled Angus and "Shorthorn Herd Book and the Shropshire Flock Book."

Mr. Sandford's steward, Castlereagh, writes:—"I am a holder of the Royal Agricultural Societies' Diploma, "obtained by examination in practical and theoretical work, and I have been trained and studied at the "Government farm, Albert Institute, Glasnevin, Dublin, under the late Professor Baldwin."

† For number of males who emigrate see Summary, Appendix 7. Of the men who emigrated from Mayo in 1892, 76·2 per cent. were under 25 years of age. The percentage in Roscommon was 52·4, in County Cork 49·8, and in Westmeath 46·3.

"off as at the beginning. A man employed in agriculture is considered at the bottom "of the social scale. This is the general opinion among the young men. They "prefer a better social position." THE AGRICULTURAL LABOURER.

24. The majority of farmers in these Unions cannot afford to buy machinery, and so it is difficult to obtain practical opinions as to whether the demand for labour has been lessened by its use or not. Effect of machinery on labour.

Mr. Jack, steward to the Earl of Longford, at Pakenham Hall, Westmeath, says that on the home farm, where there are 110 acres (Irish) of tillage, no reduction has taken place in the staff owing to purchases of machinery at various times. Mr. Owen Sweeny, a farmer in the Skibbereen Union, says that machinery has not dispensed with labour on his farm except at hay time and harvest.

25. There is an unanimity of opinion that the supply of women workers has been getting less and less, and that now in many districts their employment in the fields is a thing of the past. Scarcity of women for agricultural employment.

This is said to be owing to their disliking agricultural employment and preferring more variety and excitement, and living among more refined surroundings. Westport, par. 20, App. B 1.

In the Delvin Union, Westmeath, where there is not so keen a struggle for existence among the small holders, as in the counties of Mayo, Cork, and part of Roscommon, which is evidenced by there being no congested districts, no migration, and a decreasing number of emigrants in the last five years, women are getting so scarce that it is most difficult to procure domestic servants. From this Union they either emigrate or go into shops or service in Dublin. Speaking of the employment of women in agriculture, Mr. Jack, steward to the Earl of Longford, says: "At 18 years of age they get above "working on the land, and they try and do better for themselves."* Castlereagh, par. 20. Skibbereen, par. 17. Delvin, par. 15.

No doubt many of the girls in the West are attracted to America chiefly by the high wages there (see par. 18), which enable them to materially assist the rest of their family who remain at home.

To the farmer the deficiency of female labour is a pecuniary loss, for he has instead to employ male labour at a higher wage, which at many kinds of work is not more effective. A Westmeath farmer alluding to the scarcity of women workers said: "They were the sheet anchor of the farmer in harvest."

Many of the wives and remaining daughters of the small holders, work very hard on their own land, especially if the men migrate during a portion of the year to England.

Doubtless the women who go to Scotch farms have to work hard and undergo hardships there, particularly if the weather is inclement; but it must be borne in mind that when they are fed by the farmer they get much better food than they do at home, and that between June and September they can make more money than they could earn as a general servant in 12 months in their own neighbourhood.

Some girls enjoy the trip to Scotland, as it gives them a change from the monotony of a life on a small holding.

26. On the question as to whether the labourers are as efficient now as they were some 15 years ago, opinion is greatly divided. In the Appendices to my reports on the four Unions I have given the opinions of many employers of labour, and also of some labourers, and it will be seen that the majority of witnesses consider that the men do not do so good a day's work as formerly. Efficiency of men's work as compared with the past.

Among those who differ from this view are, however, several stewards on large estates, whose evidence is of value, as they are practical men, who have had large experience as regards labour, frequently in several districts; and also because they are as a class extremely well educated and intelligent.

But possibly their views, which, as a rule, are contrary to those of the farmers, are due to the fact that the labourers employed on large estates are frequently better off than those on farms, as they have rather a higher rate of wage, more regular employment, in many cases privileges, such as cheap cottages with land, and perquisites, such as firing and milk.

In the Westport Union two men of great experience, Mr. Powell, agent to the Marquis of Sligo, and Mr. Larminie, agent to the Earl of Lucan, say the men's work has deteriorated, in which opinion the majority of the farmers in all parts of the Union agree; but Lord John Browne's steward and Mr. Houston's manager, both Scotchmen, consider that this is not the case. Westport, par. 23, App. B 2.

* The proportion per cent. of women under 25 years of age who emigrated in [illegible] was in Mayo 55·0, in Roscommon 51·2, in County Cork 49·8, and in Westmeath 42·7.

THE AGRICULTURAL LABOURER.

Castlereagh, par. 116, App. B. 2.
Skibbereen, par. 19, App. B. 1.
Delvin, par. 17, App. B. 1.

In the Castlereagh Union The O'Conor Don's steward, and Mr. Sandford's steward, think there has been no falling off in the men's skill or capacity; in fact, the latter is of opinion that those who go to England improve from being trained by English farmers; whereas the farmers and the older labourers hold contrary opinions.

In the Skibbereen Union The O'Donovan's steward, a Lancashire man, does not see any signs of deterioration in the work of the men on that estate, though he thinks that this is not the case generally in the district. The farmers are strangely divided on this subject, which makes it difficult to form any definite opinion.

In the Delvin Union three stewards, all either of English or Scotch extraction, on large properties, consider the men's work on these estates to be perfectly satisfactory; but that, as a general rule, labour has deteriorated in the district, whereas the farmers and older labourers generally agree that the men do not do as good a day's work as formerly.

In the Castlereagh Union I heard many complaints from employers that the men will not come punctually to their work in the morning. It seems to be a frequent practice for them to come at 7 a.m. in the summer instead of 6 a.m., and not uncommon for them to come as late as 8 a.m. In the Delvin Union I heard complaints of a similar nature, but they were not so general.

Reasons for deterioration in men's skill and capacity.

27. There are several reasons advanced for the deterioration in the men's skill or capacity, and foremost, among them is the emigration, which must be draining the country of many strong and intelligent young men.* Another is that the decrease of tillage land gives the men less opportunity of learning farm work; and, again, that the scarcity of labour in the summer time enables the men, who are now more educated and consequently more able to assert their rights, to make better terms for themselves as regards the amount of work they do.† Another is, that education is making the men dislike agricultural employment, and prefer town life (*see also* paragraph 23); and another, that the people are not so physically strong, owing to the bad effects of modern diet compared with that partaken of 20 years ago. (*See* paragraph 31.)

Probably all of these reasons are sound, but as far as distaste for agricultural employment is concerned it is worthy of remark that those who migrate seldom seem to take to field work in America, but prefer to get occupation in the towns.

In England, where the reason of emigration cannot be urged, the same complaints are made by employers of the deterioration in the men's skill and capacity, and many ascribe it to the lack of interest shown by the young men in agricultural work.

Efficiency of men's work as compared with other districts.
Westport, par. 24, App. B. 3.
Castlereagh, par. 17, App. B. 2.
Skibbereen, par. 20, App. B. 2.
Delvin, par. 15, App. B. 2.

28. It is a difficult matter to find men who have a practical knowledge of labourers' work in several counties, and as a rule only landlords and stewards have this experience, for farmers generally know very little of other districts but their own. The evidence seems to show that of the four counties, the Mayo men are the hardest workers and capable of the most endurance.

In some cases the evidence is very conflicting, though most employers agree that the men require supervision. Mr. A. Hurd, engineer and contractor's agent, who has been employed in the construction of the Colloney and Claremorris Railway, Mayo, and also on the Skibbereen and Baltimore Railway, County Cork, thinks the Mayo men are physically finer and much the better workers of the two, whereas Lord John Browne's steward, Westport, thinks the Cork men more efficient, and that they require less looking after.

Mr. Redding, steward to Mr. Sandford, Castlereagh, who has had experience of labourers near Belfast, in Tyrone, County Dublin, County Kildare, County Wicklow and Queen's County, is of opinion that the Roscommon men, considering they have been worse fed than the men in any other of these counties, are harder workers though less intelligent. Mr. FitzSimmons, steward to The O'Conor Don, near Castlereagh, is of opinion that the Roscommon men, when compared with the Tipperary and Louth men, are hardier and physically stronger, but less intelligent. He thinks, moreover, that capacity to endure hardships and fatigue is one of the characteristics of the men in the West, but that another is a tendency to idleness without supervision. Another witness considers the men in the adjoining counties of Mayo and Galway are better.

* Two dissent from this view; Mr. Redding, steward to Mr. Sandford (Castlereagh), says:—"The "emigration has affected the quantity, not the quality of labour. Possibly it has been an advantage as the "idlest have gone." Mr Bennett, farmer (Skibbereen), says:—"The emigration has not affected me. It "has left quite enough good men for any purpose."

† The Rev. F. Teele, Delvin, says:—"The men are more enlightened, and do not kill themselves with work now."

‡ Mr Fitzsimmons, steward to The O'Conor Don, says:—"At harvest time we cannot grumble at the men "if they come to work after 7 a.m. as they have us in their power."

The Agricultural Labourer.

Mr. Binyon, steward to The O'Donovan, Skibbereen, considers that the Cork men are quite as good if not better and heartier, than the Queen's County and Waterford men.

As regards the Westmeath men, a steward, who has had considerable experience in England and Ireland, expressed the opinion that they and the Meath men were the worst he had ever met, and a land agent stated that the Westmeath men compared unfavourably with those in Mayo. A farmer, comparing the work performed in Westmeath with that in the North of Ireland, says as follows: "Within a few miles north "of this place good labour begins and goes right on up to the North. Wherever you "find North of Ireland men you touch on industry. How it is I know not, but it "is the case."

Efficiency of Irishmen's work as compared with that of Englishmen and Scotchmen.

29. In comparing the work of Irishmen with that of Englishmen and Scotchmen the comparison cannot be said to be unfavourable to the former, and especially if at the same time their diet is contrasted, (see paragraph 30), though, generally speaking, employers say that Irishmen require more supervision than Englishmen or Scotchmen, and that they have a tendency to work by fits and starts.

In Mayo, Mr. McDonnell, a Scotchman, manager to Mr. Houston, has had excellent opportunities of comparing the capacities of Scotchmen and Irishmen, as at one time there were a good many Scotchmen on the farm, though now they have Scotch shepherds as overseers, and the rest of the men are Irish. Mr. Houston says of the Irishmen: "They work as well under the Scotch shepherds as the Scotchmen did when "we had more of them. They did not do so much at first, not because they were not "willing but because they had to be taught. The work and stuff is in the people, "but they want proper training."

Also employers in England speak well of the capacities of Irishmen who go over there.

Mr. Hindmarsh, a large farmer in Northumberland, who chiefly employs Donegal men for harvest, and Mr. Pearson, a large farmer at St. Michael's-on-Wyre, Lancashire, who often employs Mayo men, consider that when Irishmen are employed at such work as they have been accustomed to, such as reaping or potato lifting, they are as good if not better than Englishmen. Mr. Pearson says that at piece-work the Irishmen beat Lancashire men hollow, but very little work is done there by the piece, except potato lifting, which is a class of work the Irishmen excel in. Mr. Pearson also finds that the Irishmen who come to him regularly, get through as much in a day as his own men, and at a push are more willing, but that the "roving" men are inclined to do as little as possible.* Mr. Hindmarsh says that the Irishmen he employs are not so efficient as the Northumberland men, except at reaping, and that they require more supervision.

Mr. F. Walker, agent to Lord Wenlock, at Eskrick, near York, comparing the work of Irishmen and Yorkshiremen, says that the former when at work will do far more than the latter; but, he adds, their "spree" and not being able to depend upon them spoil them for regular men. He, however, speaks very highly of the Irishwomen, and says that "two Irish girls getting 2s. a day could do more work than any two men "in the district planting potatoes, leading hay or corn stacks, or pretty nearly "anything."

The Hon. A. Parker, agent to the Earl of Cadogan, comparing Irishmen's work with that of Cheshire men, says that there is no great difference as regards the quantity or quality of their work, and a Warwickshire farmer who employs about 20 for about five months in the year, says he finds the Irishmen, as a rule, tidy men and especially handy with their hoes.

Effect of diet on men's capacity

30. In making comparison between the work of men in different districts, I venture to think that the question of diet should fairly be taken into consideration. Witnesses in Ireland of considerable experience state that feeding has much to do with the

---

* Mr. Wilkinson, farmer and bailiff to the late Lord Winmarleigh, Garstang Union, Lancashire, writes: "The two Irishmen I employ have come over for 13 years. They get 1s. a day and we find them a "roof. They pay for their food, and buy milk and butter from us at cost price. They chiefly live on "tea, bread, and milk. I believe they take back 10l. each. They come in June when we are ready for "weeding, and stay over harvest. I find they work hard. (These men do not stay for potato lifting, at "which high wages can be earned at piece-work.)"

THE AGRICULTURAL LABOURER.

distinctions observable in the men's capacity for work,* and their opinions may be summed up in the blunt language of a Lancashire farmer, who gave evidence on the same subject when I was reporting in the North of England for the Royal Commission on Labour. "No man can work with an empty belly. What goes in at the "stomach comes out in the work. If you want to keep an Englishman up to his "work and in good humour, keep his belly full of good meat."

Effect of tea drinking and modern diet on the health and strength of the people. Westport, par. 31. Castlereagh, par. 37, App. B 4. Skibbereen, par. 41, App. D 1. Delvin, par. 76, App. E 1.

31. Evidence is overwhelming that the food now partaken of by the people, though of more refined quality and more in accordance with modern ideas, is not nearly so strengthening, and in consequence the actual physical capacity of the people is deteriorating.†

White bread and tea have now taken the place of the humble but more strengthening oatmeal stirabout and milk. In the words of a Westmeath labourer, "The children "are spoilt in their youth from not having any milk. The people are killing them-"selves with tea, and do not do so much work in consequence. Stirabout and milk "used to be a grand thing for them."

A farmer in the same county speaking of the deterioration in the men's strength, which in his opinion is chiefly due to the modern diet, said:—"You could not get a "man to carry a sack of 30 stone of wheat on his back 100 yards like they used to. "If a man had 20 stone on his back now he could not cross the road with it."

The tea drinking is especially condemned by the doctors as injurious to health. Dyspepsia and its allied diseases, and also mental diseases, are said to be traceable to it. The people seem to take tea at all their meals, and frequently drink it very strong and bitter, not only because they use a great deal of it, but because they let it stand so long before the fire. In the farmhouses a hired man would think he was very shabbily treated unless he had tea with his meals.‡

III.—Conditions of Engagement.

Regularity or irregularity of employment. Westport, pars. 21, 25.

32. In the Westport Union employment is always irregular, except for the herds and hired men, because the medium and large sized farms are nearly all in grass. Agricultural labourers do not exist as a class, but small holders or their sons supply their place, their holdings being either so small, or so unproductive, that they are obliged to get such work as they can in Ireland or go to English or Scotch farms for certain portions of the year. It is impossible to give any idea as to how many days these men work in a year for Irish farmers. Many who are thus employed would like far more work than they are able to get, while others who have more land voluntarily absent themselves at times in order to attend to their own crops. Two intelligent young men, sons of small holders who work for Lord John Browne, an employer as generous as any in the district, told me they thought they lost about 60 days in the year from wet weather.

Westport, par. 18, App. A. 5, A(a) O.

Castlereagh, par. 18. Skibbereen, par. 21.

In the Castlereagh and Skibbereen Unions work is more continuous for ordinary labourers, because there are many farmers who have a regular farm staff to whom they give employment, wet or dry, all the year round.

---

* Mr. A. Reed, engineer and contractor's agent, lately employed on the Collooney and Claremorris Railway, co. Mayo, and also the Baltimore Railway, co. Cork, says, "I consider the Mayo men a good class, but they "don't come up to the average English navvy. A man fed upon eggs, bread, and tea cannot do as much "work as a man who has beef and beer three times a day."

Mr. William Gray, walking ganger on the Achill Railway, co. Mayo, who has had 30 years' experience in collecting gangs of men from English counties for railway work in England and Ireland, speaking of the Irishmen in the West, says, "Some of them are fine looking men, but they have no muscle from underfeeding."

Mr. Flynn, a small holder on Clare Island, who has been an overseer on works near Dublin, says, "I have "worked in gangs in Northumberland, on public works, at house building, on chemical works, and on farms in "the North of England, and I have seen Irishmen working under all these conditions. After three months, "when they had sweated the water out of their bodies, and had good food, they could work as well as "Englishmen."

Mr. Redding, steward to Mr. Sandford, Castlereagh, says, "The men round here find themselves better now "that rents have been reduced. If a man is not fed properly he is not worth anything. If I were a farmer I "would feed all my men to ensure getting good work. The last couple of years I have noticed the effects of "better feeding on the men."

† Witnesses in the North of England also say that the splendid race of men there, who formerly lived on porridge, milk, and wholesome bread, are deteriorating in health and strength, because they now prefer tea and white bread.

‡ A farmer's wife in Roscommon says, "I would give the men bacon instead of tea three days a week, but "they will have the tea and not the bacon."

There are, however, in both Unions a certain number of odd men whose employment is irregular in wet weather and in the winter; and there are also a certain number of small holders, or their sons, who are unable to make a sufficient living from their holdings, and these, in the Castlereagh Union, migrate for certain periods of the year to English farms, and in the Skibbereen Union they take part in the mackerel fishery.

In the Delvin Union, work is more regular than in any of the other three Unions, both because there are many farmers who employ a regular staff of men all the year round and because there are several large properties where a considerable number of men have constant work. There are, however, a number of odd men there who find work difficult to get in the winter, but in the villages in the neighbourhood of the Earl of Longford's estates at Pakenham Hall and Killucan, those out of employment are found work by the Earl of Longford, which is, of course a great boon to them.*

33. Generally speaking, the engagement of ordinary labourers, whether odd men or those regularly attached to the staff of a farm, is by the day, but there are exceptions in all the four Unions as regards the latter class. In those cases where regular men are paid partly in kind, such as a certain amount of land, the grass of cows, sheep, &c., their engagements, though nominally daily or weekly, are looked upon by both parties as of indefinite length, and in practice continue for long periods unless any serious disagreement occurs. In the Westport Union the engagement is always a daily one, probably the only exceptions are Mr. Vesey Stoney's men at Rosturk Castle, who have a yearly engagement, and some of Mr. Houston's labourers, who have a house free, some tillage land, and the grass of cattle, as part payment of their wages.

In the Castlereagh Union there are also exceptions to the daily engagement, as certain farmers engage their regular staff by the week, but in the Skibbereen Union a weekly engagement of the ordinary staff of the farm is more common, and there are a few rare instances where men are engaged by the year.

In the Delvin Union a daily engagement is the most usual, though here again there are both farmers and landowners who engage their men by the week.

34. The engagement of ploughmen is usually a weekly one. There are, however, but few of these as a class, as there are so few farms or estates where there is a sufficient amount of tillage land to require them. In the Delvin Union there are more than in the other three Unions. These men have always regular work and usually stay in their places for long periods.

35. Herds are usually engaged by the year, but the notice to quit their situations varies considerably, sometimes it is a monthly notice, occasionally two months, and at other times a quarterly, half-yearly, or yearly notice.

In many it is very difficult to determine what is the legal term of engagement, for the herds frequently stay for years in the same situation, and it is not uncommon to find cases where they have been born on the farm or property, and that their fathers and grandfathers "herded" for the same employer. Consequently no definite arrangements are made as regards notice, as neither master nor man consider the possibility of parting company.

The mode of their payment, which is chiefly in kind, such as the right to graze cattle and sheep, almost necessitates their continuing in the same employment, and another reason is that they must be thoroughly acquainted with the lie of the ground, especially on the large mountain farms in the West.

In the Castlereagh Union it is not an uncommon practice for a man to rent one or two grass farms and to put a herd in charge of each. In these cases the agreements are usually in writing, the term of engagement being for 12 months, notice to quit being frequently a monthly one.

In the Delvin Union there are 48 herds or shepherds. These men are usually engaged by the year, with a half-yearly or quarterly notice.†

---

* In the few instances where farms or estates have a sufficient amount of tillage land to employ a ploughman, he has regular employment and is engaged wet or dry, and this is also the case as regards cattlemen or carters employed on estates.

† In the Westport Union many employers refer to the engagements of the herds as monthly ones, but I think they really are yearly ones with a month's notice. Their wages or allowances are always referred to as so much a year. Agreements in writing are seldom made, and hence, if a legal dispute arose the employers might find the herds were yearly tenants of their cottages. In the Castlereagh and Delvin Unions agreements are sometimes made in writing for the herds to quit their cottages on the same notice as they have agreed verbally or otherwise to quit their employment upon.

The Agricultural Labourer.

Engagement of hired men. [illegible]

36. Hired men are usually engaged by the year, but if employers or employed desire to part company before the expiration of the time, as a rule neither seem to raise any difficulties. In the Delvin Union some of the hired men enter into agreements to quit at shorter notices, but, as in the other Unions, legal difficulties as to notice are not often raised by either side.

Engagement of cattlemen, yardmen, and carters. Westport, par. 20 & 21. Castlereagh, par. 10. Skibbereen, par. 21. Delvin, par. 23.

37. As a general rule no cattlemen, yardmen, or carters are employed in any of the four Unions except on estates. Their engagement is usually a weekly one, but occasionally for a longer period.

In the Castlereagh Union there are cattlemen on some of the larger farms, but in these cases no herds are employed. As these men and also ploughmen are frequently given houses, land and the grass of cows free, or at a cheap rate as payment in kind, or perquisites, there is the same inducement, even necessity, for them to remain in their situations as in the case of herds and sometimes in the case of ordinary labourers on the staff of a farm (pars. 23, 33).

Hours of ordinary labourers, regular meals, and meal-times in summer. Summary, App. 3.

38. Generally the hours of ordinary labourers in summer in the Westport, Castlereagh, and Skibbereen Unions are from 6 a.m. to 6 p.m. or from 7 a.m. to 7 p.m., with half an hour for breakfast and an hour for dinner. In the Delvin Union they are from 7 a.m. to 6 p.m., with an hour off for dinner, the men having to breakfast before starting for work. Thus the actual working hours in the first three Unions are 10½ and in the Delvin Union 10.

There are, however, certain exceptions in the three first-named Unions to the ordinary arrangement of the working hours. In the Westport Union where the hours are from 6 a.m. to 6 p.m. an hour is frequently allowed off for breakfast as well as dinner, which makes the total working hours 10, and in a few cases where the hours were from 7 a.m. to 7 p.m. the men had to get their breakfast before they came to work and were allowed an hour for dinner, and thus their total working hours were 11.

In the Castlereagh Union there are cases where the working hours are from 7 a.m. to 6 p.m., and then the men have either to breakfast before they arrive, or if not a shorter period than an hour is allowed for dinner. On some farms 10 or 15 minutes is allowed for tea at 4 p.m. in addition to the usual meal hours, and on others this meal is deducted from the breakfast and dinner time.

In the Skibbereen Union an hour is sometimes allowed for breakfast as well as dinner. On one small farm of 92 acres I found the hours were from 6 a.m. to 7 p.m., with an hour off for meals.

In the Castlereagh Union employers almost universally complain that the men come very late to their work in the morning. When they are supposed to commence at 6 a.m. they frequently do not come until 7 a.m. or even 8 a.m. Sometimes they stay later in the evening to compensate for this, but more often they leave off at the usual hour. In the Delvin Union many employers make the same complaint, though not so often as in the Castlereagh Union, but still it is by no means uncommon for the men to arrive half an hour or an hour late. Of course, this custom, which is said to be a growing one, must be taken into consideration when estimating the actual working hours.

I heard of no grumbling on the part of the men as to the length of hours in any of the four Unions.

Hours of work of ordinary labourers (regular meals and meal-times) in winter. Summary, App. 3.

39. The hours of work in winter depend on the duration of the daylight, and also if an employer has stock, so that men can be employed milking or cleaning out sheds, &c. after dark. Where men are exclusively employed in the fields the shortest winter hours are from 8 a.m. to 4.15 p.m. with an hour off for meals, and in some cases half an hour is also allowed for breakfast.

Westport, par. 28. Castlereagh, par. 18. Skibbereen, par. 27. Delvin, par. 26.

In the Castlereagh, Delvin, and Skibbereen Unions, but more particularly in the latter, there are farms and estates where definite summer and winter hours are agreed on, and dates fixed for them to commence.

Thus one farmer in the Skibbereen Union fixes the summer hours from March to September, and gives his men an actual working day of 10½ hours. From September to March they commence work at 7 a.m. and 8 a.m. and leave off at 6 p.m. with an hour and a half off for meals, thus making an actual working day of 8½ or 9½ hours. Another large farmer commences his winter hours about the same period of the year, and his men work from 8 a.m. to 5 p.m. with two hours off for meals. This represents an actual working day of only seven hours. Another farmer there fixes his winter hours from 7 a.m. to 7 p.m. with two hours off for meals, thus making a total working day of 10 hours.

In the Delvin Union on three properties the actual working hours in the winter are 7½ hours, eight hours and eight hours respectively.

The Agricultural Labourer.

Hours of work of ploughmen, summer and winter. Castlereagh, par. 23. Delvin, par. 29.

40. Ploughmen nominally have the same hours as ordinary labourers, but they usually have two hours for meals instead of 1½. As, however, they have to feed their horses in the middle of the day, their meal hours are not really longer. A ploughman who has to feed and clean his horses and also the stable, has extra work before he commences his nominal day's work and also after it is finished, but sometimes he has not this to do. In the summer the horses are turned out in the fields, usually close to the farm buildings. There are but few ploughmen as a class in any of the unions, but there are more in Delvin than in any of the others.

Hours of work of herds, summer and winter. Westport, par. 18. Castlereagh, par. 23. Delvin, par. 28.

41. It is, of course, impossible for herds who have the charge of sheep and cattle to have any definite hours. On some of the mountain farms in Mayo the herds have sheep and cattle on large tracts of mountain land under their care, which gives them a great deal of walking at certain seasons of the year. Again, in the Castlereagh Union, where it is a frequent practice for a herd to be put in charge of a grass farm, he is more in the position of a farmer and has to look after the premises and the stock under his care as occasion requires without regard to fixed hours. During sheep-washing, clipping, and hay time, their work is often arduous, and at lambing time, or when cattle and sheep are ill, they have long hours and often broken rest.

As a rule, the herds are a contented, well-mannered body of men. An employer of labour in Delvin informed me that socially the herds considered themselves much above ordinary labourers.

[illegible]

42. The hours of work of hired men are the same as those of ordinary labourers. In some cases, no doubt, these are rather longer, as a man living in the farmhouse is liable to be called upon to go out at odd times to see after cattle if sick, or to do other jobs which are urgent. On some of the smaller farms where no herds or cattlemen are kept, the care of cattle and horses falls to their lot, and in such cases the hours would be longer than those of the daymen employed exclusively at out-door work. On the other hand, they are living close to their work and so have no walk in the morning to get to it.

[illegible]

43. The hours of work of those men in charge of animals who are only employed on estates or large farms, are often rather longer than those of ordinary labourers, especially in the winter, as the nature of their employment enables them to work in the sheds after dark.

[illegible]

44. The hours of work of women and girls when employed, which is seldom, and also those of boys, are usually the same as those of the ordinary labourers.

[illegible]

45. A very small proportion of men are employed on Sunday to look after cattle, sheep, and horses.

On farms where herds are kept the charge of animals falls exclusively to them, but on smaller farms the hired men or the farmers themselves feed the animals and do other necessary work connected with them.

On estates where cattlemen, yardmen, and carters are kept, one or two of them attend to the animals. Sometimes they take it in turns and sometimes the same men do it always. In the summer time when the cattle and horses are turned out, they practically have no work. The men try to save themselves as much as they can by preparing the food for Sunday the day before.

It is impossible to state generally how long men in charge of animals are employed on Sundays, as their duties vary so. For instance, a herd in the mountainous districts of Mayo, in charge of cattle and sheep on several thousand acres of rough land, would often have as much to do on Sundays as week days, while a hired man on a small farm, or a cattleman or a yardman on a large estate who is assisted by others may be occupied from two to six hours every Sunday, or perhaps every alternate one.

IV.—Wages and Earnings.

Wages of ordinary labourers (regular men and odd men) summer and winter. Westport, par. 17. Castlereagh, par. 29.

46. The current rate of weekly wages in the Westport Union for ordinary labourers in summer is 9s., but in a few cases they get 10s. Frequently men are given 6s. a week, and in a few cases 7s. 6d. and their breakfast and dinner. In the winter cash wages are between 7s. and 8s. a week, though some employers pay 9s.*

In the Castlereagh Union wages in the summer are 9s., though a few employers pay up to 12s., and in the winter they pay from 7s. 6d. to 9s. a week.

On a few farms the wages are 9s. or 10s. summer and winter.

It is frequently the practice for men to be paid 6s. a week summer and winter, and supplied with breakfast and dinner.

* In all the unions the wages are usually quoted as daily and not weekly.

In the Skibbereen Union the wages near the coast in the summer are higher than they are inland as they are affected by the demand for men at the mackerel fishery. They run from 9s. to 12s. a week, and in some cases breakfast and dinner is provided as well. In the inland districts wages are about 8s. a week, or if food is supplied, 6s.

In this union it is not uncommon to pay the men partly in kind, and in these cases the men are frequently better off than those on cash wages.

In the winter the wages are often 9s. a week, or 6s. with food; 8s. a week is usually the lowest cash wage paid.

In the Delvin Union the wages in summer for men in regular employment are 8s. or 9s. a week, and on a few properties 10s., but oddmen can command 2s. a day. In some cases food is supplied for which 2s. or 3s. a week is deducted.

In winter the wages paid on the farms to the ordinary staff are 7s. to 8s. a week, but on certain properties they are up to 9s. or 10s. Odd men in winter get from 1s. 2d. to 1s. 6d. a day.

47. The weekly wages of ploughmen in the Westport, Castlereagh, Skibbereen, and Delvin Unions are 11s. or 12s. a week with a house free and sometimes other perquisites.

48. Cattlemen, yardmen, and carters usually have from 9s. to 12s. a week summer and winter, and frequently get perquisites in addition and sometimes a house rent free.

49. Women in the Westport Union are paid about 4s. 6d. a week; in the Castlereagh Union 1s. a day and their food, and girls get 6d. to 1s. a day; in the Skibbereen Union 1s. a day; in the Delvin Union 1s. a day; during harvest 1s. 6d. to 1s. 6d. a day, and when putting turf into barrows after men have cut it, 2s. a day. Girls are paid about 10d. a day.

50. In the Westport Union boys are paid at first on leaving school 5s. to 6s. a week in the Castlereagh Union 3s. to 4s. 6d. a week, in the Skibbereen Union from 4s. 6d. to 5s. a week, in the Delvin Union from 3s. to 4s. a week.

51. Very little piece-work, task-work as it is usually called in Ireland, is done in any of the unions I visited, except mowing, and this is often done by odd men. As a rule the farms are too small, and the proportion of tillage land too insignificant for employers to adopt the system of piece-work, but apart from that it seems that both employer and employed prefer payment according to day work.* Some employers state that they find the men skimp their work at piece-work, and thus require more supervision than they care to give.

Besides mowing, draining, turf-cutting and making walls, fencing and ditching are sometimes undertaken at piece-work.

52. The prices paid for mowing by piece-work at hay time or harvest, depend of course on whether the crop is a heavy or light one. This work is only undertaken at piece-work by odd men. In the Westport Union men are paid 6s. to 8s. for a statute acre, and in a day of 10 hours they can earn 3s. to 4s. 6d.†

In the Castlereagh Union 7s. to 10s. is paid for mowing an Irish acre, and an average man can earn from 3s. 6d. to 5s. in a day of 12 hours.‡

In the Delvin Union a man is paid 5s. 6d. for a statute acre and can earn about 4s. in a day of 10 hours.

53. The ordinary staff of a farm, as a rule, receive no extra payment or allowance at hay-time or harvest, but in all the unions there are exceptions. Frequently odd men receive a higher cash wage than the regular men during these times. If engaged at mowing they get about 2s. 6d. a day, and if they undertake mowing by piece-work, they are paid according to the prices mentioned in par. 52.

The wages for mowing in the Westport Union by day work are 2s. 6d. a day; in the Castlereagh Union 2s. 6d. a day and often food in addition;§ and in the Skibbereen Union, 2s. to 2s. 6d. a day; in the Delvin Union 2s. 6d.

* Mr. A. Reed, engineer and contractor's agent on the Ballinacourty Railway, Skibbereen, informed me that there he found that the men would not take piece-work, though they could have thereby earned more, because they seemed afraid they would somehow be taken advantage of.

† Lord John Browne writes from Westport, "Mowers are not plentiful. The people say it is too hard work "and unlucky."

‡ Mr James Clancy, Firmount Park, says that his men mow twice as much in a day when at piece-work as they do at day-work.

§ One large farmer gives his extra men and all his own staff 2s. 6d. a day with food, or 3s. and no food.

Owing to there being so much grass, mowing extends over many weeks, and then odd men can earn considerable sums, especially if engaged on piece-work.*

54. As a general rule perquisites are not given to ordinary labourers, but there are exceptions, chiefly on estates or the larger farms in the Castlereagh, Skibbereen and Delvin Unions.

Such perquisites include turf, coal, milk, food, potato ground, tillage and meadow land free or at a cheap rate; the carting of manure, the grass of cows or sheep free or at a cheap rate.

In those cases where men are given their breakfast and dinner in part payment of wages, they are really receiving in money and money's worth more than the current rate of wage. As a rule 3s. a week is deducted for food, but there are instances where the deduction is only 1s. 6d. or 2s. In any event it is difficult to see how a farmer can provide two meals a day for 6d.† This practice of giving food in part payment of wages is more common in the Castlereagh and Skibbereen Unions than in the Westport and Delvin Unions.

Of course the food supplied in the farm houses varies according to the means of the occupants, but there are many instances where the allowance is generous both as regards quantity and quality, and far superior to that which the men, whether small holders or labourers would get in their own homes. In some farms they are given beef or mutton three or four days a week, which on many small holdings would not be seen three or four days a year.

55. There is another form of perquisites to which I must refer, and that is the letting of good cottages with land, at a cheap rental. In the Delvin Union there are several owners of property who let excellent cottages with land, provided with good outhouses, sheds for cows, and styes, for a rent far below their market value (*see* paragraph 75).

56. Perquisites of the nature mentioned in the preceding paragraphs 54 and 55 are not unfrequently given to ploughmen, cattlemen, yardmen and carters.

57. As a general rule ordinary labourers are paid their wages entirely in cash, but there are exceptions in all the unions. I have already referred in paragraph 54 to the practice, which is more prevalent in the Castlereagh and Skibbereen Unions than in the other two, of paying part of the wages in food, although, as I have pointed out, those who get their breakfast and dinner at the farm house at a cost of 3s. a week, or less, are being fed at a very cheap rate, still the married men usually prefer to take home all their wages in cash.

In the Castlereagh and Skibbereen Unions there are a good many instances of men receiving a low rate of cash wage and having payment in kind, such as cottages, meadow or tillage land, turf, potatoes, and manure.

In some of the more remote districts in Mayo it is not an uncommon practice for the small holders, or their sons, to work for the village shopkeeper, who often rents some land, and to be paid either in shop goods or to set off their labour against the account already run up.‡

58. Ploughmen, cattlemen, yardmen, and carters, frequently receive part of their wages in kind. It is sometimes difficult to say whether the payments in kind made to these men are in lieu of a certain part of their cash wages, or whether they are given as perquisites. No doubt in some cases they receive perquisites (paragraph 56) and in other cases certain definite payments in kind are agreed upon as part of their remuneration for services rendered. Thus a cottage free, which these men often have, and turf, come under the denomination of payments in kind and not perquisites.

Herds are almost invariably paid the greater part of their wages in kind in all these Unions. These payments usually consist of free cottages, land, the right to graze cattle, horses and sheep, also free turf, milk, butter, &c.

59. Men are seldom paid extra for working overtime, but they are not frequently required to do this, except sometimes at hay and corn harvest. Some employers allow the men to come later next morning if they have worked beyond their usual time the night before.

---

* In the Delvin Union mowing at hay and corn harvests lasts about 12 weeks.

† Mr. [illegible], a farmer on Cape Clear Island, considers that his men each cost him 10s. a week in food. They get salt beef four or five days a week, and bacon and fish the other days. They also get potatoes, milk, bread, butter, and tea.

‡ In a certain county I visited, a parish priest told me of a relieving officer who gave outdoor relief to those who agreed to work on his land.

D 2

THE AGRICULTURAL LABOURER.

In the Westport Union the Earl of Lucan and Lord John Browne pay a quarter day's wages for an hour or two hours overtime.

In the Delvin Union the Earl of Longford's men are paid 1s. 4d. for two hours overtime at harvest, and Major Pollard Urquhart's men are given porter.

Wages earned in other employments besides agriculture. Westport, par. 42. Castlereagh, pars. 36, 37. Skibbereen, pars. 11, 41. Delvin, par. 12.

60. As the four unions are purely agricultural districts, there are few occupations except agriculture at which money can be earned.

In all the unions, but particularly in Westport, a considerable trade in turf is carried on by the small holders, who bring large quantities of it in creels on donkeys' backs to Westport for sale. Also an enormous number of eggs are bought from the small holders in three unions by egg merchants, who send them to London, Liverpool, Manchester, and other large centres. In the Westport Union the people living on the coast sell seaweed to those who are further inland, besides using it as manure themselves. A little seaweed is sold in the Skibbereen Union, but the people usually keep it for their own land.

In the Westport Union a good deal of kelp is made from the seaweed by the peasants. This is used in the manufacture of iodine and also of soap. Some people doubtless make a small addition to their income by making and selling "potheen."

In the Westport Union something is made by fishing, but there it is said that the want of suitable harbours, piers, boats, nets, and gear render fishing impracticable as an industry.

In the Westport, Castlereagh, and Skibbereen Unions a little money is made by weaving, spinning, knitting, and sewing.

Skibbereen, par. 14.

In the Skibbereen Union a successful mackerel fishery is carried on in the summer and autumn, which gives a great deal of remunerative employment.

Westport, par. 40. Castlereagh, par. 37.

From the Westport and Castlereagh Unions a great many of the small holders and their sons and daughters go to England or Scotland to work on farms, some of them remaining away for as long as nine months in the year. (*See* paragraph 14.)

Annual earnings of ordinary labourers (regular men). Summary, App. 1.

61. It is a matter of considerable difficulty to ascertain the actual annual earnings of ordinary labourers attached to the staff of a farm, whether they are cottagers, or small holders, or their sons, because so few farmers keep books, and the men themselves keep no record, though they can make a rough estimate by deducting Catholic holidays and a certain number of days for sickness and wet weather, if they have lost any.

In many cases it would be misleading to quote the annual cash earnings of a small holder or his son as instancing his pecuniary position, for he may have voluntarily stayed away from his employment a number of days in the year to work on his own land, or perhaps for the purpose of going to England or Scotland, or in the Skibbereen Union, for the fishing.

The following are instances of the annual earnings of men who work for the same farmer. Some lose time in wet weather and some do not:—

Westport, par. 12, App. A, 5.

In the Westport Union Lord John Browne's men average about 23*l.* a year, though a few make up to 26*l.* by piecework. Some of them are small holders' sons and others living in cottages at 10*d.* a week.

A reference to Westport, Appendix A. 5, will show the annual earnings of two youths, the sons of two small holders, on about 6 acres of tillage land, and with the right of grazing cattle on a mountain. One earned 13*l.* 13*s.* 9*d.* and the other 11*l.* 17*s.* They both lost time in wet weather, in sickness, and on Catholic holidays.

Castlereagh, par. 38, App. A. 3.

In the Castlereagh Union a large farmer gives from his books the annual earnings of two men, who pay no rent for their cottages. One came to 20*l.* 13*s.* 1*d.*, and the other to 21*l.* 18*s.* 6*d.*

On Mr. Sandford's property a weekly labourer, with a cottage free and half an acre of land, earned in a year 23*l.* 8*s.*; another with a cottage, half an acre of land, and half an acre of turf, 21*l.* 5*s.* Another weekly labourer with no house or land, 31*l.* 4*s.*, but he had 12*s.* a week. Another who could build and earned 14*s.* a week made 32*l.* 11*s.* 3*d.* This man rents a house and 6 or 7 acres of land.

On The O'Conor Don's property the annual earnings of a weekly labourer came to 22*l.* 8*s.* 5½*d.*

Skibbereen, par. 12, App. A. 2.

In the Skibbereen Union I was unable to obtain the annual earnings of the labourers from books, but they may be fairly estimated at between 20*l.* and 23*l.* 10*s.* In this Union perquisites and payment in kind are not uncommon.

Delvin, par. 46, App. A. 4.

In the Delvin Union the annual earnings may be estimated at between 20*l.* and 22*l.* on the farms.

The Agricultural Labourer.

The annual earnings of six of the Earl of Longford's men have been supplied to me, and they vary from 19*l.* 8*s.* 8*d.* to 28*l.* 10*s.* The two men who earned these sums were absent on their own business for 24 days and 8 days respectively.

Annual earnings of odd men.

62. The annual earnings of odd men are impossible to obtain from books as they work for several different farmers in the year, and themselves keep no record. They are generally small holders, or their sons; but in the Castlereagh, Skibbereen, and Delvin Unions there are a certain number who have to make their livelihood exclusively by agricultural employment. The odd men who live in the towns in these unions are frequently badly off, because their employment is irregular, and because they often live in infamously bad houses with no land.

The odd men in the Skibbereen and Delvin Unions are often paid a higher rate of wage in the summer than the men in the staff of the farms in all four unions; they can also earn 2*s.* 6*d.* a day, sometimes with food in addition, for mowing, and between 3*s.* 6*d.* and 5*s.* a day if this work is undertaken by the piece (*see* paras. 49, 53).

In the Westport Union I could obtain no evidence as to the annual earnings of odd men, but two made the following statements:—

Owen Corcoran (aged 47) says:—"I have no land and only my own labour to "depend on. I am now labouring for Mr. Burke (a farmer) at 8*s.* a week, but if he "don't pay me 9*s.* after to-morrow I'll quit. I think he'll give it to me. Last "summer I cut 20 acres of hay for him at 6*s.* From the middle of last November "(for about three months) I was working on my own account cutting rods for "thatching houses. I also worked from March 1 to May 1, 1892, on the Achill "Railway. I then earned 16*s.* a week at piece-work."

Pat Corcoran (aged 21) lives on a small holding of a few acres with his mother, brother, and sister, says:—"I get my living by working for farmers here for about "six months. For the last three years I have been harvesting in England. I go in "June and stay until potato lifting is over at the end of November. I don't work "here (for Mr. Burke, a farmer) in the winter, but for my mother, who has four acres, "half tillage and half grass."

The odd men in Castlereagh told me they averaged three or four days a week all the year round. Assuming they work four days a week at the following payments, 156 days at 1*s.* 3*d.*, 108 days at 1*s.* 6*d.*, and 48 days at 2*s.* 6*d.* for mowing, their annual earnings amount to 17*l.* 10*s.* In this estimate I have made no allowance for mowing by piece work at which between 3*s.* 6*d.* and 5*s.* can be earned in a day of 12 hours. An odd man who worked on Mr. Sandford's property in 1890 earned 16*l.* 8*s.*

Castlereagh, par. 18. Skibbereen, par. 42. Delvin, par. 47.

In the Delvin Union odd men's annual earnings may be estimated between 22*l.* and 30*l.* These men get a great deal of mowing by piece work, and also earn good wages turf cutting.

Annual earnings of ploughmen. Westport, par. 63. App. A. 3. Castlereagh, par. 38. Skibbereen, pars. 31, 34. Delvin, par. 48. App. A. 1.

63. The annual earnings of ploughmen in the Westport Union may be put at about 31*l.*, and they sometimes get a house extra. There are very few of these men in the Union.

In the Castlereagh Union ploughmen earn between 26*l.* and 30*l.* and often get a cottage and firing free in addition.

In the Skibbereen Union ploughmen can earn between 23*l.* and 30*l.*, and they often get perquisites in addition.

In the Delvin Union ploughmen earn from 23*l.* to 27*l.* They often get allowances in addition, such as cheap cottages, cheap land, free turf, or the grass of a cow.

[illegible]

64. In the Westport Union carters earn between 22*l.* and 26*l.*

In the Castlereagh Union yardmen and cattlemen earn between 26*l.* and 31*l.* In addition they usually have turf free and some of them have free cottages.

In the Delvin Union two of the Earl of Longford's cattlemen earned last year 33*l.* 3*s.* 6*d.* and 21*l.* 12*s.* The former rents a very good house and five acres of land for 4*l.* 15*s.* and gets the grass of a cow for 2*l.* 12*s.* (value 5*l.*)

Annual earnings of hired men. Westport, par. 33. App. A. 3. Castlereagh, pars. 14, 39. Skibbereen, par. 33. Delvin, par. 32.

65. Hired men usually earn between 8*l.* and 16*l.* a year, 10*l.* to 14*l.* being the usual wage. In the Skibbereen Union I met two men who had 12*l.* and the grass of a sheep each. Hired men are always found their lodging, board and washing. Hired boys or lads are paid from 2*l.* and upwards. A hired lad between the age of 14 and 18 is usually paid between 6*l.* and 10*l.* a year.

In paragraph 54 I have referred to the food supplied in the farm house, to which in most cases no exception can be taken as regards quantity or quality, though of course it varies according to the circumstances of the employers. As a general rule the hired men get much better food than the small holders or day men can provide for themselves. It does not seem probable that a farmer can give a man three meals a day under 1*s.*,

D 3

THE AGRICULTURAL LABOURER.

and some say a hired man costs them up to 10s. a week to feed, but taking the former figure, the hired men receive 18*l*. worth of food in the year in addition to their wages. As drinking among the farm servants is fortunately of rare occurrence, the hired men are in a position to save something, as clothes and boots can now be obtained both cheap and durable.*

Earnings of herds.

66. It is very difficult to state what the annual earnings of the herds are, owing to their being usually paid the greater part of their wages in kind, and also because their wages vary according to their duties and responsibilities. I have in the appendices to my reports given instances of these payments in kind and put money values on them which were either supplied by the herds or their employers.

I endeavoured to show what the actual incomes of the herds were at the end of the year, but I found the difficulties too great of correctly estimating the profits on their cattle, calves, sheep, pigs, wool, &c. which they sold, and the value of milk, poultry, eggs and bacon, turf and wool which they consumed or used at home. I have therefore only given the annual profits on cattle, and the present prices of calves, foals, sheep, lambs and pigs, in the several districts, supplied to me either by herds or farmers.

Westport, par. 31, App. A. 1.

In the Westport Union the annual wages in cash and allowances, of seven herds, vary from 30*l*. to 57*l*. 7*s*. One of these herds calculated that his gross income came to 80*l*. a year, but that after he had paid two assistants, he was worth about 47*l*.

Castlereagh, par. 30, App. A. 4.

In the Castlereagh Union the annual earnings in cash, and allowances, of five herds vary from 31*l*. 10*s*. to 70*l*. 16*s*.

Mr. Flanagan, of Tomona, Tulsk, reckons that the annual earnings of herds, who are paid according to a scale agreed on after a strike in 1881 (Castlereagh, paragraph 55), are as follows:—A herd on a farm under 100 acres 48*l*., on a farm over 100 and under 150 acres 68*l*., and on a farm over 150 acres 76*l*.

If the profits these men make on their cattle, calves, sheep, pigs, foals, &c. could be ascertained, and the value of the produce consumed by themselves estimated, the result would show that their actual incomes are very comfortable ones.

Delvin, par. 23, App. A. 3.

In the Delvin Union the annual earnings in cash and allowances of eight herds, vary between 29*l*. and 80*l*., but what their actual incomes really amount to can only be very roughly estimated.

The present time is a bad one for the herds, as the prices of stock and sheep are so low, but those who keep pigs have doubtless done well with them.†

Salaries of stewards. Summary, App. 1.

67. The income of stewards depends much on the size of the estate or farm on which they are employed.

In the Westport Union there are only *four* stewards. Lord John Browne informs me, that generally speaking, a steward on a small estate in Mayo gets about 30*l*. a year, a house, a small bit of land, generally the keep of a cow and sometimes fuel.

A steward employed on a property, whose position was more that of a foreman, estimated his income, which was paid partly in cash and partly in kind at 39*l*.

Lord John Browne's head steward gets 100*l*. a year, a house, half an acre of land and manure, and the keep of cow.

In the Castlereagh Union the stewards' incomes vary from 50*l*. to 90*l*.

One steward, paid partly in cash and partly in kind, near Castlereagh gets 90*l*., a house, the grass of two cows, and fuel.

In the Skibbereen Union a steward tells me his wages are 58*l*. 10*s*., a house, 4 tons of coal, 2 lbs. of butter a week, and as much milk and potatoes as he requires.

In the Delvin Union stewards are usually paid between 80*l*. and 100*l*. a year, paid partly in cash and partly in kind.

The Earl of Longford's steward at Pakenham Hall gets 120*l*., a house, vegetables and potatoes, and some dairy produce.

Family earnings.

68. It is frequently the case that several men from the same family on a small holding go out to different farms, or perhaps to the same employer to work for wages, but their attendance is not always regular, partly because during certain periods of the year they have to attend to their own land, or perhaps because their services are not always required.

In the Westport Union I came across a good many instances of a father and two or even three sons working irregularly for the same employer, and one or two of the sons and a daughter going to English or Scotch farms as well for a certain time.

---

* Mr. Michael Kelly of Castlereagh, a large wool buyer, who is also a tradesman and farmer, says that a warm suit of clothes costs [illegible]. Strong boots are about [illegible] a pair. Many of the people in the West have their clothes, shirts, stockings, &c. made at home, spun from the wool of their sheep and woven by weavers in the village.

† Michael MacDonagh, a cattleman in Mayo, says:—"The herds are twice as well off as the tenants."

In the Castlereagh Union Mr. Flanagan, of Tomona, gives me the combined earnings of a small tenant and his sons in his employ as 63l. 14s. 3d., and another with two sons as 68l. 16s. 2d. A man and two sons in the employment of Mr. Sandford, Castlereagh, earned in 1892 47l. 9s. 1d. They were provided with a cottage, half an acre of land and half an acre of turf bank.

In the Skibbereen Union a family regularly employed by the Dean of Ross, consisting of a man and his four sons, aged 21, 18, 15, and 10 years, earn 1l. 10s. 6d. a week between them, or 79l. 6s. a year, unless they lose money through illness. In addition they have a house free, as much ground for potatoes as they can manage, and the use of a cow for 3s. a week with all grass, hay and straw provided, and the right to the calf.

In the Delvin Union a family, consisting of a man and three sons aged 20, 18 and 15 in the employment of the Earl of Longford, earned, in 1892, 69l. 4s. 11d. They were absent 98 days in the year on their own business and not through illness.

Another family in the same employment consisting of a man and two sons aged 16 and 13, earned 53l. 10s. in the same year. These men were absent about 14 days in the year on their own business and not through illness.

Both these families have good cottages on Lord Longford's property for 3l. 5s. a year, including 1 acre 3 roods of land, and they each have the grass of a cow for 2l. 12s., value 5l., and turf free.

V.—Cottage Accommodation.

69. There does not appear to be any scarcity in the supply of cottages. In many parts, especially in the Skibbereen Union, old ruined houses and cottages bear testimony to the decreased population since the great famine. In 1891 there were in the Westport, Castlereagh, Skibbereen and Delvin Unions 282, 172, 289, and 150 uninhabited houses respectively.

Since 1891 a good many Union Cottages have been built by the guardians in the Skibbereen and Delvin Unions, and this has probably increased the number of uninhabited houses in those unions. In the former there are now 42 in course of construction and in the latter 27.

70. In the Westport Union the houses or cottages are chiefly situated in hamlets, or villages, and are often crowded together as if there were a lack of space, which certainly does not appear to be the case. As the people build their own houses they can choose their own sites on the holdings within certain limits, so they evidently prefer the present system. Doubtless they are frequently influenced by the proximity of the road or track.

In the Castlereagh Union a great many of the houses are in villages.

In the Skibbereen Union, although many of the houses are situated in villages, a number are built in more isolated spots, and there are some on farms, besides the Union Cottages.

In the Delvin Union, though a great many are built in villages, there are more detached houses than in any of the other unions, which is due partly to the erection of Union Cottages, partly to there being cottages on some of the farms, and to several large estate owners having built cottages on their estates.

71. As a general rule men who work regularly for the same employer have not far to go to their work, as small holders or labourers usually work for employers who live near their homes.

Generally speaking, two miles is the greatest distance the men live from their employment. Certainly the majority of those I met lived within a mile.

Doubtless odd men, who chiefly live in villages and who work whenever they can get employment, have sometimes to walk long distances, and there are more of these men in the Delvin Union than in the others.

72. Speaking generally, from the evidence I was able to collect, and from my own observations, I believe that the houses in the Westport Union are much the worst. Next in order of demerit come the houses in the Castlereagh and Skibbereen Unions, but on the whole the housing is better in Skibbereen, owing to the Labourers' Acts having been put into operation.

The best houses are in the Delvin Union. There the small holders' houses are better than those in the other three unions, and they have the additional advantage that no cattle or pigs are allowed to be kept in them, which is frequent in the Westport Union, and by no means uncommon in the Castlereagh and Skibbereen Unions. Again, the guardians in the Delvin Union have built Union Cottages, and there are several large estate owners who have erected excellent houses on their properties, without regard to obtaining a direct return on their outlay.

73. In the Westport Union there are practically no labourers' cottages in the ordinary sense of the word, as the men who work as agricultural labourers are either small holders or their sons. Almost the only class of men who live entirely by working for wages are the herds, whose houses are as a general rule much superior to the ordinary houses of the small holders.

The houses of the people are frequently deplorable, but there seems to be little chance of improvement so long as the present system of the tenants building their own houses continues. It is of course impossible for a man who is but an illiterate small holder, or labourer, with no knowledge of building, to make himself a decent house, and even if he had the knowledge, monetary considerations would compel him to run it up for the minimum cost. I also venture to think that this system has been to a certain extent responsible for friction between landlords and tenants in cases of eviction for non-payment of rent for the holdings, because the latter consider, no matter what the merits or demerits may be of each particular case, that it is a great injustice to force a man to leave the house he has built with his own hands.

Another stumbling block to improvement in house accommodation lies in the fact that there are no good houses in the union, and so the people have nothing better than the present ones to imitate.

I have in paragraph 5 of this report and also in paragraph 10 and Appendix A. 11 of my report on the Westport Union, given a full description of these cottages.*

74. But ill-constructed, badly repaired, and comfortless, as many of the cabins are in the Westport Union, they cannot be compared in wretchedness, in my judgment, to some of the miserable hovels inhabited by labourers in the comparatively small country towns of Castlereagh and Skibbereen.

A cabin in the country districts, however humble, has, as a rule, four advantages: fresh air, water, turf, and land, which provides potatoes and vegetables, and enables a cow, pig, and fowls to be kept. The cottages in these towns have none of these advantages, with the exception perhaps of water. There is frequently less space in them, and as regards repair their state is often worse than that of the worst cabin. Moreover, the rents of these places, which in some cases are quite unfit for human beings to inhabit, are often as much as 6*l.* 10*s.* a year, which represents the rent of a holding as large as 25 or 30 acres within a mile or two of Castlereagh, though of course much depends on the land. Still, I think that a man who rented four Irish acres of good land a mile from Castlereagh at 4*l.* 10*s.* and spent 37*l.* in building a house on it, would be getting much more for his money than the man who hired a wretched hovel in the town without a scrap of garden at 2*s.* 6*d.* a week (6*l.* 10*s.* a year).

The following are two examples of cottages in the town of Castlereagh:—No. 1 is very old and in bad repair, it is situated down a side alley and contains one room with no back door, measuring 14 feet by 14. In this room live and sleep a man, his wife, two grown up daughters, and a small boy. There is not a scrap of garden, and no closet. Rent, 2*s.* 6*d.* a week.

No. 2 is also very old and in very bad repair, it has two rooms on the ground floor both 14 feet by 14. In the living room sleep two sons aged 21 and 16. In the bedroom, in the same bed, sleep a man, his wife, two girls aged 11 and 6, and a baby, while on the bare clay floor of the same room immediately under the window, there sleep a female lodger with her two children, a boy of eight and a baby. Rent, 2*s.* a week.

In the town of Skibbereen there are some cottages equally bad, but those I visited were only rented at 1*s.* or 1*s.* 6*d.* a week, though I was told by labourers there were some at 2*s.* 6*d.*

---

* Lord John Browne, who has seen my report on the Westport Union, County Mayo, writes as follows with reference to the cottages:—"I think you are mistaken in conveying that it is usual for cattle, pigs, &c., to be "kept in the houses and rooms inhabited by the people. You must have chiefly visited the very poorest villages "and houses. In such, where the people have been 'left alone by the landlords,' they have much subdivided "the land, resulting in a state of poverty and congestion, for which there is no remedy except emigration or "migration. But, generally speaking, the people have stables and pigstyes separate from their houses. A "very large proportion of the country people's houses have three rooms, i.e., a kitchen and two bedrooms."

Lord John Browne, as a resident of long standing, as Chairman of the Grand Jury, and as an ex-Chairman of the Board of Guardians, is a most valuable witness as regards this question, and if, as it seems, I have given in my Westport report, paragraph 10, and Appendix A. 11, a too unfavourable impression of the condition of the houses in the district, I can only say that I came to these conclusions, after an exhaustive inquiry in all parts of the union.

In the little town of Delvin, which is far smaller than either Castlerea/gh or Skibbereen, there are several very old houses in bad repair. Two of them I visited have no windows at all, so when the door is shut they have neither light nor air.

75. It is satisfactory to be able to say that both in the Castlereagh and Skibbereen Unions, and more particularly in the Delvin Union, there are good cottages on some of the properties.

In this latter union the Earl of Longford, Major Pollard Urquhart, Sir M. Chapman, Mr. Fetherstonhaugh, and the Hon. G. Greville Nugent, have excellent labourers' cottages with a quarter of an acre to six acres of land each at very cheap rents.

The Earl of Longford's 30 cottages on his Pakenham Hall Estate are models of what cottages should be, and can be compared with those on such well-managed properties as the Duke of Grafton's, the Marquess of Bristol's, and the Earl of Cadogan's in the eastern counties of England. They are built in blocks of two or four at a cost of 350*l.* the pair, or 700*l.* for a block of four, and are made of brick with slated roofs. They each contain two rooms and a larder on the ground floor, and three bedrooms above. Each house has, at a convenient distance, a cowshed built of brick and slate, a pigstye, a hen-house, and a closet. There is also a garden of one rood or a rood and a half, and in addition, good meadow land varying in size from about three to six statute acres. The rents of these cottages, including the land, are from 3*l.* 5*s.* to 5*l.*

76. The Skibbereen and Delvin Unions are the only unions visited by me in which the Labourers' Acts have been put into operation, there being no union cottage in the Westport or Castlereagh Unions.

The Westport Union, where many of the houses are probably as bad as can be found anywhere in Ireland, would seem *primâ facie* to be a locality where such acts would be taken advantage of by the people, but there are several reasons for their not being put into operation in this Union, or indeed, throughout the province of Connaught. On this point I quote the opinion expressed to me by a gentleman who has a most intimate knowledge of the conditions under which the peasantry in the West of Ireland exist: "I do not think that the Act has not been put into operation because the people do not "come under the definition of 'agricultural labourers.' As a matter of fact, it would "be a very simple matter for any small occupier to 'qualify' as an agricultural "labourer within the meaning of the more recent Labourers' Acts. But the truth is "the people themselves never seem to make use of the Act. They could not get an "increase to their holding as an allotment, and therefore all they could get would be "the cottage, and they would infinitely prefer to live in their own thatched cabins on "the holdings to paying a second rent to the guardians for a slated cottage provided "under the Act.

"In some instances a son of a small occupier, when he marries, would perhaps "prefer getting a cottage or allotment, to emigrating or living with his parents, but "if he succeeded in acquiring compulsorily half an acre from one of his neighbour's "small holdings, a feud would be given birth to, which decades of skull splitting would "not allay.

"But furthermore, the financial state of these western electoral divisions is such "that the guardians and ratepayers would discountenance any additional charge being "put on the rates, and it is very doubtful whether the authorities would like to "sanction schemes for increasing the congestion and pauperism of the districts, by "allowing houses to be built for the sons of the occupiers of small holdings, who could "not get employment in the locality."

77. In the Skibbereen Union the guardians have built 163 Union Cottages, and another 42 are in the course of construction. Some houses have all the rooms on the ground floor while others have two storeys. The former have three rooms and a scullery, and are let at 9*d.* a week, and the latter have two living rooms and two bedrooms and are rented at 1*s.* a week. They also have closets and pigstyes, and half an acre (statute) of garden, and it is proposed to provide some of the new ones with an acre at the same rental.

In the Delvin Union there are 154 Union Cottages, and in addition 27 are now building. Of those already built, 114 have half a statute acre of land with a pigstye and closet each, while 40 have an acre and 25 perches, with a cowhouse and closet. Of the 27 now building, 25 have a statute acre of land with cowhouses and closets.

The advantages of having a comfortable house with sufficient land to keep a pig, and to provide potatoes and vegetables, while the ratepayers are liberally contributing towards the rent, are obvious, and, moreover, their existence must tend to raise the standard of cottage building in the country, and give the people more ambition to acquire decent homes. The extension of the operation of these Acts doubtless depends on the willingness of the ratepayers to do what so many English landlords have done, and are doing, namely, to put their hands in their pockets, and give a subscription towards paying the rent for those who otherwise could not possibly afford to inhabit houses of such a class.

78. In my report on the Skibbereen Union, I have referred to complaints made by farmers as to damages caused by the depredations of the labourer's animals on their land. No doubt in some cases this is a source of serious mischief and annoyance. A parish priest pointed out that a man, who with but half an acre keeps a cow, must feed it at his neighbour's expense. He stated that the people drive both cows and donkeys on the farmer's land at night, or when they are at market, and that consequently the farmers were justified in grumbling.

Another complaint some farmers make of the Act is that they find it an annoyance to have men put upon their land who will never do a day's work for them. One farmer said that he considered it a very one-sided arrangement that he should have a man on his farm for whose cottage he was, as a ratepayer, paying, without the advantage of securing his services.

It was also stated that labourers were sometimes put upon farms for the purpose of annoying political opponents.

79. In the houses both of small holders and labourers, which frequently do not consist of more than two rooms, overcrowding must of necessity frequently exist. In the appendices to my reports on the four unions I have given various instances of this, taken at random in course of driving through the country.

The most extreme case I met with was on Cape Clear Island, where, in a house consisting of a living room, two bedrooms, and two lofts, nineteen people were living, eight of whom were sixteen years of age and upwards.

80. Although so many of the houses in the country districts have but two rooms, in which the family have to live and sleep, and which are also used by cattle or pigs, the ventilation is as a rule not bad. This is because both the rooms are on the ground floor, with the front door, and sometimes a back one as well, opening directly into them. Again, a peat fire burns day and night, which creates a good draught, especially as many of the chimneys are very wide ones. Probably the peat smoke, which is often so thick in the houses, counteracts much of the stuffy smell which might otherwise be noticed, and at the same time acts as a wholesome disinfectant for the impurities arising from the excrement of cattle, pigs, or horses. After having had a large experience of cottage bedrooms in Norfolk and Suffolk, when reporting there for the Royal Commission on Labour in the summer of 1892, I can unhesitatingly say that the bedrooms in the older cottages in England are far worse ventilated than any of the rooms in an Irish cottage or cabin, notwithstanding the presence of cattle and pigs.

81. Throughout the Westport Union it appeared to be the general rule for livestock and poultry to be kept in the houses.* The same custom is common in the Castlereagh and Skibbereen Unions, but not so extensively, while in the Delvin Union it is extinct, owing to the action of Board of Guardians.

It is to be regretted that all Boards of Guardians do not take the same steps. In the Westport Union, where no union cottages have been built, and where many of the cabins are wretched in all respects, it would at any rate be an improvement, and I venture to think a feasible one, to keep animals out of the houses.

In my report on the Westport Union, I suggested that probably many of the people in the west of Ireland would regard such a proceeding as an unnecessary revolution, and further that many of the people might be too poor to make sheds outside. But the building of a stone wall, in a country where stone is so plentiful, between the living room and the space inhabited by the cattle, and the opening of a new door, would be but a small expense, and this it seems could be accomplished by putting the Labourers' Acts into operation.† At any rate such a condition might be imposed in the case of all new houses, as is already done in the Union Cottages in other districts. I also doubt whether the social condition of these people could be really improved, so long as they are allowed to build these miserable cabins, with no supervision from a sanitary authority, and to be allowed to keep animals of every description in them.

---

* *See* note to paragraph 73.

† In the memorandum on the Labourers' Acts prepared by Mr. William C. Little, Senior Assistant Commissioner, paragraph 27 says:—

"The power of taking over existing houses which are capable of repair with the object of fitting them for habitation has, it seems, been little used, the total number acquired and repaired up to the 31st of March last being only 35."

Two doctors informed me that skin diseases were attributable to the keeping of cattle in the houses, and one of them very strongly deprecated the custom on sanitary grounds.

The Agricultural Labourer.

Drainage. Westport, par. 59. Castlereagh, par. 46. Skibbereen, par. 51. Delvin, par. 57.

82. There is no system of drainage in any of the country districts. Surface drains of some sort are usually made by the owners of the houses, but they are frequently full of stagnant water and sewage, and consequently offensive. The small holders in the Westport, Castlereagh, and Skibbereen Unions keep their manure heaps directly opposite their front doors, which it is not in the least necessary for them to do, but they find it less trouble to fling the old bedding and manure out of the door instead of carrying it elsewhere, which is another bad result of keeping livestock in the house. In wet weather foul manure water flows from the heaps against the house and sometimes trickles inside, thus causing an unpleasant smell. In some cases where the manure has been taken away, large deep pools of stagnant drainage water are left, to which the people appear profoundly indifferent.

In some of the towns the system of drainage might be improved. The sanitary inspection in the towns of Castlereagh and Skibbereen might with advantage be more thorough, for I saw drainage water and refuse heaps close to labourers' cottages, which ought not to have been allowed there.

Closets in the houses of the small holders and labourers in the country districts, and also in the towns, are conspicuous by their absence. In localities where there is no system of drainage, no sanitary supervision, and a total indifference among the people to sanitary matters, this may possibly be an advantage, and be the means of avoiding fevers and other diseases. In the towns, however, where there is some system of drainage, and where sanitary supervision could more easily be exercised, it seems a reprehensible state of things that houses should be built without them, and it must cause much inconvenience, especially in cases of illness.

Closets are always attached to the cottages built by the guardians both in the Skibbereen and Delvin Unions, as is also frequently the case in those now built by landowners on their estates. At the present time the people are so long accustomed to their absence that they cannot be induced to use them for the proper purpose, and they are very constantly used as hen houses, pigsties, or for storing potatoes and turf, or perhaps locked up.

Water supply. [illegible]

83. In the country districts the people seem well supplied with good water near their houses. On this subject I heard very few complaints indeed as regards quantity or quality, though in some cases people had to go some distance for it.

Ownership and tenure. Westport, par. 62. Castlereagh, par. 44. Delvin, par. 61.

84. In the Westport, Castlereagh, and Skibbereen Unions there are, as I have previously stated, but few labourers' cottages. Very few are ever let with farms, except in the case of the herds' houses; the landowners who happen to have any preferring to keep them in their own hands and let them direct. The herds under tenant farmers hold their houses from them as part payment of their wages and their occupation of them ceases with their employment.

In the Delvin Union there are some farms with labourers' cottages let with them, but as a general rule the estate owners there let the cottages direct to the labourers.

In this union I asked several men who rented cottages on properties where they were employed, if they had any objection to having their employer for their landlord, and they all replied in the negative, saying they had good cottages with the additional advantages of having them kept in proper repair, and of not being unduly pressed for rent.

The cottages in some of the towns and villages not unfrequently belong to small owners, and in these cases are often conspicuous for a high rent and absence of proper repairs.

Conditions of tenure. Westport, par. 58. Castlereagh, par. 44. Delvin, par. 59.

85. A labourer or a herd living in a cottage let to him by a tenant farmer, or by an estate owner, is of course bound to quit it when he leaves his employment, a condition which is necessary for the employer, and still more so for the convenience of the labourer's successor. In the Unions I visited, there were no landholders who had more cottages for labourers than they absolutely required to house those working for them.

Period of tenure. Westport, par. 58. Castlereagh, par. 19. Delvin, 62.

86. The period of tenure greatly varies in all the unions. The length of the tenancies of the herds corresponds with the length of their engagements.

Ordinary labourers, and men in charge of animals in country districts, hold their cottages for periods varying from a week to a year, those living on properties generally getting the longer notices. The cottages in towns are most frequently held on monthly tenancies.

In the case where a cottage with land is given in part payment of wages, though the notice is nominally a weekly or monthly one, the nature of the agreement creates a necessity for the tenant to remain in his situation as long as possible.

The cottages built by the guardians are let by the month.

87. In the Castlerea, Skibbereen, and Delvin Unions, rents greatly vary, but their amount is no guide to the accommodation provided, to the state of repair, or to the amount of land let with them.

For instance, take some of the miserable hovels with two rooms and no garden in the town of Castlerea, let at rents up to 2s. 6d. a week, and compare them with some of Mr. Sandford's two-roomed cottages half a mile away, made of stone, plaster and slate, and provided with half an acre of land at 1s. 6d. a week,* or compare their rentals with those of the small holdings outside the town. (See Castlerea, paragraph 49.)

Again, take some of the labourers' cottages in Skibbereen let for 1s. to 2s. 6d. a week (see paragraph 74) and compare them with the excellent cottages built by the guardians with three or four rooms, a scullery, outhouses, and half an acre or an acre of land apiece at rents of 9d. or 1s. a week.

Or, again, in the Delvin Union, take the instance of inferior cottages in Castle Pollard, with little or no garden, rented at between 3l. and 5l. a year, and those of the Earl of Longford's a mile away, costing 350l. a pair to build, provided with a rood of garden and three acres or more of meadow land for 3l. 10s.

In the Skibbereen and Delvin Unions I met labourers who said the rent of the Union Cottages was too high. Of course any rent seems high to a man who may be earning 7s. 6d. a week irregularly in the winter, but to grumble at the rent when considered with regard to its proportion to the cost of building seems absurd. It must also be borne in mind that the labourers are provided with land which enables them to grow vegetables, and keep pigs, goats, hens, and ducks, privileges which are worth more to them than the rent they pay.

In the Delvin Union some of the tenants of the Union Cottages got a year into arrear and in some cases two years. The guardians have had to evict several for non-payment of rent.

88. The cost of cottages built according to modern ideas is considerable. The Earl of Longford's, built of stone, brick and slate, which were the best I saw, cost 350l. a pair, or 700l. a block of four, including outhouses, sheds, pigstyes, and closets. Some new ones in the same union recently built by Major Pollard Urquhart, made of laths, plaster and slate, cost 75l. each, or 150l. the pair.

The union cottages cost on an average about 106l. each to build, and the land about 32l. 10s., bring the total cost of each to 138l. 10s. (For annual cost to ratepayers see Delvin, note to paragraph 60.)

In the Westport Union a labourer's cottage costs between 50l. and 60l., and a herd's house about 65l. A small holder's house costs about 16l., excluding the cost of labour. The people build their houses themselves, with the assistance of their friends.

In the Skibbereen Union some good cottages recently built by Captain Morgan, of Bunalun, cost him between 90l. and 120l. apiece.

The actual cost of building the Union Cottages erected there comes to 75l. each, but the total cost, which includes payment for the land and other expenses, is 120l.

89. When the valuation of a holding is 4l. or under, the landlord pays the rates, but when it is over 4l. landlord and tenant each pay half, while the tenant always pays the county cess. In the case of cottages let to labourers, the landlords, or the guardians in the case of those built under the Acts, always pay the rates.

VI.—Land, Gardens, Cow-Acre, Cow Grass.

90. In the Westport, Castlerea, and Skibbereen Unions, the small holders and cottagers seldom have flower gardens, the space generally occupied by the garden in English cottages being monopolised by the manure heaps, and also used as a run by pigs and fowls, but then, of course, the small holders, and in many cases the labourers, have land adjacent on which they grow potatoes and vegetables for consumption.

In the towns of Castlerea and Skibbereen many of the wretched houses there have not a scrap of garden or even of back yard, and thus all the washing has to be done in the house, and the potatoes, tools, &c. have to be stored there, while the rooms are not nearly so well ventilated as those which have a back door opening out into a garden or yard.

---

* One of these tenants sublets his half acre for 3l. a year.

THE AGRICULTURAL LABOURER.

In the Delvin Union the cottages in the country districts are usually supplied with gardens. The cottages on some of the estates have gardens, or land between half an acre and six acres in extent.

The Union Cottages in the Skibbereen and Delvin Unions mostly have half an acre of land and some as much as an acre.

[illegible]

91. In all the four Unions those who want land hire "con-acre" from farmers. As a rule about half an acre to an acre is taken, but sometimes more.

Of course the price depends on the quality of the land and also whether it is manured by the lessor or lessee, and whether one or two crops are taken off it.

[illegible]

92. In some cases both landlords and farmers let the labourers have some land or potato ground free, or at a cheap rental. It is not an uncommon thing to meet with farmers who plough their men's land or who lend their plough and carts for manure.

There are instances of landlords and in some cases of farmers, particularly in the Delvin Union, who let land with the cottages and charge very little or nothing for it.

Cow grass. Delvin, par. 62.

93. In the Delvin Union there are landlords and farmers who are willing to keep a cow for their men, or give the grass of one or more, at considerably less than the usual price.

For instance, the Earl of Longford allows any of his men to have the grass of a cow for 12 months at 2*l*. 10*s*. (value 6*l*.). As they have from 3 to 6 acres of land with their cottages, they can get plenty of hay for their cattle in the winter. Also they can have the grass of a two-year-old at 2*l*. a year (value 2*l*. 10*s*.), the grass of a yearling at 1*l*. 5*s*. (value 1*l*. 10*s*.), and the grass of calves at 5*s*. each.

[illegible]

94. It was frequently stated in these Irish Unions, as in those I visited in the North of England, that small holders and their sons and daughters have to work far harder and for longer hours than labourers. Mr. Jack, steward to the Earl of Longford at Pakenham Hall, informs me that the small farmers on 25 acres in that neighbourhood keep one horse and borrow another from a neighbour, if they require it.

Livestock kept. Westport, par. 61. Castlerea, par. 43. Skibbereen, par. 61. Delvin, par. 72. Summary, App. A. 10. A. 11.

95. In the Castlerea, Skibbereen, and Delvin Unions it is usual for labourers who have sufficient ground to keep pigs, fowls, ducks, geese, and sometimes cows and goats.* In the Westport Union the labourers, who are small holders, or their sons, of course keep live stock, as they are their chief means of livelihood.

In the districts I visited in Ireland more labourers keep livestock than in those I visited in the eastern and northern counties of England. Possibly the reasons for this are that the Irish labourer is worse paid, and hence he has to add to his income by every other possible means; that he has in many districts either more land of his own or there is waste land on which his pigs or fowls can wander, and also the large egg trade with England ensures a ready sale for his eggs in the market towns.

Occupiers of Union Cottages invariably keep livestock of some description and fowls, as they have half an acre of land or more, and are provided with styes and some with cowhouses.

It will be seen in Summary, App. 11, that the number of livestock and poultry, with the exception of pigs, has considerably increased since 1882, but prices, except in the case of pigs, have greatly decreased.†

VII.—Benefit Societies and Trade Unions.

Benefit societies. Westport, par. 59. Castlerea, par. 51. Skibbereen, par. 56. Delvin, 73.

96. There are no benefit societies of any description in the unions I visited, but if there were it is doubtful if many of the people, particularly in the west, could afford to belong to them. Referring to this subject a herd at Westport said to me:—

"Many of the people would think if they insured their lives they would be hurrying on their death or an illness. That is the sort of people the Irish are."

Irish villages or parishes entirely lack the parish societies, clubs, charities, and other organisations which do so much to assist the poor in England.

In going round the houses of the small holders and labourers it is not infrequent to see people, who are desperately poor themselves, supporting old relations, not necessarily father and mother or grandfather and grandmother, but those of a more remote degree.

The Agricultural Labourer.

On the estates of the Earl of Longford in West Meath, and The O'Donovan in Cork, much is done to promote the comfort and welfare of the labourers. In both cases the men are paid their wages when sick, and when too old to work are pensioned off, and on the Earl of Longford's property a clothing club and a tea club exist, a night school with a competent master, and also a reading room are provided free, while any medical attendance required by those living within the gate lodges can have it gratis.

Trade unions. Westport, par. 59. Castlereagh, par. 55. Skibbereen, par. 58. Delvin, par. 74. Strikes.

97. No trade unions of any sort exist among the agricultural labourers. Possibly this is partly due to the fact that so many of the labourers are small farmers or farmers' sons, who, in their turn, during certain portions of the year are employers of labour themselves, and that in so many instances there is but little social distinction between the employers and employed. Other reasons may be that there are no large arable farms which employ large staffs of regular men, and also that there is not the same system of village life as in England which gives such facilities for organisation.

98. In the Castlereagh Union, and the neighbouring district, there was a strike of herds in 1881 with the object of obtaining higher wages, and in order to resist their demands the employers combined and formed a defence fund. The strike, however, was of short duration as the employers practically acceded to the men's requests, and since that time there has been no discontent or friction. In the neighbourhood of Castlereagh there have been one or two cases of threatened strikes on individual farms for higher wages, which speedily collapsed.

Skibbereen, par. 59.

Ten or twelve years ago there were a few strikes on certain small farms for higher wages, which resulted in some cases in their being raised, but since that time nothing of the sort has been repeated.

In the Westport and Delvin Unions I did not learn that any strikes had ever taken place.

VIII. Relations between Employers and Employed.

Relations between employers and employed. Westport, par. 62, App. B. 4. Castlereagh, par. 64, App. B. 2. Skibbereen, par. 60, App. B. 3. Delvin, par. 75, App. 5.

99. The relations between the labourers and the farmers and stewards appear to be perfectly friendly, as a reference to the evidence of both masters and men in the Appendices to my report will show.

I frequently asked labourers of all classes how they got on with their employers, and what grievances they had, and the majority of them replied, "We get on all right "with our masters, except on the question of wage." Perhaps it is but natural that when a man receives 9s. a week in summer and 7s. 6d. in winter, out of which he has to pay 1s. a week or more for rent, that he should feel aggrieved at the man who pays him this wage. As to the length of hours, the food and lodging provided in the farm houses, or the treatment of the men by the farmers, I could hear no complaints.

In some cases it was most satisfactory to hear how well the two classes agreed together. For instance, a young man, a small holder near Castlereagh, referring to Mr. Vaugh, said: "The men round here are as friendly with him as if they were his own family."

On the other hand, employers usually speak well of the men, though some notice a tendency on the part of the young men to resent being spoken to when in fault, such as coming late in the morning or "skimping" their work.

No doubt a good deal depends on the personal interest an employer takes in his men's welfare outside the commercial bargain he makes with them, whether they in their turn take an interest in his welfare. This has been Mr. Vaugh's experience. He says, "Treat them well and feed them, and then I find they work as well behind your back as before your face."

IX.—The General Condition of the Agricultural Labourer.

General condition of the agricultural labourer.

100. Generally speaking the labourers in the four Unions must have a great struggle for existence. In fact it is marvellous how those in irregular employment can feed and clothe their families at all; when even on farms where employment is regular, of which there are many in the Castlereagh, Skibbereen and Delvin Unions, the problem of making both ends meet must frequently be a difficult one to solve.

It is, however, satisfactory to be able to state that though the wages are low, and many of the houses are bad, the condition of the people has, on the whole, improved during the last 20 years, with the exception of those in the Westport Union.

General condition of the labourers in the Westport Union.

101. In consequence of there being no tillage farms of any size in the Westport Union, there is no continuous employment for labourers. Hence there is no class of men who earn their entire livelihood by working for wages, and their place is taken by small holders or their sons.

As a matter of fact, the most regular employers of the Westport Union labourers are Lancashire, Warwickshire, and Cheshire farmers, who frequently give them work in England for six or nine months in the year. The men return to their families for a few months in the winter, when they do very little, except, perhaps, to assist in ploughing and sowing their land.

The people frequently spin their wool and make clothes for themselves. Large numbers of them are illiterate.

It is very difficult to convey any accurate idea of the position of the small holders. It much depends on the earnings some member or members of their families can make in England, Scotland, or America. Without this extraneous assistance many of them could not support their families on their holdings, even if the rent were paid, situated as they are on unprofitable land, which is rendered the more unproductive by unskilled methods of tillage (see Westport, App. A. ii).

Speaking of those living in the mountain glens, the annual report of the Congested Districts Board for 1892 gives the following pitiable account of their condition:—

"In such mountain glens are to be found people who endure the most comfortless and cheerless lives of all the inhabitants of congested districts in Ireland. In a good year they are little more than free from the dread of hunger, while a complete or partial failure of their crop involves as a consequence proportionately greater or less suffering from insufficient food."

It is stated by those who know the district well that there has been but little improvement, if any, in the condition of the people during the last 20 years, though there was a marked improvement in the preceding period of 20 years. That this should be the case seems strange in face of the following facts, that during the past 10 years the population of the Union has decreased 8·8 per cent. and that during that period the number of cattle and sheep in the country have increased 7·7 and 53·6 per cent. respectively, that rents have been reduced, that wages have slightly risen, and that the prices of food and clothing have materially declined. In my report on the Westport Union (paragraph 61) I have given various reasons why the general condition of the people has not improved notwithstanding these advantages, among which I have mentioned the decline in prices of cattle, sheep and wool, the importation of American flour, the abandonment of the linen trade and the manufacture of flannel, frieze and stockings, and the decreased earnings of those who work in England owing to the conversion of arable land to grass and the introduction of machinery.

102. The labourers in the Castlereagh Union, though better off than those in the Westport Union, frequently live in ill-constructed and dilapidated houses, and suffer from want of employment. The fact that 40·1 per 1,000 of the population were migratory labourers in 1892, and that 17·3 per 1,000 emigrated prove that there is not sufficient employment in the union to support the population. Unlike the Westport Union, there are both landlords and farmers who give regular employment and perquisites in addition to wages.

Clothes are usually purchased in the town of Castlereagh. The people seem more educated than those in the Westport Union. Although it is of frequent occurrence to find cattle in the houses the custom is not so general as in the Westport Union.

During the past 20 years the condition of the labourers and peasantry has improved in the following particulars:—Wages have generally increased by 1s. a week and in some cases by 2s. or 3s.; the prices of food and clothing are considerably cheaper, material reductions have been made in rents, there has been a large increase in the number of stock, and the people have improved their dwellings, though there are no Union Cottages, and but few built by landlords.

Still taking things as they are, the wife of a herd, who is much better off than a labourer, said to me, "It is tight work to live, it is just scraping along," and I feel sure that this generally describes the position of the labourers in this district.

103. The labourers in the Skibbereen Union are in much the same position as those in the Castlereagh Union, but they have the advantage of Union Cottages and also the assistance of the mackerel fishery in the spring and autumn, which possibly may be one reason for there being no migration to English or Scotch farms. It is certainly the case that many of the small holders do not exist solely on the produce of their holdings, and that they receive considerable sums from their relatives and friends in America.

The cottages are about the same as those in the Castlereagh Union, but 153 good cottages have been built by the guardians. It is not uncommon to find live-stock in the houses, though none are kept in the Union Cottages. Clothes are usually bought in

Skibbereen. The diet of the people usually consists of potatoes, fish, bread, butter, tea, and milk. In many parts there are numbers of illiterates.

During the last 20 years wages have increased by 3s. a week, and in some cases 4s.; cottage accommodation has improved owing to the operation of the Labourers' Acts, and in addition the improvements I have noticed in the Castlerea Union have also taken place in this one.

105. The position of the labourers in the Delvin Union is generally much superior to those in the other three Unions. This is not because the rate of wages is higher, but because work is much more regular, perquisites are more frequently given, and cottages are far superior, as the ordinary houses of the country are better built, and no cattle are kept in them, and because good cottages have been erected by both guardians and landlords. Further the land is much more productive.

There is no migration to England and Scotland, and the number of emigrants from the county have been decreasing the last six years. In 1892 they were only 8·7 per 1,000, or about half the proportion of those from the other three unions.

The chief diet of the people is bread, potatoes, bacon, eggs, cabbage, butter, stirabout, tea, and milk. Education is more advanced than in any of the other unions.

During the past 20 years wages have risen between 1s. and 3s. a week, cottage accommodation has greatly improved, owing to building being undertaken by both guardians and landlords, in many cases rents have been reduced, and there has been a large increase in the number of stock in the county.

106. A comparison between the position of the labourers in the districts I visited in Ireland and that of those in the eastern counties in Norfolk and Suffolk may be of interest.

In all the four Irish Unions a man regularly employed on a farm earns about 22*l.* a year. His house may cost him 1*s.* or 1*s.* 6*d.* a week with quarter to half an acre of land, on which he keeps a pig and fowls, and grows potatoes and vegetables. In some cases he may get perquisites such as the grass of a sheep free, or cheap turf, or perhaps a cottage free.

I will now take the worst position as far as I can ascertain it of a man in the Swaffham Union of Norfolk, that is one who loses time in wet weather, gets no piece-work, perquisites, or a garden, and pays a high rent for his cottage:—

	£	s.	d.	£	s.	d.
48 weeks at 11s.*				26	8	0
4 weeks' harvest				7	10	0
				£33	18	0
Less 1s. a week loss by wet weather†	2	12	0			
Rent for cottage at 2s. a week with no garden‡	5	4	0			
				7	16	0
				£26	2	0

It will thus be seen that the Irish labourer after paying his rent of 1*s.* a week has 19*l.* 8*s.* in cash and gets potatoes and vegetables from his garden, and also the profits from his pig and fowls, while the English labourer has 26*l.* 2*s.*, and has to buy his vegetables.

I will now take the position of the labourers on the Earl of Longford's estate at Pakenham Hall, Westmeath, as being the most satisfactory of any who came under my notice in Ireland, and compare it with that of those in the eastern counties in England who are regularly employed on farms or estates where no time is lost through wet weather, where piece-work is given, and where good cottages with gardens are let at a moderate rental.

Two of the Earl of Longford's men, aged 35 and 50, earned in 1892, 25*l.* 3*s.* 9*d.* and 22*l.* 0*s.* 4*d.* The former was paid 10*s.* a week and the latter 8*s.* to 9*s.* 4*d.*, and they both have free turf. They were each absent from their work for 12 days in the year on their own business, otherwise they lost no time. They both have excellent cottages,

* When I visited that district in August 1892 the current rate of weekly wages was 12s., but I understand it has since been reduced to 11s.

† Labourers usually put their possible losses from wet weather at 1s. a week during the year.

‡ Allotments of one eighth of an acre are let about half a mile from the town of Swaffham at a rental not exceeding 2l. an acre. The Union is generally very fairly supplied with them.

with pigstyes and outhouses, and a rood of garden. The former has in addition 1 acre and 3 roods of meadow, and pays 3l. 5s. for house, garden, and land; the latter has 3 acres 1 rood, and pays 8l. 10s. for house, garden, and land. Both these men have the grass of a cow at 2l. 12s. (value 5l.), and they could if they chose keep more at the same rate.

I now give the annual earnings in 1892 of labourers employed on large farms in the Thingoe Union, Norfolk, and Swaffham Union, Norfolk, when wages were 12s. a week.

Employer.	District.	Annual Earnings.	Rent of Cottage.	Garden.
Mr. [illegible] (the Marquis of Bristol's property).	Little Saxham (Suffolk)	35l. to 41l. 7s.	1s. a week.	20 rods to ¼ acre.
Mr. G. [illegible]	Gazeley (Suffolk)	36l. 14s. to 40l. 7s.	1s. 3d. to 1s. 6d. a week.	15 to 20 rods.
Mr. R. [illegible]	Westley (Suffolk)	35l. 17s. 4d.	About 2s. a week	20 rods to ¼ acre.
Lord Amherst of Hackney	Didlington (Norfolk)	35l.	2l. 2s. to 4l. 10s. a year.	Up to ¼ an acre.
Mr. [illegible]	Ashill (Norfolk)	35l.	3l. to 4l. 10s.	10 rods to ¼ acre.
Mr. Clark	Swaffham (Norfolk)	36l.	3l. 10s. to 4l.	¼ acre.

It will thus be seen that the English labourers are much better off, although no doubt Lord Longford's labourers make considerable profits from cattle, pigs, and fowls, which they either keep on the land they rent with their houses, or on Lord Longford's at a cheap rate.

Now, an English labourer in the eastern counties in the position I have described, with an income of 26l. 2s. a year after paying for his cottage, thinks himself very badly off, and so he is, but it is interesting to consider how an Irish labourer on 22l. or 23l., out of which he has to pay 32s. for rent, can support a wife and family.

The Irish labourer does it in this way. He eats a cheaper class of food, spends little or no money on drink,* and dresses worse. He also keeps live stock and poultry, has often the advantage of cheap or free turf, and probably in many cases gets help from America.

The advantage of live stock and poultry to a labourer with a family can be illustrated by referring to the case of one of Lord Longford's ploughmen. This man and one of his boys earn 13s. 6d. a week, which represents a yearly income of 31l. 12s. after paying 3l. 10s. rent for an excellent house and two or three acres of land. His family consists of his wife and eight children, making ten to clothe and feed.

It will be seen that the earnings of this man and his boy come to considerably more than the earnings of most labourers, and yet he says:—"Last year we did not make "both ends meet, and if it had not been for our cow, pigs, and hens we could not have "done. If a labourer has a family he could do with 4 or 5 acres on which he could "keep cattle, and this would be an advantage."

106. In addition to higher wages, the labourers want what is the next most important consideration to them, better homes. Districts already overburdened with rates

probably cannot afford to be further impoverished by building cottages, but they can, without much additional expense, put in motion the machinery they already possess and make the existing houses more habitable (see paragraph 81).

Supervision could be exercised over the building of houses, representations could be made as regards repairs, and regulations could be framed forbidding cattle, pigs, and poultry to be kept in the dwellings. Pools of stagnant manure water in front of cottages, bad drains, and offensive heaps of refuse in towns could be removed.

I ventured to say in my English reports, and I say so with much greater emphasis as regards Ireland, that there should be a periodical Government inspection of the houses, because there no public opinion is brought to bear on sanitary matters. Local bodies and their officers may be biassed in their decisions or hampered in the performance of their duties by many considerations and influences, financial or political; and I think that until the supervision of sanitary matters is undertaken by the Government the houses of the people in the Westport, Castlerea, and Skibbereen Unions must remain as they are for an indefinite period of time.

107. The condition of the people has improved in the last 20 years in the following particulars*:—

1. Wages have increased between 1s. and 4s. a week.

2. The prices of food and clothing are considerably cheaper. Hence the labourer buys more expensive food and dresses better.
3. Cottages have slightly improved in the Castlerea Union; have improved to a greater degree in the Skibbereen Union owing to the erection of Union Cottages, and have materially improved in the Delvin Union owing to cottage building both by guardians and landlords and to regulations excluding cattle.
4. Work is less arduous, owing to the introduction of machinery, to the better class of implements now used, and to the working hours being more defined to fixed limits.
5. Education is said to have considerably improved, though a large proportion of the people are still illiterate.†

6. Rents of holdings have in many instances been considerably reduced.‡

* The valuation of the four unions in 1871 and 1881 was as follows:—

X.—Conclusion.

108. In concluding this report I must refer to the very great assistance I received from landowners, clergy, land agents, farmers, and also labourers, who, as these pages will show, readily provided me with facts and figures. Their cordial co-operation, so necessary for the purposes of this inquiry, was the more necessary in my case because I was a stranger to them and to the country; and if they or others should think that an Irishman, and not an Englishman, would have better understood the characters and customs of the people, I trust that they will, at any rate, believe that I undertook this inquiry with the earnest desire of approaching every question without considerations of class, party or creed.

I have, &c.
(Signed) Arthur Wilson Fox,
Assistant Commissioner.

NOTE.—The following evidence of the Irish Poor Law Inspectors in 1869 and of Professor Baldwin, an Assistant Commissioner appointed by the Royal Commission on Agricultural Interests (Richmond Commission), 1879–1882, to make local inquiries, will be of interest, as it refers to the condition of the labourers as far back as the year 1849, in the unions I visited in 1893. I have extracted this from the memoranda prepared for the Royal Commission on Labour by Mr. William C. Little, Senior Assistant Commissioner:—

EVIDENCE OF POOR LAW INSPECTORS, 1869.

Poor Law Inspector.	District.	Evidence.
Dr [illegible]	[illegible] to [illegible]; [illegible] to [illegible]. (Includes Westport Union.)	I have to state that the wages of agricultural labourers have doubled since 1849.
Dr Hall	Longford to [illegible]; [illegible] to [illegible]. (Includes the Delvin Union.)	During the last 20 years the rate of wages in the Delvin Union has been doubled. The average increase in wages of agricultural labourers in the 13 unions in my district, taken collectively, during the last 20 years, has been a little more than 50 per cent.
Dr. [illegible]	[illegible] to Skibbereen; [illegible] to [illegible]. (Includes the Skibbereen Union.)	Within the last 20 years the wages of agricultural labourers have been fully doubled throughout my district generally, but in many localities the increase has not exceeded 75 per cent. These localities are on the seaboard of the unions of Skibbereen, Skull, Bantry, and Castletown.
Dr [illegible]	Boyle to [illegible]; [illegible] to [illegible]. (Includes the [illegible] Union.)	I beg to report that the general rate of wages for agricultural labourers in my district is about double what it was 20 years ago. Formerly 6d. or at most 8d. was the usual rate; now a good labourer in regular employment earns about 1s. a day.

EVIDENCE OF PROFESSOR BALDWIN, ASSISTANT COMMISSIONER (Richmond Commission), 1879 to 1882.

Professor Baldwin, Assistant Commissioner.	Chief Inspector of the Government agricultural schools and model farms in Ireland. Has made inquiries in every part of Ireland.	If you take all Ireland, the average wages of the agricultural labourer would not be more than [illegible] a week, excluding everything. It varies in the neighbourhood of large towns.

SUMMARY REPORT.

APPENDICES.

APPENDIX TO SUMMARY.

APPENDIX

ANNUAL EARNINGS and CURRENT RATE of WAGES

[illegible]	[illegible]		[illegible]	[illegible]	[illegible]		[illegible]	[illegible]
[illegible]	[illegible]				[illegible]			
	[illegible]	[illegible]			[illegible]	[illegible]		
[illegible]	[illegible]	[illegible]	[illegible]	[illegible]	[illegible]	[illegible]	[illegible]	[illegible]
[illegible]	[illegible]	[illegible]	[illegible]	[illegible]	[illegible]	[illegible]	[illegible]	[illegible]
[illegible]	[illegible]	[illegible]	[illegible]	[illegible]	[illegible]	[illegible]	[illegible]	[illegible]
[illegible]	[illegible]	[illegible]	[illegible]	[illegible]	[illegible]	[illegible]	[illegible]	[illegible]
[illegible]	—	—	[illegible]	—	—	—	[illegible]	—
[illegible]	—	—	[illegible]	[illegible]	—	—	[illegible]	[illegible]
[illegible]	—	—	[illegible]	[illegible]	—	—	[illegible]	[illegible]
[illegible]	[illegible]	[illegible]	—	[illegible]	[illegible]	[illegible]	—	[illegible]
[illegible]	[illegible]	[illegible]	—	—	[illegible]	[illegible]	—	—
[illegible]	—	—	[illegible]	[illegible]	—	—	[illegible]	[illegible]

I.

of all Classes of Labourers in four Unions.

[illegible] Union, Co. Cork.				[illegible] Union, co. [illegible].			
Daily or Weekly rate of Wages.		Annual Earnings.	Remarks.	Daily or Weekly rate of Wages.		Annual Earnings.	Remarks.
Men.	Women.			Men.	Women.		
[illegible]	[illegible]	[illegible]	—	[illegible]	[illegible]	[illegible]	[illegible]
[illegible]	[illegible]	—	[illegible]	[illegible]	[illegible]	[illegible]	[illegible]
[illegible]	[illegible]	[illegible]	[illegible]	[illegible]	[illegible]	[illegible]	[illegible]
[illegible]	[illegible]	[illegible]	[illegible]	[illegible]	[illegible]	[illegible]	[illegible]
—	—	[illegible]	—	—	—	[illegible]	—
—	—	[illegible]	[illegible]	—	—	[illegible]	[illegible]
—	—	—	[illegible]	—	—	[illegible]	[illegible]
About 1s. a day	About 1s. a day	—	[illegible]	[illegible]	[illegible]	—	[illegible]
[illegible]	[illegible]	—	—	[illegible]	[illegible]	—	—
—	—	[illegible]	[illegible]	—	—	[illegible]	[illegible]

APPENDIX 2.

RATE of WEEKLY WAGES on certain Properties and Farms in the Castlereagh, Skibbereen and Delvin Unions from 1873 to 1893.

Years.	Roscommon. Castlereagh Union. Mr Sandford's Property.	Co. Cork. Skibbereen Union. Mr. James Jones' Farm. Drimoleague.	Westmeath. Delvin Union. Earl of Longford's Property.
1873	7s. per week.	4s. and house and garden free.	7s. 6d. per week.
1874	7s. "	4s. " "	7s. 6d. "
1875	7s. "	4s. " "	7s. 6d. "
1876	7s. "	4s. " "	7s. 6d. "
1877	7s. "	4s. " "	7s. 6d. "
1878	7s. "	5s. " "	7s. 6d. "
1879	7s. "	5s. " "	7s. 6d. "
1880	10s. to 12s. "	5s. " "	7s. 6d. "
1881	10s. to 12s. "	5s. " "	7s. 6d. "
1882	10s. to 12s. "	5s. " "	7s. 6d. "
1883	10s. to 12s. "	5s. " "	7s. 6d. "
1884	10s. to 12s. "	5s. " "	7s. 6d. "
1885	10s. to 12s. "	5s. " "	7s. 6d. "
1886	10s. to 12s. "	5s. " "	7s. 6d. "
1887	10s. to 12s. "	6s. " "	7s. 6d. "
1888	10s. to 12s. "	7s. " "	7s. 6d. "
1889	10s. to 12s. "	8s. " "	7s. 6d. "
1890	10s. to 12s. "	8s. " "	8s. to 10s. "
1891	10s. to 12s. "	8s. " "	8s. to 10s. "
1892	10s. to 12s. "	8s. " "	8s. to 10s. "
1893	10s. to 12s. "	8s. " "	8s. to 10s. "

Note.—The wages on Mr. Sandford's property, Castlereagh, and the Earl of Longford's, Delvin, are higher than those paid on ordinary farms.

With reference to the rise of wages during the past 20 years in the Westport Union, Lord John Browne writes:—"There being, properly speaking, no agricultural labourers in most of Mayo, the men of small "tenants act as such, particularly in those times of year (chiefly spring and harvest) in which there is any "demand for agricultural labourers. The wages paid at those times vary a good deal, according as the "weather is wet or dry, but are frequently 2s. to 2s. 6d. a day. But as there are no large or even middle-"sized tillage farms in Mayo, there is too limited an extent for us to be able to deduce from it any regular scale "of agricultural labour prices.

"Wages at other times of year have risen about 1s. a week during the last 20 years, and may be put now "at 8s. or 9s. a week.

"I do not think, therefore, that the table you wanted could be made out for Mayo."

For perquisites and allowances given to the Earl of Longford's men see Delvin, par. 46.

APPENDIX 3.

ACTUAL HOURS of WORK in Summer and Winter in the Four Districts of Inquiry by Mr. Wilson Fox.

Description of Labourers.	Westport Union (County Mayo.)	Castlereagh Union (Counties Roscommon and Mayo.)	Skibbereen Union (County Cork).	Delvin Union (County Westmeath.)
	Summer Hours.			
Ordinary labourers (including the regular staff of a farm, whether cottagers or hired men, and also odd men)	10 to 11 hours.	10½ hours.*	10 to 10½ hours.	10 hours.*
	Winter Hours.			
	7½ to 10 hours.	7½ to 10 hours.*	7 to 10 hours.	7½ to 10 hours.*

APPENDIX 5.

TABLE of Population in 1871, 1881, and 1891 in the Four Districts of Inquiry by Mr. Wilson Fox.

Poor Law Union.	Population in 1871.	Population in 1881	Population in 1891	Decrease per cent. between 1871 and 1881	Decrease per cent. between 1871 and 1881	Decrease per cent. between 1881 and 1891	Increase per cent. between 1881 and 1891	Excess of Births over Deaths 1881 to 1891.
Castlerea - - -	43,616	43,443	37,474	·67	0	15·7	0	3,029
Delvin - - -	11,709	10,742	9,465	[illegible]	0	13·7	0	990
Skibbereen - - -	31,856	32,290	25,430	0	2·85	11·8	0	2,454
Westport - - -	40,827	40,974	37,393	0	·89	9·7	0	4,393

Compiled from the Census Tables.

APPENDIX 6.

NUMBER of EMIGRANTS from the Counties of Roscommon, Westmeath, Cork, and Mayo, for [illegible] to [illegible].

County.	Number of Emigrants.												
	[illegible]	[illegible]	[illegible]	[illegible]	[illegible]	[illegible]	[illegible]	[illegible]	[illegible]	[illegible]	[illegible]	[illegible]	[illegible]
Roscommon	[illegible]	[illegible]	[illegible]	[illegible]	[illegible]	[illegible]	[illegible]	[illegible]	[illegible]	[illegible]	[illegible]	[illegible]	[illegible]
Westmeath -	[illegible]	[illegible]	[illegible]	[illegible]	[illegible]	[illegible]	[illegible]	[illegible]	[illegible]	[illegible]	[illegible]	[illegible]	[illegible]
Cork - -	[illegible]	[illegible]	[illegible]	[illegible]	[illegible]	[illegible]	[illegible]	[illegible]	[illegible]	[illegible]	[illegible]	[illegible]	[illegible]
Mayo - -	[illegible]	[illegible]	[illegible]	[illegible]	[illegible]	[illegible]	[illegible]	[illegible]	[illegible]	[illegible]	[illegible]	[illegible]	[illegible]

APPENDIX 8.

Number of Houses in the Four Districts of Inquiry by Mr. Wilson Fox, in 1841 and 1891.

Unions.	1841. Inhabited, uninhabited, and building.	1891. Inhabited.	1891. Uninhabited.	1891. Building.	1891. Total.	Proportion per cent. of Uninhabited to Inhabited Houses in 1891.	Decrease per cent. of Houses between 1841 and 1891.
Castlereagh - -	10,793	7,180	177	4	7,360	3·2	31·9
Delvin - -	3,712	1,887	180	18	2,129	4·8	42·8
Skibbereen -	10,039	4,744	299	15	5,053	5·9	49·7
Westport - -	14,521	6,509	252	6	6,797	3·7	53·25

Taken from the Census Tables.

APPENDIX 9.

Persons engaged in Agriculture in 1891.

Poor Law Unions.	Farmers, Graziers. M.	Farmers, Graziers. F.	Farmer's or Grazier's Sons, Grandsons, Brothers, Nephews. M.	Farmer's or Grazier's Sons, Grandsons, Brothers, Nephews. F.	Farm Bailiffs. M.	Farm Bailiffs. F.	Agricultural Labourers, Cottagers. M.	Agricultural Labourers, Cottagers. F.	Herdsmen, Shepherds. M.	Herdsmen, Shepherds. F.	Farm Servants (Indoor). M.	Farm Servants (Indoor). F.	Others engaged in or connected with Agriculture. M.	Others engaged in or connected with Agriculture. F.	General Labourers.* M.	General Labourers.* F.
Castlereagh	[illegible]	[illegible]	[illegible]	[illegible]	[illegible]	[illegible]	[illegible]	[illegible]	[illegible]	[illegible]	[illegible]	[illegible]	[illegible]	[illegible]	[illegible]	[illegible]
Delvin -	418	[illegible]	413	—	14	—	[illegible]	[illegible]	[illegible]	—	[illegible]	[illegible]	[illegible]	—	[illegible]	—
Skibbereen	[illegible]	[illegible]	[illegible]	—	6	—	[illegible]	[illegible]	—	—	[illegible]	[illegible]	[illegible]	[illegible]	[illegible]	[illegible]
Westport	[illegible]	[illegible]	[illegible]	—	[illegible]	—	[illegible]	[illegible]	[illegible]	[illegible]	[illegible]	17	13	—	[illegible]	[illegible]

* Possibly many of these are agricultural labourers.

Taken from the Agricultural Statistics (Ireland).

APPENDIX 10

Livestock in 1891.

Poor Law Unions.	Horses.	Mules.	Asses.	Cattle.	Sheep.	Pigs.	Goats.	Poultry.
Castlereagh - -	2,025	647	3,634	34,023	33,180	10,677	3,616	166,133
Delvin - -	2,808	50	696	16,771	60,825	8,140	1,243	44,605
Skibbereen - - -	3,468	34	918	60,260	17,236	10,231	1,202	96,779
Westport - - -	6,712	18	2,859	30,642	77,296	6,067	904	107,465

Taken from the Agricultural Statistics (Ireland).

APPENDIX 11.

INCREASE or DECREASE in Livestock and Poultry in the Counties of Roscommon, Westmeath, Cork, and Mayo, between 18[illegible] and 1891.

Counties.	Increase or Decrease since 18[illegible].	Horses.	Mules and Asses.	Cattle.	Sheep.	Goats.	Pigs.	Poultry.
Roscommon	18[illegible]	9,121	10,1[illegible]	102,[illegible]	1[illegible]	11,0[illegible]	27,[illegible]	4[illegible]
	1891	[illegible]1,159	12,21[illegible]	1[illegible]	1[illegible]	14,787	27,0[illegible]	[illegible]
	Increase	1,[illegible]	2,0[illegible]	[illegible]	[illegible]	4,7[illegible]	—	[illegible]
	Decrease	—	—	—	—	—	4[illegible]	—
Westmeath	18[illegible]	11,1[illegible]	4,075	101,[illegible]	116,[illegible]	6,[illegible]	[illegible]	2[illegible]1,1[illegible]
	1891	1[illegible]	5,3[illegible]	10[illegible],1[illegible]	157,1[illegible]	7,717	1[illegible]	[illegible]
	Increase	[illegible]	[illegible]	[illegible]	[illegible],181	1,0[illegible]	—	1[illegible]
	Decrease	—	—	—	—	—	[illegible]	—
Cork	18[illegible]	[illegible]	1[illegible],7[illegible]	[illegible]	2[illegible]	[illegible]	171,6[illegible]	1,[illegible]
	1891	[illegible]	15,310	417,[illegible]	41[illegible]	[illegible]	1[illegible]	1,1[illegible]
	Increase	4,0[illegible]	4,[illegible]	34,[illegible]	1[illegible]	3,[illegible]	—	17,[illegible]
	Decrease	—	—	—	—	—	[illegible],195	—
Mayo	18[illegible]	18,0[illegible]	[illegible],810	1[illegible]	[illegible]	[illegible]	[illegible]	[illegible]
	1891	16,7[illegible]	[illegible]	17[illegible]	[illegible]	6,[illegible]	[illegible],316	751,[illegible]
	Increase	—	3,0[illegible]	[illegible]	1[illegible]	[illegible]	[illegible]	1[illegible]
	Decrease	1,[illegible]	—	—	—	—	—	—

Compiled from the Agricultural Statistics (Ireland).

APPENDIX 12.

PROPORTIONS per cent. under CULTIVATION of the Four Districts of Inquiry by Mr Wilson Fox.

Poor Law Unions.	Crops, including Meadow and Clover.	Grass.	Fallow.	Woods and Plantations.	Turf Bog.	Marsh.	Barren Mountain Land.	Water, Roads, Fences, &c.
Castlerea	[illegible]	[illegible]	·1	1·1	17·5	[illegible]	1·[illegible]	[illegible]
Belmullet	[illegible]	[illegible]	—	[illegible]	[illegible]	1·[illegible]	·[illegible]	1·[illegible]
Skibbereen	[illegible]	[illegible]	·1	1·[illegible]	[illegible]	[illegible]·7	1[illegible]	[illegible]
Westport	[illegible]	[illegible]	·1	·[illegible]	[illegible]·7	7·[illegible]	[illegible]	[illegible]

Taken from the Agricultural Statistics (Ireland).

APPENDIX 14.

Cultivation of the Four Districts of Inquiry by Mr. Wilson Fox.

Description of Crops in 1891.

Poor Law Union.			Corn, Beans, and Peas.								Other Crops.										Hay only.			
Castlereagh	[illegible]	[illegible]	[illegible]	[illegible]	—	[illegible]	[illegible]	[illegible]	[illegible]	[illegible]	[illegible]	[illegible]	[illegible]	[illegible]	[illegible]	[illegible]	[illegible]	[illegible]	[illegible]	[illegible]	—	[illegible]	[illegible]	[illegible]
Delvin	[illegible]	[illegible]	[illegible]	[illegible]	—	[illegible]	[illegible]	[illegible]	[illegible]	[illegible]	[illegible]	[illegible]	[illegible]	[illegible]	[illegible]	[illegible]	[illegible]	[illegible]	[illegible]	[illegible]	—	[illegible]	[illegible]	[illegible]
Skibbereen	[illegible]	[illegible]	[illegible]	[illegible]	[illegible]	[illegible]	[illegible]	[illegible]	[illegible]	[illegible]	[illegible]	[illegible]	[illegible]	[illegible]	[illegible]	[illegible]	[illegible]	[illegible]	[illegible]	[illegible]	—	[illegible]	[illegible]	[illegible]
Westport	[illegible]	[illegible]	[illegible]	[illegible]	[illegible]	[illegible]	[illegible]	[illegible]	[illegible]	[illegible]	[illegible]	[illegible]	[illegible]	[illegible]	[illegible]	[illegible]	[illegible]	[illegible]	[illegible]	[illegible]	[illegible]	[illegible]	[illegible]	[illegible]

Taken from the Agricultural Statistics (Ireland).

APPENDIX 15.

Cultivation of the Four Districts of Inquiry, by Mr. Wilson Fox.
Produce of the Crops in 1891.

Poor Law Unions.	Corn, Beans, and Peas.						Other Crops.								Hay.	
	Wheat.	Oats.	Barley.	Bere.	Rye.	Beans.	Potatoes.	Turnips.	Mangel Wurzel and Beetroot.	Carrots and Parsnips.	Cabbage.	Vetches.	Rape.	Flax.	Clover, Sainfoin, and Grasses under rotation.	Permanent Pasture.
	Cwts. of 112 lbs.	Cwts. of 112 lbs.	Cwts. of 112 lbs.	Cwts. of 112 lbs.	Cwts. of 112 lbs.	Cwts. of 112 lbs.	Tons.	Tons.	Tons.	Tons.	Tons.	Tons.	Tons.	Stones of 14 lbs.	Tons.	Tons.
Castlereagh	[illegible]	[illegible]	[illegible]	—	[illegible]	—	[illegible]	[illegible]	[illegible]	[illegible]	[illegible]	[illegible]	[illegible]	—	[illegible]	[illegible]
Delvin	[illegible]	[illegible]	[illegible]	—	[illegible]	—	[illegible]	[illegible]	[illegible]	[illegible]	[illegible]	[illegible]	[illegible]	—	[illegible]	[illegible]
Skibbereen	[illegible]	[illegible]	[illegible]	[illegible]	[illegible]	—	[illegible]	[illegible]	[illegible]	[illegible]	[illegible]	[illegible]	[illegible]	—	[illegible]	[illegible]
Westport	[illegible]	[illegible]	[illegible]	[illegible]	[illegible]	[illegible]	[illegible]	[illegible]	[illegible]	[illegible]	[illegible]	[illegible]	[illegible]	[illegible]	[illegible]	[illegible]

Taken from the Agricultural Statistics (Ireland).

APPENDIX 16.

Number of Holdings in the Four Districts of Inquiry by Mr. Wilson Fox, and their size in Statute Acres.

Not exceeding—

Poor Law Unions.	1 Acre.	—5.	—15.	—30.	—50.	—100.	—200.	—500.	Above 500 Acres.	Total Number of Holdings.
Castlereagh	[illegible]	779	[illegible]	1,714	[illegible]	191	116	66	7	[illegible]
Delvin	[illegible]	[illegible]	[illegible]	[illegible]	[illegible]	[illegible]	[illegible]	[illegible]	11	[illegible]
Skibbereen	[illegible]	166	[illegible]	[illegible]	[illegible]	[illegible]	115	[illegible]	6	[illegible]
Westport	[illegible]	[illegible]	[illegible]	[illegible]	[illegible]	[illegible]	[illegible]	77	[illegible]	[illegible]

Taken from the Agricultural Statistics (Ireland).

ROYAL COMMISSION ON LABOUR.

THE AGRICULTURAL LABOURER.

IRELAND.

REPORT

BY

MR. ARTHUR WILSON FOX
(ASSISTANT COMMISSIONER),

UPON THE

POOR LAW UNION OF WESTPORT
(MAYO).

TABLE OF CONTENTS.

I.—Introduction.

II.—Supply of Labour.

III.—Conditions of Employment.

IV.—Wages and Earnings.

V.—Cottage Accommodation.

VI.—Benefit Societies and Trade Unions.

VII.—Relations between Employer and Employed.

VIII.—General Condition of the Agricultural Labourer.

THE AGRICULTURAL LABOURER.

[illegible]

To Geoffrey Drage, Esq., Secretary,
Royal Commission on Labour.

I.—Introductory.

Westport, County Mayo, Ireland,
March 15th, 1893.

Sir,

1 I have the honour to present to you my report upon the condition of the agricultural labourer in the Westport Union of Mayo.

2 My enquiries occupied me for a period of about five weeks, commencing the 10th of February. This was a longer period than I spent in any of the districts I had previously visited in England, but owing to the great size of the union* and the absence of railway communication, I found my task by no means a light one.

3 I obtained the information contained in this report in the following manner:—

I drove to nearly every part of the union, and interviewed a great number of small farmers and labourers, either in their houses, or at work on the land.

Although I cannot speak too warmly of the friendly way in which I was everywhere received by the people, I am bound to say there was a tendency, particularly in the poorer districts, on the part of some to understate their financial position, and I think this was due to the fact that they had the idea that I should be able to procure them work, or in some way to benefit them if their cases were considered to be bad. At the same time it is quite apparent that in many districts the people are extremely poor, and that their life is one long struggle for a livelihood.

I also carefully inspected a number of cottages in various parts, and while doing so I had ample opportunities of gaining information from the people.

Through the courtesy of the chairman of the board of guardians, Mr P J Kelly, I was given the opportunity of attending a meeting of the board, where I met representatives from all parts of the union.

At the following villages I held meetings, which were numerously attended by the inhabitants:—Murrisk, Louisburgh, Kilmeena, and Drummin. (Appendix D.)

Among those from whom I obtained information I would especially mention Lord John Browne, Sir Thomas Brady, the Rev. Bernard McDermott, Administrator (Westport); Mr. R. Powell, agent to the Marquis of Sligo; Mr. Lawrence, agent to the Earl of Lucan; Osborne Thompson, agent to Mr. Mitchell Henry; Mr. Livingstone, Westport; Mr. Hamlin, R.M.; Mr. Thomas O'Donnel, Westport; Mr. R. Lynch of the Land Commission Board; the Rev. P. O'Connor, P.P., Achill; and the Rev. W. Joyce, P.P., Louisburgh.

4 The union is situated on the west coast of Mayo, and consists of 21 electoral divisions, comprising [illegible] acres, with a valuation of [illegible]. It extends on the coast from Tullaghan Bay on the north to Killary Bay on the south. On the north-east it is bounded by the Belmullet Union and Ballina Union, on the east by the Castlebar Union, and south-east by the Ballinrobe Union.

5 The district is purely an agricultural one, there being practically no other industries except a little fishing on the coast. The only large employer of labour in the union is Mr. Livingstone, of Westport, who is extensively engaged in the importation of American flour and Indian corn. He has a regular staff of about [illegible] men, besides which he gives considerable employment in carting goods and unloading vessels.

Before the growing of corn was given up in this country, Mr. Livingstone bought large quantities of grain in the district, which he ground in his mills, now closed, as are also the large corn granaries at Westport Quay.

As the three principal landowners are non-resident there is little or no employment given by them in the district.

Between 18[illegible] and 1850 there was an extensive linen trade, and nearly all the people grew flax and made linen, which they sold in the Westport market. They also made considerable quantities of flannel frieze and stockings for sale. These industries have now almost entirely died out.

6 The principal market town of the union is Westport. The market day there is on Thursdays, and is chiefly held for the sale of cattle, sheep, pigs, potatoes, and vegetables.

There are also numerous fairs for the sale of live stock and agricultural produce. Westport, Achill Sound, and Mulranny each have 12 fairs in the year. At Ballyvary there are six, and four at both Louisburgh and Aughagower.

7 The north part of the union is mountainous, and there is also a great deal of bog land. In the centre to the east of Achill there is a considerable quantity of green land. South-east of Westport there is both grass and tillage, and the soil is a good clay. South-west of Westport along the coast of Clew Bay as far as Louisburgh, the land is very poor and thickly populated. The neighbourhood is mountainous, and comprises Croagh Patrick, which reaches the elevation of 2,510 feet.

In the south the soil in the cultivated districts is clay, but there are large areas of bog and mountain land. Several of these mountains reach an elevation of between 2,000 and 2,[illegible] feet.

The scenery, especially along the coast, from which views of the many bays, islands, and headlands, and also of the Connemara and Mayo mountains can be obtained, is magnificent.

8 The principal crops grown in the district are potatoes, oats, and turnips. (Appendix A. 13.)

Most of the small holders grow about an acre to an acre and a half of potatoes which provide the principal article of food for the family, and it becomes apparent in travelling through this district what a serious state of things a failure in the potato crop must produce.

In the hilly districts there is a mountain breed of cattle, and on the low lands crosses of shorthorns and polled Galloways.

The sheep in the mountains are Scotch black-faced, and in the other parts Border Leicesters and their crosses. (Appendix A. 14.)

9. The average farm of the countryman may be put at 15 acres (Irish), though there are many smaller.*

---

* In 1891 the [illegible] Union, consisting of [illegible] electoral divisions, was amalgamated with the [illegible] Union. (See Appendix A. 1.)

* The Earl of Lucan has on his estate [illegible] tenants, [illegible]

The following are the sizes of the holdings on the [illegible] property:—

Under	[illegible] acres (Irish)	[illegible]
[illegible]	[illegible]	[illegible]

[illegible]

[illegible] There are about [illegible] grazing farms between [illegible] and [illegible] acres, and there is one in the south, rented by Mr. [illegible], of [illegible] acres. (Appendix A. [illegible].)

Landowners. 10. The principal landlords in the district are the Marquis of Sligo, the Earl of Lucan, and Sir Roger Palmer, who own respectively in the county of Mayo about [illegible] acres, [illegible] acres, and [illegible] acres.

Population. 11. In 1891 the population of the Westport Union was [illegible] persons. (Appendix A. 1.) Between 1881 and 1891 the population has decreased from [illegible] to [illegible], being a decrease of [illegible] or [illegible] per cent., although the excess of births over deaths was [illegible]. The parish of Achill increased between 1851 and 1881 from [illegible] to [illegible] persons, or [illegible] per cent., but in 1891 had decreased to [illegible], or [illegible] per cent.

From 1841 and 1891 the population of the county of Mayo decreased from [illegible] to [illegible], or [illegible] per cent., and had further decreased in 1891 to [illegible], or [illegible] per cent.

Between 1841 and 1891 the males in the county of Mayo decreased from [illegible] to [illegible], or [illegible] per cent., and the females from [illegible] to [illegible], or [illegible] per cent.

Pauperism. 12. The number of indoor paupers in 1891 was [illegible], and of those in receipt of outdoor relief [illegible]. The average number of paupers in the workhouse for the year ending September the 29th, 1891, was [illegible].

Rates. 13. The valuation on which the rate is struck is [illegible]. The rates vary in the different electoral divisions from [illegible] to [illegible] in the pound. In [illegible] electoral divisions they are between [illegible] and [illegible] in the pound; in three they are between [illegible] and [illegible], and in [illegible] they are between [illegible] and [illegible] in the pound.*

The number of holdings in the union at and under a valuation of [illegible] is [illegible], or [illegible] per cent. of the total number.

Congested districts. 14. It will be seen from the preceding paragraphs that many parts of the union are extremely poor. Of the [illegible] electoral divisions [illegible] are scheduled as congested. (Appendix A. 1.) Section [illegible] of the Act for the improvement of the congested districts in Ireland (1891) thus defines a congested district:—

"Where at the commencement of this Act more than [illegible] per cent. of the population of a county, or in the case of the county of Cork of either riding thereof, live in electoral divisions of which the total rateable value, when divided by the number of the population, gives a sum of less than one pound ten shillings for each individual, those divisions . . . shall form a separate county (in this Act referred to as a congested district county)."

Now, in the Westport Union, the proportion of the valuation to each person is about [illegible], and so if the union was considered as a whole, it would all come within the definition laid down in section [illegible].

Mr. P. J. Kelly, the chairman of the board of guardians, is of opinion that the Congested Districts Board should not always proceed on the basis of taking electoral divisions as the area for determining whether a locality should come within the definition of section [illegible], but that in some cases smaller areas should be chosen. Under the system now adopted, he says that sometimes very poor districts, which ought to be scheduled as congested, do not come within the Act, because a small and more prosperous part of the electoral division in which they are situated, is the means of excluding the division, when considered as a whole, from the operation of section [illegible].

Mr. Kelly is also of opinion that when calculating the rateable value of the divisions for the purposes of the Act, that the non-residential holdings should not be taken into account.

By referring to Appendix A. [illegible] it will be seen that the poor law valuation per head of the population in Mayo is very low when compared even with that of other counties in which there are congested districts.†

The Congested Districts Board have recently undertaken many practical operations for permanently improving the condition of the people. These are set out at length in their [illegible] report for [illegible].

Three operations have included the employment of an instructor to teach the people the best system of cultivating plots or portions of the holdings;‡ experimenting in planting trees on the west coast to ascertain if waste land could be profitably turned to account; improving the breeds of livestock by bringing stallions, bulls, rams, and boars into the districts; and improving the quality of the poultry by introducing some useful breeds.

Also the board has recently purchased an estate in the county of Galway for [illegible], in order to divide some grazing lands among the occupiers of those neighbouring small holdings. They have also paid great attention to the development of the fishing industry, both with regard to the fresh and cured fish trade. With this object the board established seven trained crews to instruct some of the Connemara and Arran people in the management of large boats and nets, for the purchase of which the board is willing to make loans to suitable persons; and to demonstrate to the local fishermen what earnings might be theirs if the industry was skilfully carried on.

On the north and north-west coasts [illegible] stations are either opened, or are about to be opened, for the curing of fish for the English and Scotch and American markets. Moreover, instruction in net mending has been arranged for in certain centres.

The board, with a view of developing or stimulating industries have advanced money to certain enterprises, namely, the Foxford Spinning Factory, Mayo, the Balla [illegible] Knitting Factory, Mayo, and the [illegible] Dairy Company, County Cork. For the purpose of providing a market for goods in congested districts, the board have agreed to make a grant for that purpose.

An agency for the sale of goods is to be instituted in Manchester, and the board are endeavouring to stimulate the factory and cottage industry of the making of shirts and underclothing by sewing machines and hand sewing, and also to develop the manufacture of home spun tweeds.

The board are also undertaking certain works in South Connemara, such as building piers, landing stages, bridges, and making roads, and they are anxious to contribute other works of a similar character, if they can obtain a sufficient sum of money.

15. Under the Seed Supply Act (1890) the Board of Works advanced in 1891 [illegible] to the union, of which they spent [illegible] and refunded [illegible].

The first instalment of [illegible] was due on August 1st, 1892, and of this sum the board of guardians paid [illegible]. The second instalment and the balance of the first will all be due on August 1st, 1893, amounting in all to [illegible].

The Board of Works have threatened to suspend the rates by April 1st, 1893, owing to the nonpayment of the first instalment.

It will be seen in paragraph 13 that the electoral divisions of Achill and Ballycroy are [illegible] of the total rate, and as the rates in Ballycroy North, Ballycroy South, Achill, and Corraun Achill are respectively [illegible], [illegible], [illegible] and [illegible] in the pound, the prospects of obtaining the balance due from these districts do not seem very bright.

16. Extensive relief works, rendered necessary by the partial failure of the potato crop, were undertaken in various unions on the west coast in the latter part of 1890 and in 1891. In the Westport Union a great many works were opened, and for a period of [illegible] weeks, commencing February [illegible], 1891, an average of [illegible] persons employed on them per week, involving a total expenditure of [illegible] on wages.

These works comprised making, repairing, fencing, and draining roads, building bridges, making and repairing piers, making boat slips and landing slopes,

* Ballycroy, South, is [illegible]
Achill, [illegible]
Corraun, Achill, [illegible] (See Appendix [illegible])

† When the occupier's valuation does not exceed [illegible], the landlord pays the rates, but when it exceeds [illegible] the landlord and tenant each pay half the rates. The [illegible] which the county cess, which has increased of late [illegible]

‡ The [illegible] [illegible]

* The [illegible] Report for [illegible] says:—"We believe we are not [illegible] [illegible] the [illegible] [illegible] the congested districts [illegible] the [illegible] of the [illegible] could be improved [illegible] to [illegible]"

‡ PURPOSES OF THE BOARD.

The board is empowered to take such steps as it thinks proper for [illegible] congested districts, in connexion with the following subjects or [illegible], namely:—

1. Agricultural development.
2. Forestry.
3. Breeding of live stock and poultry.
4. Sale of seed potatoes and seed oats.
5. Amalgamation of small holdings.
6. Migration.
7. Emigration.
8. Fishing and matters subservient to fish[illegible]
9. Weaving and spinning.
10. Any other suitable industries.

and deepening the bed of rivers, &c. Many of these undertakings, and especially those connected with the improvement of roads, have greatly added to the convenience of travelling in the district.

In addition the construction of the railway under the Light Railways Act from Westport to Achill Sound, a distance of 28 miles, has been the means of giving a great deal of employment, to which I shall refer hereafter in paragraph 12.

17. The Labourers Acts have never been put into operation in this union.

No doubt the fact of there being scarcely any married men who earn their livelihood exclusively by agricultural employment is one reason, though there are doubtless many persons who come within the definition of an agricultural labourer (48 & 49 Vict. c. 77, s. 4.)

But even assuming there was a desire for cottages on the part of those qualified to rent them, which there is not, probably because the people prefer remaining in their present cabins to paying rent for cottages, the question whether the already over-burdened rates could bear the additional expense, seems doubtful in the extreme.

18. The emigration from Mayo to America is very extensive, and it is the exception to find a family in the Westport Union from which no member has emigrated, or who at any rate have not relatives who have done so.[*]

It seems that when one member of a family has gone there, attracted by the accounts sent home of high wages and the prospect of a successful life, others follow, and are frequently enabled to do so through the generosity of those already in America, who send tickets over for the passage from England. There is no doubt that large numbers could not afford to go without this assistance, for the parents and relatives at home often find it difficult to provide the necessary outfit for the intending emigrants.[†]

The fidelity, loyalty, and generosity displayed by those who have gone towards those who remain cannot but command both admiration and respect. It is the most common occurrence to find that sons and daughters, some of whom are mere children, are regularly remitting from America money to clear the debts of the village shop, to buy a cow, or to pay the rent for the holding, which is seldom sufficiently large or productive to support the family. (Appendix B 1.)

Nearly all the young women emigrate from the Westport Union, and in consequence it is difficult to get domestic servants, and almost impossible to find women to work in agricultural employment. Out of the 3,793 persons who emigrated from Mayo in 1892, 2,147 or 56·6 per cent. were women, and of these women 1,927 or 89·8 per cent. were unmarried. Of these 1,927 unmarried women 1,728 or 89 per cent. were under 25 years of age.

A great number of the girls who emigrate find employment in mills or factories, while some take situations as domestic servants, and others become dressmakers.

I interviewed one young woman of 21 years of age who had recently returned from America to see her friends. She had been employed as a cook in America since the age of 15, and was earning 15s. a week and her board and lodging. She informed me that girls could always find situations either in service or in factories, without difficulty. In the factories she said that girls earn 7½ dollars a week, and up to 10 dollars a week by piece-work.

This girl, in her well-fitting cloth dress and jacket, looked strangely out of place in the small cottage where I found her, and she herself said that her home surroundings seemed very poverty stricken after her experience in America.

Of the 1,677 men who emigrated from Mayo in 1892, 1,456 or 86·8 per cent. were single, and of these single men 1,111 or 76·3 per cent. were under 25 years of age.

It is constantly said that the country is being drained of the best young people, but unless some other industry than agriculture can be found for the young men and women who are growing up, it is difficult to see what alternative they have. When the members of a family reach a certain age, it becomes obvious that the holding which might support two persons cannot support eight or nine, and to obtain any employment at home is practically an impossibility.

Manufactures there are none. Fishing does not appear to be an industry by which a living can be made at present. Agricultural employment is scanty, partly because there are but few farmers whose holdings are large enough to require extra labour, and partly because most of the large farmers have reduced their tillage land to a minimum quantity on account of the impossibility of growing corn at a profit.

Many a young man I met told me that his ambition was to emigrate, as it was impossible to better his position in Ireland, and that it was only the want of funds which prevented his doing so at once. It would certainly seem better for them to do so, and thereby to get the chance of earning a good livelihood in America, than to remain in Mayo insufficiently fed, insufficiently employed, and learning habits of indolence from their enforced idleness.[‡]

19. The principal islands off the coast comprised in the union are Achill, Clare, Inishturk, and Inishbiggle.

Achill Island (35,288 acres), which is now joined to the mainland by a bridge, contains about 4,897 inhabitants. The parish of Achill, which is partly on the mainland, contains 6,333 persons.

The people there are engaged in agriculture and fishing.[§] Nearly all the able-bodied men and unmarried women leave Achill for England and Scotland between April and July to work on farms, many of them remaining away for some months in the year. (Appendix C, 12.) Thus Achill is in reality the winter quarters for labourers employed on English and Scotch farms. During the winter months the island contains far more people than it can possibly support, and they can try as "employment," which in such a place is practically impossible to obtain.

In the spring of 1891 Achill and Ballycroy received about 2,081l. worth of seed potatoes, payable in two instalments on August 1st, 1892, and August 1st, 1893. Of the first instalment they only paid 891l., leaving due on August 1st, 1893, 3,854l.

Some of the people have emigrated to Australia, but a great many men and women have gone to America. The great hope for the future of Achill and the surrounding country lies in the railway from Achill Sound to Westport, now within a near prospect of completion, undertaken on the advice of the Right Hon. A. J. Balfour, when Chief Secretary for Ireland. By means of the railway this over-populated and isolated portion of the country will be enabled to communicate with the outside world, and the fishing industry, which I understand from the Thomas Brady may have a future of increasing importance when properly developed, will have an accessible market at Westport, and indeed all along the line to Dublin, and from thence to England. Again the men and women who go to work on English or Scotch farms will be saved a weary tramp of over 30 miles to Westport, while greater facilities for reaching this spot, so beautiful as regards scenery, and so attractive as regards sport, may increase the number of tourists and visitors, whose presence will bring both money and employment.

The construction of this railway in the last two years has given a considerable amount of work, not only to some of the Achill men, but to those all along the route between Achill and Westport. This has been very highly appreciated by the people and has proved a great boon to them. It has also had the effect of driving up agricultural wages in the district, and of giving employment to many who would otherwise have gone to England or Scotland.

Clare Island (4,133 acres) contains 101 inhabited houses, and a population of 537 persons. The soil there appeared to be very poor. The inhabitants are engaged in agriculture and fishing. They have about 80 boats and curraghs, but few are of any value. I was informed by Mr. Flynn, the rate collector, and also by the people themselves, that they could not exist without the harvest money they make in England and Scotland,[‖] and what their relatives and friends send

[* In 1892 the number of persons who emigrated from Mayo was 3,793, or [illegible] of the population.]

[† The [illegible] people apply the rents for this purpose, [illegible] to do so.]

[‡ [illegible]]

[§ [illegible]]

[‖ [illegible] "[illegible] to England and Scotland, they would die much faster."]

from America.* (Appendix C. IV.) The people spin their wool, and make their blankets, flannel, and frieze.

Potato seed to the value of about 170*l.* was advanced to Clare Island under the Seed Supply Act, 1880, of which they have repaid only 33*l.*

Inishturk Island, 9 miles from the coast (1,440 acres), contains 25 inhabited houses and 27 families, or a population of 137 persons. The people live by agriculture and fishing, and on the money they receive from those members of their families who are in America. They have nine boats and seven canoes. The holdings vary in extent from 3 to 15 acres of tillage, but there is a considerable quantity of commons. The land looks poor and unproductive.

As the islanders have to row their cattle 7 miles to Roonah Point, and drive them from thence 23 miles to Westport Market, they are carrying on farming operations under considerable difficulties.

Inishbiggle Island, off Achill, belongs to the Achill Mission, and contains about 427 acres. There are 30 holdings upon it, comprising 140 acres, and the population is 135. The people are engaged in agriculture and also collect whelks, which are sent in great quantities to London. Some of them go to England and Scotland for harvest.

Achillbeg (300 acres), off the extreme south point of Achill Island, has a population of 170 persons.

There are also 33 other islands in Clew Bay, whose total population amounts to 620 persons, the number of inhabited houses being 103.

20. In describing the different classes of farm labourers employed it is difficult to give an accurate impression how few labourers in the ordinary sense of the word there are. Throughout this large union there are very few farms or properties where men, regularly employed all the year round in agriculture for wages, are to be found, except the herds.†

This is chiefly due to the fact that very little of the land is now under tillage owing to the impossibility of growing corn at a profit and the country is divided between small farms or holdings of from 5 to 20 acres, and grazing farms sometimes of a considerable size.

There thus being hardly any farms with a sufficient amount of tillage land to regularly employ a staff of labourers all the year round, the tenants of small holdings, or their sons, are called in to work by the day when labour is required. These men are only too anxious for the opportunity of such work, as many of them cannot live on the produce of their own holdings, and have either to look to what they can earn by working occasionally as labourers in Ireland, by going to English or Scotch farms for some portion of the year, or to what they can get from their friends and relatives in America.

The different classes of labourers employed are as follows:—The herds, who look after both cattle and sheep. These men are by far the best paid of any, and in fact are much more comfortably off than members of the small holders. A good deal of responsibility attaches to their work, for they are frequently put in charge of a distant farm and sometimes do not see their employer for a long period.

The ordinary labourers, who are, as I have already stated, usually small holders or their sons, and whose employment, especially in the winter time, is very irregular.

Also there are a few ploughmen and carters, and one or two gardeners stewards who supervise the men's work, and have the general management of the farm.

There are also a few hired men and boys who live and board in the farm-houses.

* Mr. [illegible] says: "The people on Clare Island could not live if they had the land [illegible] [illegible] [illegible]. They certainly could not [illegible] [illegible] [illegible] [illegible] [illegible] [illegible] [illegible] England. All [illegible] [illegible] [illegible] America."

† The [illegible] [illegible] [illegible] [illegible] [illegible] [illegible] [illegible] [illegible] [illegible] [illegible] [illegible] [illegible] [illegible] [illegible] [illegible] Westport Union [illegible] [illegible] [illegible] [illegible] [illegible]:—

	Male	Female
[illegible]	[illegible]	[illegible]
[illegible]	[illegible]	[illegible]
[illegible]	[illegible]	[illegible]
[illegible] labourers, cottagers	[illegible]	[illegible]
[illegible]	[illegible]	[illegible]
[illegible]	[illegible]	[illegible]
[illegible] connected with [illegible]	[illegible]	[illegible]
[illegible]	[illegible]	[illegible]

‡ [illegible] [illegible] [illegible] [illegible] [illegible] the [illegible] [illegible] agricultural labourers.

Practically no women are employed.* All who can be spared from home either go to America to work in factories, or to become servants, or else go to work on farms in Scotland for several months in the year between the spring and autumn.

I did, however, visit a few places where women are employed. Mr. Vesey Stoney's steward informed me that he sometimes has 14 or 15 working in June, July, August, and September. Their work chiefly is to cut turf, spread and carry it, pick potatoes, collect seaweed, and help in the harvest.

There is but little employment for boys, there being no weeding or other light work such as is frequently found for them in an arable country.

II.—The Supply of Labour.

21. The supply of labour is amply sufficient for all requirements, or in fact it greatly exceeds the demand. Wherever I went I heard the same story that the lack of employment was one of the greatest disadvantages from which the whole countryside was suffering. I believe that five out of six of all the men I interviewed from Ballycroy in the North to Louisburgh in the South asked the question, "Will the Government find us employment?"

But this great desire for employment does not arise because there are agricultural labourers in the ordinary sense of the word seeking for work, but because the country is populated with a peasantry the bulk of whom are attempting the impossible, namely, the support of themselves and their families, usually large ones, on holdings of an insufficient size, frequently composed of unproductive land and often reclaimed [illegible] [illegible] by their inability to farm it properly. These men are therefore farming under conditions which in many cases render it impossible for the holding to be a self-supporting business, and any number of them, or their sons, are ready and willing to add to their means of support by working for wages on a farm, on a railway, on relief works, or at any other kind of employment that may happen to turn up.

Of course the fact that hundreds of men throughout the Westport Union spend from three to nine months in England for the purpose of earning money there is the best proof of the impossibility of obtaining employment at home.

In a few districts I heard complaints that labour was rather difficult to get when hay harvest was in full swing, and higher wages had sometimes to be given to cause men to come, but at that particular period a great number of men and women are away in Scotland and England, and those who remain are all saving to get in their own hay.

22. There certainly has been a decrease in the supply of labour in the last 10 or 15 years, as the population has considerably lessened, owing to so many young men and young women going to America. (Appendix B. 1.) However, the decrease has not affected the employers, who, owing to the lowness of prices, have of late years been keeping as much land as possible in grass, and for the same reason have been economising in the labour they employ as far as possible.

It is scarcely not surprising to find the young men and young women leaving a district, where, at the best, they can but eke out a hard and uncomfortable existence in squalid houses and on unproductive land, for a country which affords them both higher wages and brighter prospects. It is sometimes asserted that if the people could obtain land they would remain in Ireland and earn their livelihood by cultivating it. If that be the case, the Irish people are different to the English, who, in the counties I reported on are rapidly developing a distaste for the monotony and lack of excitement of agricultural life. But I am inclined to think that the Irish and English people are taking the same view, for in Ireland, as in England, the majority of the employers agree that the men take less interest in agricultural work than formerly, and certainly the majority of the young men I interviewed, who had expectations of going to America, informed me that they would seek work in the towns rather than in the country.

23. As mentioned in the previous paragraph, a great many employers say that the men do not work as well as formerly. Others, however, take a contrary view, so no general rule can be laid down. (Appendix B. 8.)

* [illegible] [illegible] [illegible] [illegible] of small holders very frequently [illegible] [illegible] [illegible] [illegible]. In the [illegible] [illegible] [illegible] [illegible] [illegible] [illegible] [illegible] England and Scotland, the [illegible] [illegible] [illegible] [illegible] [illegible] frequently [illegible] [illegible] [illegible] [illegible].

Probably the emigration of so many active young men to America, which is draining the district of numbers of the best labourers, and the fact that many of the younger men who remain take but little interest in agricultural employment, are reasons which justify the adverse criticism of the employers.

24. To compare the capacity of labourers in one district with that of those in another is a very difficult matter, because it is almost impossible to find a standard whereby to test it. It is said in Ireland, as in England, that the men who are well-fed are most capable of work, and employers frequently state that when a man returns from England or Scotland he works much better for a certain time than he did before he started, owing to the better food he obtained there.

The food eaten by the labourers and small farmers in the Westport Union is certainly not a diet on which English men would care to do a day's work on, for they eat little but potatoes and bread, have no bacon, and never see beef or mutton from one year's end to the other.

The character given to the labourers in the Westport Union by two Scotchmen, Mr. M'Donnell, manager to Mr. Houston, and Mr. Gray, walking ganger on the Achill Railway, is that they want looking after, and are not inclined to work if left to themselves, though they work well under supervision. Lord John Browne's steward, who is also of Scotch extraction, says the men in Wexford and Cork do not need so much looking after as the men in the west.

I asked a good many farmers in Northumberland and Lancashire, where I was engaged in the autumn of 1892, how the work of the Irishmen compared with that of the Englishmen, and they generally replied that the former worked as hard as the latter "at a push," but that the Englishmen were steadier and required less supervision. They also considered that the English labourer was the best all-round man, but that at certain work to which he has been accustomed, such as potato planting and lifting, or using a reaping hook, the Irishman was frequently the better man of the two. [Appendix B. 5.]

III.—Conditions of Engagement.

25. Employment is, as a general rule, very irregular, except in the case of herds. There are scarcely any employers who give continuous work throughout the year to ordinary labourers.

I met with one or two employers who gave their men work any day they chose to come, but these were very rare instances.* It must, however, be borne in mind that there are scarcely any agricultural labourers in the ordinary sense of the word in the whole district, and that when they are not working for wages they are working on their own land.

26. The engagement of ordinary labourers is nearly always a daily one. In one instance I found they were engaged by the year at a wage of 9s. a week, summer and winter. In a few cases the men are engaged by the week, "wet or dry."

Herds are usually engaged by the year with a month's notice. On one estate I visited they had a yearly system.

It is difficult to say what is the actual term of engagement of the hired men who live and board at the farmhouses. It is probably intended to be a yearly one, as a rule, by both employer and employed, but if a man wants to leave at any time or his employer desires to get rid of him, neither party seems to make any difficulty about parting company.

27. The hours of work for ordinary labourers in summer are from 6 a.m. to 6 p.m., or from 7 a.m. to 7 p.m. In many places, where the hours are from 6 a.m. to 6 p.m., an hour is allowed for breakfast at 9 a.m. and an hour for dinner at 1 p.m. or 2 p.m., though the break-fast time is in most instances only half an hour.

Where the hours are from 7 a.m. to 7 p.m. I found that sometimes the men were expected to get their breakfast before they came, though this was not always so.

28. The hours of work in winter are generally from light to dark. The shortest working hours are from 8 a.m. to 4.30 p.m., with an hour off for dinner at 1 p.m. or 2 p.m.

29. Herds who have to attend to cattle and sheep have no definite hours either summer or winter, their duty being to be with the animals under their charge whenever necessary.

30. A carter begins work in summer about 4.30 a.m. and leaves off at 6 p.m., but after that he has to feed and clean his horses. In winter his hours are from light to dark. His meal hours are the same as those of ordinary labourers.

31. Ordinary labourers have no work on Sundays, but herds and cattlemen have to look and look after cattle and sheep as usual, and their work is frequently as heavy on Sundays as on week days, particularly in lambing time and when there is stock on the ground.

Carters have to feed their horses twice a day on Sundays, and this occupies them about half an hour each time.

The men try to save themselves all the work they can by preparing food on Saturday afternoon or evening, and when cattle are out in the fields the herds and cattlemen often throw down the food for them on Saturday night.

IV.—Wages and Earnings.

32. The current rate of weekly wages of ordinary labourers is 9s. a week, though some employers give 10s.† Frequently men are paid 1s. and sometimes 1s. 3d. a day, and given their food as well.

In winter wages are often 8s. a week, and sometimes 7s., though some employers pay the same wages (9s. or 10s.) summer and winter.

33. A carter gets 9s. or 10s. a week, and a ploughman 10s. or 11s. and a house. These men have constant employment, and are engaged by the week.

34. Herds are paid chiefly in kind, and their annual wages may be put at from 10s. to 11s. 6d. a week.

If, however, the profits they make from the sale of sheep, cattle, and fowls, for which they are allowed free grazing, are considered, they may be said to be worth from 15s. to 20s. a week. It must, however, be borne in mind that a herd in receipt of high wages frequently has a son, and sometimes as many as three, helping him, and under these circumstances he is no better off than a single-handed man, and from a pecuniary point of view the sons' position is not a satisfactory one, as they are practically only working for their food and clothes.

I have given several examples of the mode of payment in Appendix A. 4.

35. As previously stated, there are some hired men in the union who live and board at the farmhouses, but they do not seem easy to obtain. Their wages range from 6l. to 12l. with everything found in the way of lodging, board, and washing. A few men get 14l. Hired boys get from 4l. to 8l.

The food they are given, of course, depends on the position of the farmer who employs them. For instance, one hired man I met on a wage of 12l. a year, employed by a large farmer at Louisburgh, told me he had mutton or bacon every day for dinner, and beef or mutton on Sundays; while another hired man, on a wage of 8l. a year, employed by a farmer who rents 60 acres, lives in a farmhouse little better than a labourer's cottage, and scarcely ever sees fresh meat from one year's end to the other, though it must be added that he has the same food as his employer.

36. Boys are paid 3s. or 4s. a week when they first begin to work.

As I have already stated, women very seldom work in the fields for wages. When they do, they are paid about 1s. 6d. a week.

37. There is hardly any piece-work in this district except at haytime, when mowing is frequently undertaken by the piece.

38. The prices for mowing, of course, depend on whether the crop is a heavy or light one, but it usually varies between 6s. and 8s. for an Irish acre (say 3s. 9d. to 5s. per statute acre).

Several farmers who give 6s. an Irish acre tell me the men earn 3s. a day in a day of 10 hours' work.

Lord John Browne's steward, who gives 8s. for an Irish acre and 5s. for an English acre, tells me that their men earn between 3s. and 3s. 6d. a day of 10 hours.

* Mr. Vesey Stoney, of Rosturk Castle, employs [illegible] the year round at 9s. a week. [illegible] Lord John Browne [illegible] [illegible]

* Lord John Browne [illegible] a week [illegible]

† The Earl of Lucan [illegible]

[illegible]. The ordinary staff of a farm are paid nothing extra at hay-time and harvest, and they usually get the current rate of wages in the summer, namely, [illegible] a week or [illegible] a week and their food. [illegible] these [illegible] are paid as much as [illegible] a week at such times, but this is the exception.

Extra men frequently do not receive more than the ordinary wages at harvest, that is, [illegible] a week, though they sometimes get 10s. or 12s. a week.

Mowers are paid 2s. 6d. a day when engaged at day work, and when working by the piece can earn between [illegible] and [illegible] a day. (See paragraph [illegible].)

On many farms the mowing extends over many weeks, as there is a considerable quantity of hay land on the grazing farms. Mr Burke, who farms [illegible] acres near [illegible], told me that his mowing lasts from the middle of July to September.

[illegible]. There are practically no perquisites given to ordinary labourers, and they get nothing except the current wages.

On Mr [illegible]'s large farm there are some outside labourers, who receive certain payments in kind in consideration for their agreeing to work on his land at 1s. a day when required and [illegible] a week at harvest. One of these men told me he only earned [illegible] in cash last year, though in a good year he had earned [illegible] or [illegible], and another said that he was only employed [illegible] or [illegible] days in the year.

The payments in kind made to these men are not strictly perquisites, as they are definitely agreed on between them and their employers as part of their remuneration for services rendered.

41. In some places overtime is paid for, though in the majority of cases it is not. When men do work overtime, that is, more than a working day of 10 or [illegible] hours, they often come rather later the next morning as a compensation.

Mr Lawrence, agent to the Earl of Lucan, informs me that he pays a quarter day's wages if the men work an hour overtime. Lord John Browne's steward pays a quarter day's wages for two hours' overtime.

[illegible]. All along the coast and also in the islands of Achill, Clare, and Inishturk, fishing is carried on to a certain extent, but it is a very general ground of complaint that the people have not sufficient boats or nets for the purpose, and it is constantly asserted that if they had, they would be able to earn a much better livelihood.

These complaints were more particularly made to me by those living on Clew Bay, and in Clare, and Inishturk Islands.

Those on the coast gather large quantities of seaweed for the purpose of manuring their land. It is quite a common thing to see the tillage land thickly spread with it. Many of these people collect seaweed for the purpose of selling to those who dwell inland.

Money can also be earned by making and selling kelp, which is made from certain seaweed commonly found on the shore. Kelp is used in the manufacture of soap and iodine. It is prepared in the following way:—The seaweed is dried and then tightly packed in a drain dug some feet deep in the earth and then burnt. It then forms a hard substance of considerable weight. The price given for it is from [illegible] to [illegible] a ton.[*] The sale of kelp is extensively carried on. A great quantity is brought in by the country people in creels or panniers on donkeys or horses to Westport on market days.

[illegible]. The annual earnings of ordinary labourers are very difficult to estimate, as the majority of them work very irregularly, and generally neither employers nor employed keep any record of the number of days in the year they have worked.

On Lord John Browne's farm, where the men have regular employment, the steward, who went into the question for me, told me "that the majority of the "men do not average more than [illegible] a year, though a "few of the best could earn another [illegible] by piece-"work."

Mr. Vesey Stoney's men and those of a few other employers who are regularly employed, get about the same.

Mr R. Powell, agent to the Marquis of Sligo, who employs six or eight men himself, tells me that his men work three quarters of the working days in the year.

The earnings of those in irregular employment greatly vary, but it must be remembered that these men when not employed for wages are frequently working on their own land or that of their relatives, or perhaps in England or Scotland for some portion of the year.

I asked three very intelligent young labourers who were regularly employed, except sometimes in wet weather, how many days they worked in the year, and one said he lost a day a week all the year round, and the other two said they lost about [illegible] days altogether.

In Appendix A. [illegible] I have given the number of days on which two men in irregular employment worked in a year for Mr McKeown, of [illegible].

[illegible]. The annual earnings of carters vary from [illegible] to [illegible]. Ploughmen's wages come to about [illegible]. (Appendix A. [illegible].)

[illegible]. The annual earnings of herds may be put at between [illegible] and [illegible], if their profits on the sheep and cattle they graze free and on their land are not taken into consideration. But if such profits are estimated they may roughly be said to be worth between [illegible] and [illegible] a year. It is, however, very difficult to estimate these profits, as they depend on whether the season is favourable, on the luck they have with their stock, and on the prices of sheep and cattle, which have been extremely low in recent years. (See Appendix A. [illegible].)

[illegible]. A very great number of men and women go to England and Scotland from Mayo to work on the farms during the year. To say that they go "harvesting" by no means describes the length of time the people stay out of Ireland, for many of them, both men and women, begin to go from the middle of March for the purpose of putting down potatoes, weeding, and doing the ordinary work on the farms, and do not return until after potato lifting is over towards the end of November or in time for Christmas. (See Appendix A. [illegible].)

Mr Tatlow, the manager of the Midland Great Western Railway, tells me that 17,[illegible] harvest tickets were issued by their company from stations in Mayo in 18[illegible]. (Appendix A. [illegible].)

Also from Westport Quay in 18[illegible] Mr. O'Malley booked by steamer to Scotland [illegible] persons, the majority of whom were women, and to England by steamer [illegible] men. (Appendix A. [illegible].)

In addition Messrs. Alexander Laird and Company, of Glasgow, carried [illegible] harvesters by their steamers from Ballina to Glasgow in May and June.

This makes a total of [illegible] persons who started from stations and ports in Mayo to England and Scotland in 18[illegible], or [illegible] per cent. of the population of the age of 15 years and upwards. (See Summary Report, paragraph [illegible].)

The women who go harvesting nearly all go to Scotland, and are employed there in putting down potatoes, thinning turnips, weeding, harvesting, and potato lifting. As previously stated the great majority of them go by sea from Westport to Glasgow (see [illegible]). Several have told me that they dread the voyage owing to seasickness, and that it is so trying to the whole woman's work.

A boat runs every alternate week from Westport and Ballina, but in busy times, i.e., in June and July, extra boats are run. A boat also starts from Sligo on certain days. The great day for the people in the south part of the union to go is June [illegible], so they attend the Newport Fair on the [illegible], where they sell their cattle, and, with part of the proceeds, pay for their fares, the remainder going towards the payment of their debts at the shops.

The women in the Connemara districts make an earlier start than this, many going about Easter time.

The men from the Westport Union chiefly go to Lancashire and Cheshire, but some go to Warwickshire and a few to Northumberland and Yorkshire. I met several men who worked for farmers in the Garstang Union of Lancashire, where I was making inquiries in November 18[illegible], and the information I had acquired there from the farmers, and also from several Irishmen I interviewed, greatly assisted me in dealing with the men I met in Mayo. One man was very much surprised when I showed him a letter from the farmer in Lancashire who employed him, giving a detailed account of the wages paid to Irishmen on his farm this last year.

The women who go to Scotland have an advantage over the men who go to England in this respect, namely,

[*] The following are the [illegible] to [illegible] in Mr. [illegible]'s [illegible]:—

[illegible]

[illegible]

[illegible]

[illegible]

[illegible] Mr. [illegible] [illegible] of Westport, informs me [illegible] [illegible] [illegible] [illegible] [illegible] [illegible] that there is a sort of system or organisation which enables them to be sure of work before starting. It is frequently the custom in Scotland for merchants to buy the potatoes while still in the ground, also undertaking the lifting and carting. To do this they communicate with some man in Ireland, called by the people a "gaffer," and request him to bring over a certain number of men. The "gaffer" then takes over the workers, and accompanies them from farm to farm, wherever the merchant, who has bought the potatoes, requires them for digging and lifting. From this the men are ensured continued employment from start to finish, which is, of course, a considerable advantage. They have, moreover, the companionship throughout of their own friends and neighbours, which is pleasant for them.

There is, however, no such system as regards the men, though I did meet one or two farmers, both in Northumberland and Lancashire, who wrote to Ireland for the men they required, and in one case the money for their journey was advanced.*

But it frequently happens that the men waste some days, or even a longer time in going from farm to farm in search of work on their arrival, which involves loss of wages, and costs them money for food and lodging that they can ill afford.† On their arrival in England they often have scarcely a penny in their pockets, and a week without employment consequently entails much hardship.

Possibly a labour bureau might be started in some of the big towns in Lancashire, such as Liverpool, Southport, Preston, and Lancaster, to which the farmers could send, stating the number of men they required, and where the Irishmen could go on their arrival in England to seek for work.

But there is another way in which the harvesters could be materially helped, and that is by advancing to those who have no means a sufficient sum to enable them to get to England or Scotland. One has only to visit some of the small holdings to understand what a sacrifice it must entail to gather money, and what an impossibility it is to others to find funds to enable two or perhaps three out of a family to make the journey. To those who start in March or April the question of finding journey money is especially difficult, for at the end of the winter they are in the worst pecuniary situation of the year.

I met several young men who told me they would start for England if they had the means. Two of these were strong lads who were merely lounging about doing nothing, and it appeared to be a very great pity that the want of a sovereign or two should prevent such men from earning in England what to them is a substantial sum.

After I left Mayo I was fortunate enough to have the advantage of an introduction to Sir Thomas Brady, and I then learnt from him that he was deeply interested in this subject, and that he had advanced considerable sums of money among the poorest classes in Mayo, to enable them to proceed to England or Scotland for the spring or harvest work.

"In this district," says Sir Thomas Brady, "I have "frequently lent 10l. to 100 persons, the loan being "repayable in six months, and these have often and "often been repaid long before the time they were due, "and in nearly all cases punctually repaid. The de-"faulters were sharply admonished but all eventually paid "up."

Perhaps Sir Thomas Brady's philanthropic enterprise may be the forerunner of some organised system of carrying out this excellent work, which without doubt must have been of very great benefit to the families so assisted. (See Appendix B. 7.)

In Appendix B 8 I have given the opinions of employers in Northumberland, Lancashire, Cheshire, Yorkshire, and Warwickshire, as to the quality of Irishmen's work compared with that of Englishmen, and the comparison does not seem unfavourable to the former, especially when the poverty of their dietary is taken into consideration. With the exception of Sir James Poulett's case (Lancashire), I am not in a position to say that the evidence I quote refers specially to Mayo men, but as harvesters go from Mayo to all these counties, the employers I have named, who are all large ones, have in all probability employed some of them.

I asked a great number of men how much money they could clear by their work in England for five or six months, and received replies varying from about 9l. to 15l., and from the information I gathered in Lancashire, I do not think this estimate is far wrong. There are, however, men who spend nearly nine months in the year in England and these probably make over 20l. clear.

I give in Appendix A. 10 the particulars of the earnings of two men who were at Maltmoney for last year, taken from the books of Mr James Pearson, a farmer at St Michael on Wyre, Garstang, Lancashire. It will be seen that their earnings each came to 20l. 10s. in about 6½ months. If the cost of their food is put at 8s. a week, and it probably does not come to more, as it will be seen they are given a Lancashire pie twice a day, and if their railway fare (return), 30s., is deducted, their net profits are 12l. 6s.*

If several men go from the same family, as is frequently the case, and each man earns a sum as this, their united earnings amount to something considerable.

In the Glendale Union of Northumberland, where I was reporting for the Royal Commission on Labour in September 1892, Irishmen are not able to earn so much as in Lancashire, as the ordinary staff of the farms there can as a rule do all the necessary work, except at harvest time, though on some farms they do some turnip thinning, but after harvest is over there the Irishmen frequently go to other districts where the harvest is later, or go further south and help at potato lifting. In Appendix A. 10 I give the earnings of six Irishmen employed on a farm near Wooler, Northumberland in 1892. These men came in June, July, and August, and left on October 1st. The most one man earned was 11l. 8s. 9½d., and the least was 5l. 19s. 1d. They were supplied with lodging and all food during harvest, but while they were [illegible] they had to find their own food, but were given skim milk. I was unable to ascertain what else these men were able to earn that year in other districts.

In Appendix A. 10 I also give the detailed earnings of nine Irishmen employed on a large farm of about 1,000 acres, in Warwickshire, supplied me by Colonel Baker, agent to the Marquis of Hertford. It will be seen that in 21 weeks every man averaged 19s. a week, with lodging and food free, but as some arrived [illegible] they did not all earn the same sum.

Mr F. Walker, agent to Lord Wenlock, informs me that near York Irishmen are paid 20s. a week at hay-time and harvest, and 17s. a week for potato lifting. The farmer provides lodging.

The Hon. A. Parker, agent to the Earl of Cadogan, referring to Irishmen employed in the neighbourhood of Chester, says that they arrive there between March and hay harvest and return to Ireland in October and November, and sometimes as late as Christmas.

First class men are paid 15s. per week and 10s. extra for hay harvest, and 20s. extra for corn harvest. Second-class men get only 12s. a week. Englishmen are paid 18s. to 20s. a week for hay harvest and 20s. extra for corn harvest.

The Irishmen there have free lodging and are given milk night and morning. On Sunday they get bread and cheese and a pint of beer each at night.

A great many of the older men say that in consequence of the introduction of machinery and the giving up of tillage farming, the necessity for the employment of so many hands at harvest has been done away with, and, for the same reason, their earnings have been considerably lessened. One man who has been to England for 30 years, told me that he used to bring back 20l., whereas now he could only bring back 10l.†

In Cumberland the use of machinery has entirely done away with the necessity of employing Irish labour.‡

* Sir W. T. [illegible]

† [illegible]

* [illegible]

† [illegible]

‡ [illegible]

The girls who go to Scotland also seem able to earn a considerable sum in a short time. One of these who went there last year from Achill from June to September, told me she cleared 6l. or 7l. besides 2l. which she spent on clothes.* It seems the general custom of those who go to Scotland to buy clothes there out of harvest money for themselves and their families.

V.—Cottage Accommodation.

47. There are scarcely any cottages in the union which come within the ordinary definition of a labourer's cottage, that is, a cottage with a small piece of garden rented by a man whose sole occupation is agricultural employment for wages. I only came across one or two instances of the above, namely, where several men on Lord John Browne's farm rent cottages in the neighbourhood of Westport at 1s. a week.

I have already given the probable reason why the Labourers Acts have not been put into operation in this Union (par. 18).

The herds invariably have cottages provided for them by their employers as part of their wages, with from one to five acres of land usually attached.

As, however, it is impossible to distinguish between the cottages of the ordinary labourer and those of the small holder, who frequently works himself for wages, I have given in Appendix A. 11 some examples of the cottages I saw and examined in various parts of the union.†

48. The houses are frequently clustered in long straggling hamlets, surrounded by a few acres of the bogs, but in some places I found them packed closely together, presumably one small improvident [illegible] [illegible] [illegible] to live as near their neighbours as possible. Space certainly appeared to be but little object in some of the larger [illegible], or on the hill sides where some of these hamlets were situated, but, as the people build their houses themselves, they choose, within certain limits, their own sites.

49. When the description of one cottage has been given it suffices for all, as they usually contain the same accommodation, and are of similar structure.

They generally belong to the tenants, who, as I have pointed out, are their own architects and are constructed of stones, with roofs covered with thatch and turf.

There is one principal room, generally about 15 × 12, with a beamed roof, generally black with smoke from the peat fire, which seems to escape into the room quite as much as up the chimney.

In a sort of niche in the wall on the right-hand side of the fireplace there is a bed, in front of which curtains are often drawn, and in this the father and mother and perhaps a child usually sleep.

At the end of the room and opposite the fireplace the cattle frequently live, sometimes two cows and two calves, with occasionally the addition of a donkey or a horse, a pig or two, and some hens. The floors are sometimes stones, sometimes concrete, but as often as not there is nothing but the bare ground.

A small room used as a bedroom generally opens out of the kitchen at the left-hand side of the fireplace. These are sometimes as big as 15 × 12, but often far smaller, and I have seen them only just large enough to put a bed into. The furniture of these rooms is extremely scanty, usually consisting of a few chairs, a table, sometimes a spinning wheel, and always a dresser upon which china and crockery is arranged, and underneath which, in the spring time, the geese appear to sit.

Such a thing as a closet is unknown, and there is no drainage whatever.‡

The manure heap is very frequently placed in front of the door. The people are either careless of the effect or find it more convenient to throw the old bedding and manure out of the door on to the heap immediately opposite.

50. The water supply in the country districts is, as a rule, pure and plentiful. I heard very few complaints on that score.*

51. The ventilation is better in the houses than might be expected, considering that large families are frequently sleeping and living in one room, which is also shared by cows and other animals, but this is because the door communicates with the outside air, and is so often open, and also because a peat fire is almost constantly burning. I do not consider an Irish cottage nearly so stuffy as many bedrooms in some of the cottages in a Norfolk or Suffolk village.

52. I have already pointed out that the people chiefly own their houses, which they have built on the land they rent from their landlord. This system, I cannot help thinking, has led to a great deal of ill-feeling between tenant and landlord, because a man who gets into arrears and fails to pay his rent considers it a very great injustice that he should be turned out of the house he has erected with his own hands, and consequently looks upon as his own property, whereas if he merely rented the cottage which was built and provided for him by his landlord, I believe he would not entertain the same feeling.

The herds' cottages are usually built by the landlord. Generally no agreement is made between the farmer and the herd as to the tenancy of the cottage, but it is mutually understood that notice to quit employment means notice to quit the cottage.

53. The great disadvantage under which a local authority labours in dealing with the cottage and sanitary questions is that the houses do not belong to landed proprietors, or other persons of means, as is frequently the case in England, upon whom pressure can be brought to bear if repairs are needed or sanitary alterations desirable, but to people who, in many cases, can scarcely find sufficient money to obtain the bare necessities of life, and who are in debt both to the landlord for their holding and the village shop for their food.

It is indeed difficult to suggest anything practical to remedy the deplorable state of many of the houses put up by the inhabitants themselves with but little skill, and at a minimum cost, in a thickly populated district which cannot support its population, and which contains electoral divisions where the rates reach the enormous figure of 5s. or 6s. in the pound.

Still the question remains, and will, I venture to think, at no distant date have to be answered by local authorities or the Government of the country, whether the people in the West of Ireland shall be allowed to build and inhabit cottages which are often unfit habitations for the cattle they contain, much less for the crowd of growing girls and boys, who share with them the shelter.

The practice of keeping the animals in the houses is greatly to be condemned, and steps ought to be taken by the board of guardians to discourage it.

Doubtless a total prohibition could not be enforced as many of the people could not afford to make other arrangements, but it could easily be made a condition in new houses that a wall should be built between the living room and the space inhabited by the cattle, and a separate door made for them to enter by.

Such a stipulation would probably be considered by the people as an unnecessary revolution, but it has been accomplished in Northumberland within the memory of those now living, and also in other parts of Ireland, and one cannot seriously question that the fact of cattle living in the same room and breathing the same air as several human beings, and fouling the floor, can be anything but unhealthy, or whether the social condition of the people can really improve so long as they live in the same room as the beasts of the field.†

54. It is almost impossible to say what rent such cottages would command. Herds who are generally provided with a better cottage than many of the small holders have built, usually value them at 3l. or 4l. a year.

55. It is difficult to ascertain the cost of building a labourer's cottage in this district, and in fact I was unable to find an instance where a cottage suitable for

* Mrs. [illegible], [illegible], [illegible] that many of the girls [illegible] [illegible] [illegible] [illegible] [illegible]. She [illegible] [illegible] [illegible] [illegible] [illegible] [illegible] [illegible] [illegible] by the [illegible] [illegible] of Achill, but they [illegible] [illegible] [illegible] [illegible] to [illegible].

† In [illegible] there were [illegible] houses in the union and [illegible] [illegible], or a [illegible] of [illegible] per cent.

‡ Dr. Aileen, Westport, writes:—"The [illegible] are [illegible]."

* Dr. Aileen, Westport, writes:—"The water supply is [illegible] [illegible] [illegible] as regards quantity and quality. In the [illegible] [illegible] of the [illegible] it is good."

† As regards the effect upon the question of cattle in the house [illegible] [illegible], Dr. Aileen, Westport, writes:—"The very [illegible] of [illegible] [illegible] [illegible] [illegible] [illegible] [illegible] [illegible] [illegible] [illegible] [illegible] [illegible] [illegible] [illegible] [illegible] [illegible] [illegible] [illegible] [illegible]."

a labourer had recently been built. Mr R. Powell, agent to the Marquis of Sligo, says that the present cost of building a herd's house is 60l., and a labourer's cottage 40l.

Mr Livingstone, agent to the Earl of Lucan, considers that a labourer's cottage, with two rooms, could be built for about 50l.

A small holder told me his house cost him 14l. to build. He paid nothing for labour, as he had the assistance of friends.

It must be borne in mind that the stone of which houses are made is very plentiful, and consequently the price of it, and the cost of carting is small.

56. When the valuation of the building is 4l. a year or under the landlord pays the rates, but when it is over 4l. the landlord and the tenant each pay half. The tenant always pays the county cess.

57. Persons who have no land, or not a sufficient quantity, sometimes rent from an occupier an acre or two, and such land is known as "conacre."

The price of conacre is fixed according to the quality of the land, but it varies from 1l. an acre (Irish) for one crop on ordinary land to 3l. if two crops are to be taken off in consecutive years.

From 4l. to 5l. an acre is charged for corn off tilled and manured land, and from 5l. to 7l. for potatoes.

VI.—Benefit Societies and Trade Unions.

58. Benefit societies appear to be quite unknown, which is much to be regretted, and there do not seem to be any insurance societies or burial clubs.

Speaking of benefit and insurance societies a herd said to me—

"Many people would think if they insured their lives they would be hurrying on their death or an illness. That is the sort of people the Irish are."

Whether they would think the insurance of cows would induce any injury on those animals, I know not, but I cannot help thinking they would find it a great boon if such insurance clubs could be started. Throughout the district every family keeps a cow, perhaps two, and the death of the cow is a very serious matter indeed, and in some cases means almost bankruptcy. Mr Moran, R.V., told me that he never saw much greater distress or despair than when he visited the house of a small holder where the only cow had just died.

Some of the great drawbacks to an Irish parish or village, when compared with an English one, are that there are no charities of any sort, no parish societies, coal or clothing clubs, no mother's meetings, parish nurses, cottage hospitals, reading rooms, or other organisations to promote the well being, the comfort or the happiness of the people.

59. Trade unions do not exist in any shape or form, as there are so few agricultural labourers in the ordinary sense of the word, to form combinations. I understand from a gentleman who was somewhat prominently connected with an organisation called the Land League, to which many of the small tenants belonged, that the methods adopted by that body to gain the ends its promoters had in view were never copied by those who went out to work for wages with the object of inducing employers to give them greater privileges.

VII.—Relations between Employers and Employed.

60. The relations between employers and employed can be described as good. I heard of very few complaints by the employers of the men's conduct and very little grumbling on the part of the men, who are almost unanimous in saying that the relations between them and their employers are satisfactory and that any difference they may have is solely on the question of wages. (Appendix B. 5.)

Some employers say that the men are getting more independent in their manner, and are not unwilling to work overtime, and also that they do not come so punctually in the morning, but I do not think that this is due to estranged relations, but is rather the outcome of the general distaste for agricultural employment, which seems growing, not only in Ireland but in England.

VIII.—General Condition of the Agricultural Labourer.

General condition of the agricultural labourer.

61. The question as to whether the condition of the agricultural labourer has improved in the last 20 years or not is a difficult one to answer generally. But I think it may be replied to in the affirmative, as far as regards those men who live exclusively by agricultural employment, though such are very scarce in Mayo. Westport

Their wages are higher by 2s. a week or more, the necessaries of life are cheaper (Appendix A. 7), and their educational facilities are greater.

But as the great majority of men who work for hire are small farmers themselves, in the case of Mayo, the positions of the farmer and the labourer cannot be separated, and an inquiry into the condition of the labourer in Mayo means an inquiry into the condition of the peasantry.

It will be seen in Appendix B. 6 that several witnesses consider that, if anything, the condition of the people has retrograded in the last 20 years, while Lord John Browne, and Mr Powell, agent to the Marquis of Sligo, consider that, though there has been no marked change for the better in the last 20 years, there was a very great improvement in the preceding period of 20 years. Mr Thomas Healy, who is intimately acquainted with the condition of the people in Mayo, confirms the view that there has been an improvement in the last 20 years, in that they "are better fed and "clad, and in many cases better housed." But he adds: "Their condition is much below the standard of "the ordinary labourer in other countries."

Now the question arises, how is it that the people are so very little better off, if at all, at the present time than they were 20 years ago? The fact that the population of the Union decreased 6.8 per cent. between 1881 and 1891, that the number of cattle in the county increased from 168,291 to 174,977, or 3.7 per cent., that the number of sheep increased from 225,519 to 263,343 or 16.8 per cent., that rents have been reduced, and that prices of food and clothing are cheaper would make it appear that the people must be more generally prosperous.

But to this question there may be several answers. In the first place the prices of cattle and sheep are much lower,[1] and the growing of corn has practically ceased, the large empty granaries and abandoned mills at Westport and elsewhere standing as monuments of a bygone agricultural industry. Further, the introduction of machinery at harvest has both lessened the demand for labour in England, and decreased the earnings of the Irishmen who formerly were adepts at handling the scythe.

The linen trade, and consequently the growing of flax, has also been given up, and the making of frieze, flannel, and stockings for sale has almost died out. It may be that this is partly due to the emigration to America of almost every able-bodied unmarried woman, but, whatever the cause, it is quite apparent that in a district where small holdings abound, any or all of these reasons may counteract the good results which would appear to accrue from a decrease in population, a decrease in rent, a decrease in the cost of food, and an increase in the number of stock.

Perhaps nothing demonstrates the poverty of the district more effectually than a reference to the number of relief works it was found necessary to undertake in 1891 to keep the people from actual want when the potato crop partially failed. (Paragraph 16.)

It is difficult for a stranger to describe accurately the actual condition of the people in Mayo. Possibly the appearance of the cabins and squalid poverty, the poverty of the soil, the ragged clothes and bare feet of men and women all appeal to him to paint the picture darker than a native of the district would do. I will therefore quote from the annual report of the Congested Districts Board for 1893 to describe the condition of those living in the congested districts:—

"In the first place, practically all the inhabitants of congested districts in Ireland are in possession of small plots of land, so that the development of agriculture and the improvement of the breeds of live stock and poultry are of primary and universal importance. Secondary sources of income vary in different districts. In many localities the results of fishing are as valuable as the produce of the land. In other districts migratory labour in England, Scotland, and elsewhere is an indispensable source of livelihood. Weaving, knitting, sewing, lace-making, sale of seaweed, sale of turf or peat, sale of illicit whiskey, remittances from relatives in America, occasional employment at home, are sources of income of greater or less importance in different localities. Residents along the seaboard have many advantages, arising from fishing, from gathering seaweed for kelp and manure, and from cheap carriage by sea for flour, meal, and other commodities; but, on the

---

[1] Mr [illegible], [illegible]

[illegible]

other hand, peat for fuel has often to be brought from a great distance by those living on the sea-shore, and rough grazing for cattle and sheep is frequently not available there. People dwelling inland rather depend almost altogether on their farms or else they regularly migrate for some months of the year in search of employment in England and Scotland, or even America as [illegible]. In some inland mountain places where the inhabitants have very small patches of land tilled in [illegible], and [illegible] where their cattle and sheep have deteriorated in breeding and diminished in numbers, where little effort is made by the men to earn money through migratory labour or otherwise, in such mountain places are to be found people who endure the most [illegible] and cheerless lives of all the inhabitants of congested districts in Ireland. In a good year, they are little more than free from the dread of hunger, while a complete or partial failure of their crop involves as a consequence proportionately greater or less suffering from insufficient food."

Again, Sir Thomas Brady says:—

"I know that the majority of the people are, I might say, in the depths of poverty. They rely on their small holdings or patches of land for support, and, if they have a favourable season their crops will enable them to tide over most of the difficulties, and pay the shopkeepers for supplies they have had on credit during the past year, but if an unfavourable season they are steeped in poverty." (Appendix B 4.)

In this district where many of the people are illiterate and the larger portion extremely uneducated, I found it impossible to obtain any accounts of their expenditure. In fact, the small holders have not the slightest conception what their annual income amounts to.

I have, however, obtained from the books of a village shop the accounts of several small holders, which really represent their annual expenditure, as they live 18 miles from Westport, and have nowhere else to make their purchases except at this shop. Two of these people live in a village, described by the sergeant of the constabulary as "a village as poor as any in Ireland."

It will be seen on a perusal of these accounts that these small holders are usually in debt, and that but little cash passes, payment being frequently made in hay, eggs, pigs, cattle, or by working as a labourer. A small tradesman in the north of the union told me that he would have a "[illegible] full of cattle" if he chose to be paid in cattle instead of cash.

From inquiries I made among the people and from village shopkeepers in various parts of the union, I ascertained that a great number of the small holders are in debt at the present time, and this is caused to a considerable extent by the serious decline in the prices of sheep and cattle. These debts are frequently reduced by cash payments sent from relatives in America, and by money made in England during the harvest.

The principal food consists of by the peasantry of tea, milk, potatoes, eggs, fish, and cabbage. When the potatoes are finished "[illegible]," meals of Indian meal, are taken instead.

Here I was told the same story as in England, namely, that tea drinking is largely on the increase, and that its effects are detrimental to the health of the people. It was also asserted, as in Northumberland, that the substitution of white for whole meal bread, and the growing distaste for porridge has decreased the stamina of the people.

Referring to this subject, Dr. Aitken, of Westport, says:—

"I consider the tea drinking of late years has decidedly a bad effect on the health of the people. Dyspepsia and allied diseases, also mental diseases are all traceable to the cause. The leading formerly was porridge for breakfast and supper and potatoes for dinner, now tea and loaf bread are substituted for the porridge, which made a more civilised diet, but I doubt if it is as healthy."

As regards the houses there also have been but little improvement. I saw a good many which had been put up of recent years but they were built on much the same lines as the older ones. As I have previously stated it seems difficult to understand how the sanitary conditions of the houses can be really improved so long as the cattle are allowed to live in them.

The dress of the people is said to be improving, and certainly on Sundays I saw people turning out of poor looking houses in good clothes. The materials of which the clothes usually worn are made are warm and serviceable, being made of pure wool spun at home.

The men generally wear flannel shirts, a thick frieze waistcoat, sometimes with flannel sleeves, and frieze coats and trousers. Their socks or stockings are made of wool spun and knitted at home. The women make their own clothes. Their petticoats are generally thick and warm.

The education of the people is improving, and I am informed that parents are showing a desire to have their children properly taught, as they learn from their friends in America how difficult it is to get on there if their education has been neglected.

However, many of the present generation are very uneducated. In 1891, 32·0 per cent. of the persons aged 5 years and upwards in the county of Mayo were illiterate. The percentage for that year in the parish of Achill was 50·2.

Lord John Browne informs me that in the town of Westport drunkenness is on the increase. In many of the country districts drinking is rare, and this is caused in a great measure by the people having no money to spend. I have been told that when these country people come into market then a very little whiskey will make them drunk, partly because they are not accustomed to it, and partly because they often take it on such occasions on an empty stomach.

There is one admirable trait in the character of the Irish people, which considerably affects the means of livelihood of those in the poverty stricken districts. I mean the family affection which prompts those, who have sought employment in America, to send assistance to their less fortunate friends and relatives in Ireland.

I have, &c.
(Signed) ARTHUR WILSON FOX,
(Assistant Commissioner).

TABLE OF CONTENTS.

A. 1.

Westport Union.

Electoral Divisions.	Area			Rates		Inhabited Houses.	Population in 1891.
	Acres	Roods	Perches	s.	d.		
Aghagower, North	3,439	1	5	1	1	149	840
*Aghagower, South	5,701	2	33	1	0	44	211
*Aillemore	7,444	2	10	2	4	[illegible]	1,[illegible]
Bundorragha	10,436	1	13	1	6	[illegible]	163
*Clare Island	3,948	2	3	2	0	[illegible]	[illegible]
*[illegible]	3,440	1	30	0	9	[illegible]	1,[illegible]
*Croagh Patrick	7,[illegible]	0	33	0	8½	160	[illegible]
*Drummin	33,[illegible]	2	11	1	1	91	546
*[illegible]	6,091	2	24	1	1	[illegible]	1,148
Erriff	26,[illegible]	3	14	0	6	97	746
*Islandeady	[illegible]	1	[illegible]	1	3	[illegible]	[illegible]
*[illegible]	15,948	3	34	1	1	73	494
[illegible]	3,[illegible]	2	[illegible]	1	0	189	718
[illegible]	6,718	3	3	1	6	271	2,[illegible]
*[illegible]	3,079	0	13	1	6	178	1,301
*Knappagh	6,340	0	35	1	1	221	1,116
*Louisburgh	5,701	2	0	0	1	[illegible]	1,441
Owennadornaun	3,444	1	20	1	3	[illegible]	77
*[illegible]	10,311	0	34	0	4½	140	676
Westport	3,331	0	7	2	6	654	4,[illegible]
*Achill	8,540	3	17	3	0	[illegible]	1,[illegible]
*Ballycroy, North	[illegible]	0	10	3	5	187	1,311
*Ballycroy, South	31,[illegible]	2	24	0	0	117	848
*Corraun, Achill	13,[illegible]	3	[illegible]	0	0	[illegible]	1,[illegible]
*Derryloughan	8,974	2	31	0	0	114	1,014
*[illegible]	[illegible]	0	3	0	0	110	1,[illegible]
*[illegible]	10,879	1	1	1	3	174	976
*Newport, East	8,[illegible]	3	32	2	0	[illegible]	1,[illegible]
*Newport, West	17,611	2	[illegible]	1	4	[illegible]	1,[illegible]
*Slievemore	17,161	1	[illegible]	0	4	73	1,010
*[illegible]	[illegible]	3	3	0	0	91	644

TABLE OF CONGESTED DISTRICTS COUNTIES.*

Congested Districts County.	Number of Congested Districts.	Number of Congested Electoral Divisions.	Area in Statute Acres.	Population in 1891.	Poor-Law Valuation.	Poor-Law Valuation per head of Population.
					£.	£. s. d.
Donegal	[illegible]	[illegible]	[illegible]	[illegible]	[illegible]	[illegible]
Leitrim	[illegible]	[illegible]	[illegible]	[illegible]	[illegible]	[illegible]
Sligo	[illegible]	[illegible]	[illegible]	[illegible]	[illegible]	[illegible]
Roscommon	[illegible]	[illegible]	[illegible]	[illegible]	[illegible]	[illegible]
Mayo	[illegible]	[illegible]	[illegible]	[illegible]	[illegible]	[illegible]
Galway	[illegible]	[illegible]	[illegible]	[illegible]	[illegible]	[illegible]
Kerry	[illegible]	[illegible]	[illegible]	[illegible]	[illegible]	[illegible]
Cork	[illegible]	[illegible]	[illegible]	[illegible]	[illegible]	[illegible]
Totals	[illegible]	[illegible]	[illegible]	[illegible]	[illegible]	[illegible]

* Valuation per head on the total population.
† Taken from the First Annual Report of the Congested Districts Board, 1892.

A. 2.

WAGES.

—	Daily or Weekly Wages.		Annual Earnings.
	Summer.	Winter.	
Ordinary labourers	Per Day. 1s. 0d. to 1s. 6d., or 1s. to 1s. 3d. with food.	Per Day. 1s. 0d. to 1s. 3d., or 10d. to 1s. with food.	[illegible] in regular employment about 1[illegible]d. and food.
Hinds†	Per Week. 10s. to 11s. 6d.	Per Week. 10s. to 11s. 6d.	[illegible] to 27l. 14s.
Ploughmen	Per Day. 2s.	Per Day. 2s.	31l. 4s.
Carters	1s. 6d. to 1s. 9d.	1s. 6d. to 1s. 9d.	[illegible] to [illegible]
Hired Men	—	—	8l. to 14l. with lodging, board, and washing.
Hired Boys aged between 14 and 18.	—	—	4l. to 8l.

* These figures represent the average [illegible] they receive as wages without any [illegible] up the profits they make from the sheep and cattle they graze free. It will be seen in Appendix A. 4 that if such profits are taken into consideration their position is a much more satisfactory one.
† A few of Lord John Browne's [illegible] up to 32l. by [illegible].

Payments or Allowances and their supposed Values	1. [illegible] under Mr F. King [illegible]	2. [illegible] under Mr R. King [illegible]	3. [illegible] under Mr R. King [illegible]	4. [illegible]	5. [illegible]	6. [illegible]	7. [illegible]
Wages	£ s. d. [illegible]	£ s. d. [illegible]	£ s. d. [illegible]	£ s. d. [illegible]	£ s. d. [illegible]	£ s. d. [illegible]	£ s. d. [illegible]
Tillage land	[illegible]	[illegible]	[illegible]	[illegible]	[illegible]	Land [illegible]	[illegible]
Grass for cattle	—	[illegible]	[illegible]	—	—	Grazing [illegible]	[illegible]
[illegible]	[illegible]	—	—	[illegible]	[illegible]	[illegible]	—
[illegible]	[illegible]	—	—	[illegible]	[illegible]	—	—
[illegible]	[illegible]	—	—	—	—	[illegible]	—
[illegible]	[illegible]	—	—	[illegible]	[illegible]	—	—
[illegible]	[illegible]	—	—	[illegible]	—	—	—
[illegible]	[illegible]	—	[illegible]	—	—	[illegible]	[illegible]
[illegible]	—	—	—	[illegible]	—	—	—
[illegible]	—	—	—	—	—	Turf [illegible]	—
Cash	—	[illegible]	—	[illegible]	[illegible]	[illegible]	[illegible]
Total [illegible]	[illegible]	[illegible]	[illegible]	[illegible]	[illegible]	[illegible]	[illegible]
Remarks	[illegible]	[illegible]	[illegible]	[illegible]	[illegible]	[illegible]	[illegible]

A 5.

Number of Days Two Children worked in a Year for Mr McKeown, Leenane.

Number of days Stephen Joyce (aged [illegible]) worked for Mr. McKeown, innkeeper and farmer, Leenane, from March [illegible], to March [illegible].

Stephen Joyce's wages are 1s. 6d. a day. He lost some time through wet weather, [illegible] weeks on account of illness, and was absent on [illegible] Roman Catholic holidays.

He lives at [illegible] with his father, mother, two brothers, and two sisters. His father has about [illegible] acres of tillage, and the run of a mountain. His rent is [illegible].

	£	s.	d.
From March 16, [illegible], to April 27, [illegible], [illegible] days at 1s 6d. per day	[illegible]	[illegible]	[illegible]
From April 27, [illegible], to July [illegible], [illegible], [illegible] days at 1s 6d a day.	[illegible]	[illegible]	[illegible]
From July [illegible], [illegible], to December [illegible], [illegible], [illegible] days at 1s 6d a day.	[illegible]	[illegible]	[illegible]
From December [illegible], [illegible], to March 16, [illegible], [illegible] days at 1s. 6d a day	[illegible]	[illegible]	[illegible]
Total earnings [illegible] days at 1s. 6d. a day	[illegible]	[illegible]	[illegible]

Number of days John McLoughlin Dan* (aged [illegible]) worked for Mr. McKeown, innkeeper and farmer, Leenane, from February [illegible], to February [illegible].

McLoughlin Dan's wages are 1s 6d. a day. He lost some time through wet weather, a month through illness, was absent on [illegible] Roman Catholic holidays, and for three weeks during his mother's illness. He lives at [illegible] with his father, mother, two brothers, and two sisters. His father's holding is about the same size as the Joyce's, but the land is not so good and the rent is only [illegible].

	£	s.	d.
From February [illegible], to March 11, [illegible], [illegible] days at 1s. 6d. a day	[illegible]	[illegible]	[illegible]
From March 11, [illegible], to April 27, [illegible], [illegible] days at 1s 6d a day.	[illegible]	[illegible]	[illegible]
From May [illegible], [illegible], to June [illegible], [illegible], [illegible] days at 1s 6d. a day.	[illegible]	[illegible]	[illegible]
From June [illegible], [illegible], to December [illegible], [illegible] days at 1s. 6d a day.	[illegible]	[illegible]	[illegible]
From December [illegible], [illegible], to February [illegible], [illegible], [illegible] days at 1s. 6d a day	[illegible]	[illegible]	[illegible]
Total earnings [illegible] days at 1s 6d a day	[illegible]	[illegible]	[illegible]

A. 6.

Account of A B. with B.C., Grocer and General Dealer.

A B is about [illegible] years old. He has a wife, a daughter about [illegible] years, two sons, one a hired man, the other works at odd times. His holding is [illegible] acres (Irish), and he has, in addition, the right of grazing on a mountain. He has a cow and calf, and seven hens. Last year he had [illegible] acres of potatoes, and [illegible] acres of oats. He grew cabbages in ridges through the potatoes.

[illegible]

* "Dan" is added to John McLoughlin's name to distinguish him from others of the same name. [illegible]

[illegible]

			s. d.
[illegible]	[illegible]	[illegible]	[illegible]

Above goods were given on condition that they were to be paid by work, so above amount was charged to ledger account, and the days taken off on March 15th, 1882.

Analysis of Expenditure in Shop Goods during Period of 12 Months, January to December 1882, abstracted from the preceding Account.

	£	s.	d.	£	s.	d.
Food:						
Bread	0	7	5			
Cake	0	0	4½			
Flour	2	1	7			
Oatmeal	0	7	8½			
Indian meal	0	8	8			
Bran	0	5	11½	3	5	3½
Bacon	0	0	11			
Fish	0	1	4			
Lard &c., butter, &c.	0	0	6	0	2	11

[8

	£ s. d.	£ s. d.
GROCERIES FOR CONSUMPTION		
*Tea (7 lbs., 10 ozs.)	1 1 1½	
Sugar (80 lbs.)	0 16 8	
Salt (8d.)	0 0 8	
Cream of tartar (5½d.)	0 0 5½	
		2 1 8
Tobacco	0 [illegible] 3	
Drapery	0 [illegible] 6	
Total amount of goods for consumption		[illegible]
HOUSEHOLD REQUISITES:		
Washing materials—Soap (1s.); soda (1½d.); starch (1d.)	0 1 8½	
Lights	0 0 11	
Blacking (1d.); oil (4d.); Logwood (5½d.)	0 0 10½	
		0 3 0
CLOTHING		[illegible]
SUNDRIES:		
Tongs (9d.); Wall paper (6d.), nails (1½d.)	0 [illegible] 4½	
Cash to Mary	0 0 6	
		0 1 10½
To add from subsequent account—Tea (3 ozs., 6d.), sugar (1 lb., 3½d.); Clothing (9s. 10½d.)		0 10 6
		[illegible]

B.C. informs me that A.B. deals with no one but himself, and that his only means of livelihood are the produce of his holding and the annual earnings of his two sons. B.C. has ascertained that the family live almost entirely on potatoes. In the village where A.B. dwells B.C. is of opinion that there are not more than two families who have meat more than twice a year.

* Tea is sold in the shop at [illegible] a pound.

Account of C.D. with B.C., Grocer and General Dealer

C.D. is aged about 50. He has a wife, three grown up daughters and two young sons living at home, and has three other children in America. He rents 10 Irish acres of land for 6l., with the additional right of the run of a mountain, on which he has about three head of cattle and [illegible] sheep.

			£ s. d.	£ s. d.
1891. March 17	Owed			[illegible]
" 17	Paid cash			[illegible]
				[illegible]
September 6	Owed			[illegible]
" 6	Paid cash*	[illegible]		
" 1	Allowance for butter	[illegible]		[illegible]
				[illegible]
November [illegible]	Owed			[illegible]
" [illegible]	Paid cash			[illegible]
				[illegible]
1892. [illegible] 27	Owed			[illegible]
" [illegible]	Paid cash			[illegible]
				[illegible]
[illegible]	Owed			[illegible]
" [illegible]	Paid cash			[illegible]
				[illegible]
November [illegible]	Owed			[illegible]
" [illegible]	Sold a heifer	[illegible]		
	Less (for luck)	[illegible]		[illegible]
				[illegible]
" [illegible]	Owed			[illegible]
" [illegible]	Given 1½ cwt. of hay at 4s. 6d. a cwt.			[illegible]
				[illegible]

* This sum was sent by two daughters in America.
† The account was then closed for some time, as B.C. refused to give further credit.
‡ [illegible]

Account of E.F. with B.C., Grocer and General Dealer

[illegible]

E.F. is aged about 45, and is unmarried. He lived with his mother, who has just died, and a niece. His sister, a servant in America, is now living in his house. His holding is about five Irish acres. Rent 4l.

		£ s. d.	£ s. d.
1891. May 1	Owed		[illegible]
" 1	By cash, per sister in America	[illegible]	
	By hay, [illegible] cwt., at [illegible] a cwt.	[illegible]	[illegible]
			[illegible]
1892. January [illegible]	Owed		[illegible]
" [illegible]	By a [illegible] of [illegible]		[illegible]
			[illegible]
November [illegible]	Owed		[illegible]
" [illegible]	By cash brought by sister returned from America		[illegible]
			[illegible]
" [illegible]	Owed		[illegible]
" [illegible]	By hay	[illegible]	
	By sale of bullock, less in the bank	[illegible]	[illegible]
			[illegible]
1893. March [illegible]	*Owed		[illegible]

* B.C. [illegible]

Account of G.H. with B.C., Grocer and General Dealer.

G.H. has five children, the eldest about 8 years old. He rents five Irish acres of land, and has also the run of a mountain. He has a cow and a calf and also [illegible] sheep, which B.C. gave him.

		£ s. d.	£ s. d.
1891.* December [illegible]	Owed		[illegible]
" [illegible]	Owed		[illegible]
1892. January [illegible]	Owed		[illegible]
" [illegible]	Credit for [illegible] days' work from October [illegible] at [illegible] a day and goods allowed on a account taken by B.C.		[illegible]
			[illegible]
" [illegible]	Owed		[illegible]
	Credit for [illegible] days' work in November, December, and January		[illegible]
			[illegible]
March [illegible]	Owed		[illegible]
" [illegible]	Less cash paid for work		[illegible]
			[illegible]
May [illegible]	Owed		[illegible]
" [illegible]	Paid cash		[illegible]
			[illegible]
" [illegible]	Owed		[illegible]
" [illegible]	Less [illegible] cwt. hay at [illegible] a cwt.		[illegible]
			[illegible]
July 19	Owed		[illegible]
	Sold a calf		[illegible]
			[illegible]
August [illegible]	Owed		[illegible]
" [illegible]	Paid cash		[illegible]
			[illegible]
October 1	Owed		[illegible]
	Paid cash	[illegible]	
	By [illegible] days' work	[illegible]	[illegible]
			[illegible]

* [illegible] G.H. [illegible] B.C. [illegible]

				£	s.	d.
18[illegible]—contd. October [illegible]	Cleared. [illegible] calf (18 [illegible] old)			[illegible]	[illegible]	[illegible]
				[illegible]	[illegible]	[illegible]
December [illegible]	Cleared. By [illegible] days' work at [illegible]s. [illegible]d.			[illegible]	[illegible]	[illegible]
				[illegible]	[illegible]	[illegible]
18[illegible]. January [illegible]	Cleared			[illegible]	[illegible]	[illegible]
	By [illegible] days' work at [illegible]s. [illegible]d. By [illegible] a [illegible]	[illegible]		[illegible]	[illegible]	[illegible]
				[illegible]	[illegible]	[illegible]
March [illegible]	Cleared			[illegible]	[illegible]	[illegible]

* [illegible]

A. 7.

Prices of Shop [illegible] in 1871 and 1893.

Taken from Mr McKeown's books at [illegible].

Commodity.	Amount.	Price in 1871.	Price in 1893.
Flour	per stone	[illegible] ([illegible])	[illegible] ([illegible])
Meal	"	[illegible]	[illegible]
Oatmeal	"	[illegible]	[illegible]
White loaf sugar	per pound	[illegible] (Crushed)	[illegible] (Crushed)
Tea	"	[illegible]	[illegible]
Coffee	"	[illegible]	[illegible]
Currants	"	[illegible]	[illegible]
Raisins	"	[illegible]	[illegible]
Salt	per stone	[illegible]	[illegible]
Pepper	per ounce	[illegible]	[illegible]

Note.—Mr. McKeown says that all clothing is cheaper now than it was in 1871 and also boots and shoes. Tobacco has slightly risen in price. In 1871 two ounces cost [illegible]d. and in 1893 they cost [illegible]d.

A. 8.

Harvestmen booked to England from certain Stations in Mayo, Seasons 18[illegible] and 18[illegible].

Mayo Line Extension and Ballaghaderreen.

Station	[illegible]	[illegible]	[illegible]	[illegible]	[illegible]	[illegible]	Total 18[illegible]	Total 18[illegible]
Ballina	[illegible]	[illegible]	[illegible]	[illegible]	[illegible]	[illegible]	[illegible]	[illegible]
Foxford	[illegible]	[illegible]	[illegible]	[illegible]	[illegible]	[illegible]	[illegible]	[illegible]
Westport	[illegible]	74	[illegible]	[illegible]	[illegible]	[illegible]	[illegible]	[illegible]
Castlebar	[illegible]	175	[illegible]	[illegible]	[illegible]	[illegible]	[illegible]	[illegible]
[illegible]	[illegible]	[illegible]	[illegible]	[illegible]	[illegible]	[illegible]	[illegible]	[illegible]
Balla	[illegible]	[illegible]	[illegible]	[illegible]	[illegible]	[illegible]	[illegible]	[illegible]
Claremorris	[illegible]	[illegible]	[illegible]	[illegible]	[illegible]	[illegible]	[illegible]	[illegible]
Ballyhaunis	[illegible]	[illegible]	[illegible]	[illegible]	[illegible]	[illegible]	[illegible]	[illegible]
[illegible]	[illegible]	[illegible]	[illegible]	[illegible]	[illegible]	[illegible]	[illegible]	[illegible]
Ballaghaderreen	[illegible]	757	[illegible]	[illegible]	[illegible]	[illegible]	[illegible]	[illegible]
Killala	[illegible]	[illegible]	[illegible]	[illegible]	[illegible]	[illegible]	[illegible]	[illegible]
[illegible]	[illegible]	[illegible]	[illegible]	[illegible]	[illegible]	[illegible]	[illegible]	[illegible]
[illegible]	[illegible]	[illegible]	[illegible]	[illegible]	[illegible]	[illegible]	[illegible]	[illegible]
Total booked from stations in Mayo							[illegible]	[illegible]
Total booked from other stations on the Midland Great Western system							[illegible]	[illegible]
Total booked on Midland Great Western system							[illegible]	[illegible]

Fares for Harvestmen from certain stations in Mayo to Glasgow or Liverpool.

From	From to Dublin North Wall.	Through fare to Glasgow or Liverpool.
	s.	s.
Killala	[illegible]	[illegible]
Foxford	[illegible]	[illegible]
Westport	[illegible]	[illegible]
Castlebar	[illegible]	[illegible]
Ballaghaderreen	[illegible]	[illegible]

A. 9.

Number of Harvestmen booked by Steamer from Westport to England and Scotland in 18[illegible].*

(Supplied by Mr. O'Malley, Westport Quay.)

Month.	England.	Scotland.
January	[illegible]	[illegible]
February	[illegible]	[illegible]
March	[illegible]	[illegible]
April	[illegible]	[illegible]
May	[illegible]	[illegible]
June	[illegible]	[illegible]
July	[illegible]	[illegible]
August	[illegible]	[illegible]
September	[illegible]	[illegible]
October	[illegible]	[illegible]
November	[illegible]	[illegible]
December	[illegible]	[illegible]
	[illegible]	[illegible]

Note.—In addition to these Messrs. Alexander Laird & Co., of Glasgow, booked [illegible] harvesters from Ballina to Glasgow in May and June 18[illegible].

A. 10.

Wages paid to Irishmen in Lancashire, Warwickshire, Northumberland, and Yorkshire.

Wages of two men who worked on Mr. James Pearson's farm at St. Michael's-on-Wyre, Lancashire, in 18[illegible].

	£	s.	d.
From June 15, hay harvest, 6 weeks at 20s. a week.	6	0	0
From July 27, farm work, 4 weeks at 15s. a week.	3	0	0
From August 24, harvest, 5 weeks at 21s. a week.	5	5	0
From September [illegible], potato lifting, 3 weeks at 30s. a week.	4	10	0
	18	15	0
An extra week on an adjoining farm at 35s. a week.	1	15	0
Total earnings of each man	20	10	0

Mr. Pearson says that one of these men has been over for 14 years and been paid at the same rate. In addition to the above wages these men got free quarters in the corn granary.

Up to potato lifting time, in September, they got a good Lancashire pie twice a day, at 9 a.m. and 4 p.m., but during potato lifting time they only got tea and coffee.

Mr. Pearson further writes:—"On the range of hills "in the Blackburn and Yorkshire districts Irishmen get "very good wages for hay harvest, i.e. [illegible]s. a week and "all their food, but they are subject to be out of work "afterwards, as there is no corn harvest, and of course "they are glad to get working at a low rate of wage, "sometimes [illegible]s. a day without food."

Wages of Six Men who worked on a Farm at Millfield, Wooler, Northumberland, in 1892.

[illegible]

Mr. Ch[illegible], writing from Millfield, Wooler, says—
"The days on which the men were receiving 2s. and 2s. 6d. were before harvest, and they then had to find their own food, except skim milk, though we found them sleeping accommodation. In harvest, i.e., the days at 3s. 6d., we supplied both food and lodging. The above may fairly be said to be about the regular wages paid in this district to Irishmen.

"The great majority of them go to this district here in time for harvest. They have from four to five weeks here, and they then generally try to get work in a later district.

"I think Nos. 1, 2, 3, 5, 6 came direct from Ireland and went on to a later district after leaving us."

Earnings of Nine Irishmen in the Summer and Autumn of 1892, on a Farm of 3,000 Acres in Warwickshire.

[illegible]

Note.—These men were provided with lodging and fuel. Their employer says:—"They usually want to borrow money as soon as they arrive here and then we always let them have, and it is a very rare thing for them to go away without repaying it. They live very cheaply and send most of their money home."

A. 11.

Particulars of Certain Cottages.

Norfolk.

[illegible]

No. in Family	Materials	Living Room	Bed-room	Remarks
A widow	Stone and thatch	[illegible]	[illegible]	[illegible]
Man, wife, [illegible]	Stone, thatch, and walls of [illegible]	[illegible]	[illegible]	[illegible]
Old [illegible]	Stone and thatch	[illegible]	None	[illegible]

NOTE.—Many of the windows in these cottages do not open, and they are often only 1 foot by 1 foot wide; the front doors are about 6 feet high. None of the houses have closets; the water supply is good. All the rooms have sloping roofs, beamed, and covered with sods of turf, over which the thatch is placed. The rooms are all on the ground floor.

[illegible]

No. in Family	Materials	Living Room	Bed-room	Remarks
Man, wife, [illegible]	[illegible]	[illegible]	[illegible]	[illegible]
Man, wife, and two children	Stone and thatch	[illegible]	[illegible]	[illegible]
A widow [illegible]	Stone and thatch	[illegible]	Two	[illegible]
Man, his mother, and sister	Stone and thatch	[illegible]	[illegible]	[illegible]
Man, wife, and [illegible] daughters [illegible]	Stone and thatch	[illegible]	[illegible]	[illegible]

[illegible]

No. in Family	Materials	Living Room	Bed-room	Remarks
Man, wife, [illegible]	Stone and thatch	[illegible]	Two [illegible]	[illegible]

[illegible]

No. in Family	Materials	Living Room	Bed-room	Remarks
Widow, her [illegible]	[illegible]	[illegible]	Two [illegible]	[illegible]
Old [illegible]	[illegible]	[illegible]	[illegible]	[illegible]
Man, wife, [illegible]	Stone and slate	[illegible]	[illegible]	[illegible]

[illegible]

No. in Family	Materials	Living Room	Bed-room	Remarks
Man, wife, [illegible]	Stone and [illegible]	[illegible]	[illegible]	[illegible]
Man, wife, [illegible]	Stone [illegible]	[illegible]	[illegible]	[illegible]

NOTE.—The rooms in all the above houses are on the ground floor. None of the houses have closets. There appears to be a sufficient supply of good water.

[illegible]

K

A 12.

CROPS and ESTIMATED PRODUCE in the WESTERN UNION in 1880.*

Crops.	Statute Acres.	Estimated Produce in 1884.
Wheat	[illegible]	1,[illegible] cwt. of 112 lbs.
Oats	[illegible]	74,[illegible] " "
Barley	[illegible]	[illegible] " "
Bere	[illegible]	[illegible] " "
Rye	[illegible]	11,[illegible] " "
Potatoes	[illegible]	[illegible] tons
Turnips	[illegible]	[illegible] "
Mangel wurzel and beetroot	[illegible]	[illegible] "
Carrots and parsnips	[illegible]	[illegible] "
Cabbage	[illegible]	[illegible] "
Vetches	[illegible]	17 "
Rape	[illegible]	[illegible] "
Other green crops	[illegible]	
Flax	[illegible]	154 stones (14 lbs.)
Clover, sainfoin, and grasses under rotation	[illegible]	[illegible] tons.
Permanent pasture and grass not broken up in rotation	[illegible]	11,[illegible] "

* Compiled from the Agricultural Statistics of Ireland, [illegible].

A 13.

OCCUPATION of WESTERN UNION, 1881.

Extent in Statute Acres under—

Crops, including Meadow and Clover.	Grass.	Fallow.	Woods and Plantations.	Turf Bog.	Marsh.	Barren Mountain Land.	Water, Roads, Fences, &c.	Total.
Acres.	Acres.	Acres.	Acres.	Acres.	Acres.	Acres.	Acres.	Acres.
[illegible]	[illegible]	[illegible]	[illegible]	[illegible]	[illegible]	[illegible]	[illegible]	[illegible]

PERCENTAGE PER CENT.

Crops, including Meadow and Clover.	Grass.	Fallow.	Woods and Plantations.	Turf Bog.	Marsh.	Barren Mountain Land.	Water, Roads, Fences, &c.	Total.
[illegible]	[illegible]	·1	·5	11·7	7·3	[illegible]	[illegible]	

APPENDIX B.

TABLE OF CONTENTS

B 1.

Emigration to America.

Name.	District.	Evidence.
[illegible]	Westport	[illegible]
[illegible]	[illegible]	[illegible]
[illegible]	Louisburgh	[illegible]
[illegible]	Louisburgh	[illegible]
[illegible]	Louisburgh	[illegible]
[illegible]	Louisburgh	[illegible]
[illegible]	[illegible]	All our girls go to America.
[illegible]	[illegible]	[illegible]
[illegible]	[illegible]	[illegible]
[illegible]	[illegible]	[illegible]
[illegible]	Clare Island	[illegible]
[illegible]	[illegible]	[illegible]

B 2.

Efficiency of Men's Work as compared with the Past.

Name.	District.	Evidence.
[illegible]	Westport	[illegible]
[illegible]	[illegible]	[illegible]
[illegible]	Westport	[illegible]
[illegible]	[illegible]	[illegible]
[illegible]	[illegible]	[illegible]
[illegible]	Castlebar	[illegible]
[illegible]	Castlebar	[illegible]
[illegible]	Claremorris	[illegible]
[illegible]	[illegible]	[illegible]

B 3.

Efficiency of the Men's Work as compared with other Districts.

Name.	District.	Evidence.
[illegible]	Westport	[illegible]
[illegible]	[illegible]	[illegible]

Name.	District.	Evidence.
[illegible]	[illegible]	[illegible]

B. 4.

EVIDENCE ABOUT THOSE WHO WORK IN ENGLAND AND SCOTLAND.

Name.	District.	Evidence.
[illegible]	[illegible]	[illegible]

Name.	District.	Evidence.
[illegible]	[illegible]	[illegible]
[illegible]	[illegible]	[illegible]
[illegible]	[illegible]	[illegible]
[illegible]	[illegible]	[illegible]
[illegible]	[illegible]	[illegible]
[illegible]	[illegible]	[illegible]
[illegible]	[illegible]	[illegible]

B. 8.

RELATIONS BETWEEN EMPLOYER AND EMPLOYED.

Name.	District.	Evidence.
[illegible]	[illegible]	[illegible]
[illegible]	[illegible]	[illegible]
[illegible]	[illegible]	[illegible]
[illegible]	[illegible]	[illegible]
[illegible]	[illegible]	[illegible]
[illegible]	[illegible]	[illegible]
[illegible]	[illegible]	[illegible]
[illegible]	[illegible]	[illegible]
[illegible]	[illegible]	[illegible]
[illegible]	[illegible]	[illegible]

B. 9.

GENERAL CONDITION OF LABOURERS.

Name.	District.	Evidence.
Lord John Browne	Westport	[illegible]
[illegible]	Westport	[illegible]
[illegible]	Westport	[illegible]
[illegible]	Westport	[illegible]
[illegible]	Westport	[illegible]

[illegible]	[illegible]	[illegible]
[illegible]	Achill	There is a [illegible] [illegible]
[illegible]	Achill [illegible]	The [illegible] people are very [illegible]
[illegible]	[illegible]	I [illegible]
[illegible]	Westport	In [illegible]
The schoolmaster	[illegible]	The children do not [illegible]
The schoolmaster	[illegible]	The children [illegible]
The schoolmaster	[illegible]	The children do not [illegible]

Westport, Co. Mayo, Ireland,
May [illegible]

My dear Sir,

I cannot reply to your questions about agricultural labourers in Mayo, because they do not exist as a class in this country. Their place is taken, with great advantage to themselves, and everybody, by the sons of the small tenant farmers.

There is no permanent employment for agricultural labourers, as there are no tillage farms, except those of a very small size, which are cultivated entirely by the tenant occupiers and their families.

The medium and large sized farms are nearly all in grass, as are the greater part of the small tenant farms, except the very smallest and poorest.

In parts of Mayo, particularly in the union of [illegible], the tenants were for many years allowed to sub-divide their farms, the result of which is that these holdings are now so small that they cannot reserve any land for grass or cattle.

The people in these places are consequently very poor.

Experience has shown that the climate of Mayo is too wet and windy for much tillage, but on the other hand it is well suited for grass and cattle.

If it were possible to establish a class of pure agricultural labourers in Mayo, thousands of the smallest tenant farmers would be [illegible] from losing the earnings of their sons in haymaking, harvesting, &c., on which they are employed in the time of year during which they have no labour work on their own land, and for a few months in the small quantity of tillage in the larger farms, much of which is in growing a few acres of turnips.

Pure agricultural labourers would, I believe, be unable to pay any rent for their houses, and would require "outdoor relief" for part of every year.

I do not think that there has been any great improvement in the condition of the poorer classes of Mayo during the last 10 years, but there was a vast change for the better in that respect during the previous 10 years.

Of late there has been a constantly increasing [illegible] on the part of those who have substantial [illegible] to embark in any industrial [illegible] undertakings or works of any kind.

[illegible], however, I regret to say greatly [illegible], and is now increasing about Westport.

Yours truly,
A. [illegible] Fox, Esq. (Signed) J. T. [illegible],
Assistant Commissioner.

11, [illegible] Place, Dublin,
[illegible] May 1893.

My dear Sir,

The general condition of the peasantry on the west coast of Ireland has improved since I first became acquainted with it—now over [illegible] years ago. They are better fed and clad and in many cases housed. They indulge in [illegible] years past in tea and [illegible] bread, which they never thought of doing in former days. But even with this [illegible], and the fact that they take more interest in passing events, and seem to feel their own position more than formerly, their condition is much below the standard of the ordinary labourer in other countries.

I believe that it is on very rare occasions and only under some special circumstances that they eat [illegible] [illegible] for their dinners. The [illegible] with the majority of the peasantry of the west coast. The deprivation of animal food is caused by the inability to purchase it. While such a state of things exists, I do not think their condition can be said to be satisfactory.

I know that the majority of the people are, I might say, in the depths of poverty. They rely on their small holdings or patches of land for support, and if they have a favourable season their crops will enable them to tide over most of their difficulties, and pay the shopkeeper for supplies they have had on credit during the past year, but if an unfavourable season, they are reduced to poverty, as there is little, if any, employment for them.

I know the people of the west coast probably as well as any man living. They are primitive in their [illegible], [illegible], [illegible] religious and moral, and on the whole strictly honest in their dealings. Of the latter I have had practical proofs, having for some years past been on the habit, through the aid of charitable friends, of lending them sums of money for various purposes—buying food, seed for their land, cattle, [illegible], &c., and, as a rule, in their payments they have proved themselves honest, though I do not intend to convey by this that all have acted in this honest manner. In the case of loans made to enable them to go to England or Scotland during the spring or harvest work I have lent some hundreds of pounds, and the total sum not repaid up to the present amounts to only [illegible] [illegible] [illegible]. Were it not for this migration to England and Scotland the people would indeed be badly off.

These people return, sometimes with as much money, earned by their own labour, as will keep their families for the greater part of a year. Without the assistance obtained from this migration and the fishing on many parts of the coast, I feel convinced their holdings of land would not support them; certainly not, except in the most humble and frugal manner, and most certainly not in such a way as one ought to feel a human being should live.

This migration from the west coast is of the greatest importance to the welfare of the districts from which the people migrate, and the return from the small outlay required for a man to embrace remunerative employment in England and Scotland, ready for them during the seasons, is such as to encourage the philanthropist to aid them largely in this migration. The money lent to them for such purposes would, I believe, be honestly repaid with interest, and such would be found remunerative in every sense of the word. I send you a copy of a letter I published on this subject in April [illegible], and also copy of a letter I received from a clergyman of one of the districts in which I made these loans.

In many places the fishing is their mainstay. They depend on its produce, not only for the necessaries of life, but for much of what many now call luxuries, such as tea, white bread, clothing, &c.

Without the fishing they would be miserably off, although the prices obtained in markets far away from railways, such as Belmullet and parts of Donegal, are barely able to cover the expenses and wear and tear of fishing gear. In Belmullet I have known a fine turbot of [illegible] lbs. weight to be sold for [illegible] [illegible]. This is nearly [illegible] miles away from a railway and over [illegible] from the chief market of Dublin. In Achill I have known fish carted to be cut up for baiting lobster pots.

It is to be hoped that the railways in progress will have some effect in improving this state of things, though, unfortunately, the thriving little town of Belmullet, where abundance of fish is sometimes to be seen in the market square, and but few persons to purchase, does not come within the purview of those places to be improved by railways, while Achill, to which a railway will shortly be opened, can never in my mind be counted on as a fishing centre or basis for a company, and certainly not so long as the fishing is carried on by curraghs or canvas and open boats; and this it must be so long as there are no sufficient harbours round the island in which to maintain craft suitable for fishing on this wild coast. I do not think, therefore, the railway will very much aid the development of the fisheries round Achill Island by the islanders, though it may give some help to improve prices when there happens to be any great capture of fish.

It will materially help the salmon fisheries round the island, but that does not affect the general population there.

The fishing in Clew Bay might be developed materially if proper harbour accommodation were given at some of the islands adjacent, in which large fishing craft could be kept, and by a judicious system of loans freely given for the purpose of obtaining such. The value of the security offered must not be too closely scrutinised, for if this be done, no loans will be given. They should be administered in the same spirit which led to the great success of the fishery at Baltimore. These remarks hold good as to the whole of the west and north-west coast.

The advantages to be derived by a locality where the fishing industry in its expansion is manifested at the case of Baltimore (Co. Cork) in the increase in the value of ordinary labour.

When the fishing season commences there, most of the people find employment in some business either directly or indirectly connected with fishing. The price of labour consequently goes up all round, and a state of prosperity exists.

This is the case for several years past in Baltimore and many other centres of fishing on the Cork and Kerry coasts.

As regards the education of the people there is no doubt it has improved very much of late years. I look, however, upon the whole system as erroneous. The head is crammed, as Wolfe says like a parrot, while the hands are left neglected. It is, to my mind, lamentable to see the present generation of boys brought up as they are without any industrial education, and, indeed, I would add, the girls also. I speak of the general system of national education.

I am, &c.
THOMAS F. BRADY.

To A. Wilson Fox, Esq.,
Assistant Commissioner.

B 7.

APPEAL sent to the PRESS by SIR THOMAS BRADY for FUNDS to enable him to advance MONEY to HARVESTMEN proceeding to England and Scotland, and for other purposes.

A WAY TO HELP THE IRISH POOR.

TO THE EDITOR,

As there may be thousands of my countrymen who, I feel assured, would be glad to help their poor countrymen in some practical manner that would not pauperise or demoralise them, will you kindly allow me space in your columns to state what I believe is the most efficient means of doing so, and what I have myself done within the past few years with money entrusted to me from America, France, England, and Ireland.

From my experience, extending over many years amongst these poor people, I believe the best way of helping the poor farmer, labourer, or fisherman in the West of Ireland is to afford him the means of helping himself. This is to be accomplished by giving him a loan of a small sum of money to enable him to purchase what he stands in need of. Whether the farmer or labourer stands in need of potatoes to sow his land, or a horse, or a cow, or a pig, or the fisherman repairs of his boat or fishing gear—let him have the means of obtaining what he wants for himself. This can be done effectually by loans. The poor people are keen enough to know how to spend their money to the best advantage, and when they know they will have to repay it, they will be more particular about the expenditure.

The system will make each man self-reliant, and impress on him the necessity and importance of honesty and punctuality—two very important conditions in the life of the poor peasant. It will, I am sure, be said by many, "But what security have you that they will repay these loans?" My answer is, "The security of themselves and their good characters, vouched for by their pastors, confidence in their honesty, and a conviction that not 1 in 50 or 1 in 100 will act dishonestly, if only the commonest sympathy be shown to them in their troubles, and a little reliance placed on them."

Let me give examples of my practical experience.

I have been in the habit for some years of making loans of 1*l.* each to the very poorest class in a part of the Co. Mayo, to enable them to proceed to England and Scotland for the summer harvest work. Thousands of people make that annual pilgrimage from the West. Without it they would never be able to exist. I am assured that as much as 8*l.* to 10*l.* are either sent or brought home to their families by each man; and I have heard of one case where, after a lengthened sojourn, as much as 33*l.* were sent home. In this small district I have frequently lent 100*l.* to 100 persons, the loans being repayable in six months; and these have, often and often, been repaid long before the time they were due, and in nearly all cases punctually repaid. The defaulters were simply postponed, but all eventually paid up.

Last harvest time an urgent application was made to me from another district in same county to give some help to a large number of poor people who were in the habit of going to England or Scotland for this work, but who had not the means, and could not raise them, to pay their travelling expenses, which are never over 1*l.* I had no funds in hand. All the money entrusted to me was out on loans. What was to be done? The poor people and their families would suffer seriously during the winter and spring if they could not get away. No one who had money and who could have given it would trust them unless I would security myself. I resolved to make an appeal to the public. I did so, and in a few days I was able to make 188 loans to 188 people. These have all been repaid [illegible], and I feel certain this will also be repaid in a short time, and the money is now lying in the National Bank of Ireland, Dublin, "Migratory [illegible] Fund," and will be lent out again as soon as the people are ready to migrate for their annual labour. The loans will be only 1*l.* each, and I could as easily and as safely have made 1,000 loans as I did only 188. At the very lowest calculation I can safely say, without the fear of exaggeration, that each 1*l.* lent brought back at least 5*l.* to 10*l.*, and the principal remains intact for subsequent year's loans, 2½ per cent. interest being charged on each loan, so as to cover the expenses of printing, postage, &c.

I have three other charitable funds working on a similar principle for other purposes, from which loans from 1*l.* to 10*l.* are made, repayable by instalments, extending over three or four years. On the audit of accounts at the end of last year the following was the result:—

American Fund. I received 1,220*l.*; I gave in loans (and free grants in some urgent cases) 3,[illegible]. Leverpool Fund. I received [illegible]*l.*; I gave in loans (and free grants) 2,100*l.* Disarcon Fund. I received [illegible]*l.*; I gave in loans (and free grants) 1,[illegible]*l.* Total received 3,[illegible]*l.* Total given in loans and grants 6,[illegible]*l.*

The "free grants" (made only in very urgent cases) since the establishment of these funds amounted to [illegible]*l.*, and the total amount of the capital now stands 3,07[illegible]*l.* So that in the few years these loans have been in existence I have been enabled, out of 3,[illegible]*l.*, to pay away in free grants [illegible]*l.*, to pay for printing, stamps, advertising, clerical expenses, &c., [illegible]*l.* [illegible], and to give loans to the amount of [illegible].

The punctual repayments of the loans, with 2½ per cent. interest, and their re-issue to others as fast as the money comes in, have enabled me to effect all this. That speaks sufficiently *for the honesty of the people*.

I want to extend my operations considerably, as there is a very great necessity for them. Will my countrymen enable me to do so, and help those of their own flesh and blood in Ireland, who are able and willing to help themselves, if they only get the chance of doing so.

To any one desirous of having it, I will send a copy of my last Report on these funds.

Any contributions to any of the funds may be sent to the National Bank of Ireland, Dublin. I am most anxious that the "Reproductive Fund" should be largely increased, as I know what enormous benefits result from its operation.

Yours truly,

11, Percy Place, Dublin, Thomas F. Brady.
1st April 18[illegible].

LETTER from a Parish Priest to Sir Thomas Brady, in answer to his appeal.

MY DEAR SIR THOMAS,

I have read in the *Press* your letter with much interest. With regard to one of your Charitable Loan Funds—the "Reproductive"—I wish to say a few words, and I think you will not deny my right to speak with a considerable amount of authority respecting it. You say that each of the loans of 1l. made under the "Reproductive Loan Fund" was the means of bringing into the country 5l., and that you are much under the mark in saying that the total loans of [illegible] produced [illegible]. Well, you are so far under the mark that you are not at all near it. I assert, without the fear of contradiction, and am prepared to produce evidence to convince you and the public that each of those loans of 1l. brought 10l. into the country. I have the facts at hand to prove to the satisfaction of anyone who wants proof that this statement is still well "under the mark." Now there is another view of the case that you have not dwelt upon, or put before the public and subscribers to this Fund. You have estimated its total productiveness in pounds sterling, no doubt a truly practical, hard-headed test, but certainly far from being complete in estimating its far-reaching character. A loan multiplying itself tenfold, made to a community in comparative comfort, should be a matter of gratitude on the part of that community, and a subject for great self-satisfaction to the benevolent donors; the recipients in such a case, however, could live on fairly well without the loan, or might obtain it elsewhere. But how does the case stand with your Reproductive Fund? The loans were made to a people steeped to the lips in poverty, and who were utterly unable to procure a similar loan. It is no pleasure to me to parade the poverty of the people; but is it not better, even at the expense of exposure, to try and relieve them, than allow them to suffer on? The first loan advanced in that parish last year was made towards the end of June. Before that date, and while you were making a noble effort on their behalf, all who could had fled to England. Let me point out to you some of the pitiable expedients many of these poor fellows had to adopt to do so. I had in my hands the pawnbrokers' tickets which showed that the men's coats, pairs of their wives' clothing, their miserable belongings, and everything that could be dispensed with, with any regard to Christian decency, were pledged to secure their expenses of travelling. Some, who could not succeed, even in this extreme way, in obtaining the necessary amount, walked scores of miles in order to save the few shillings required to take them across the strip of sea. More than one assured me, when handing him your loan, that he had not a pound of provisions for his family. How were they to live? By borrowing a quart of Indian meal from their neighbours, who could afford to lend it, until relief came from the bread winners in England.

It is impossible for these people to procure even the [illegible] support from their present wretched, worn-out patches of land, and they must necessarily supplement their efforts at home by seeking employment abroad. It is unnecessary for me to say that this is a badly congested district. A radical cure is not within my reach, but that is no reason why I should not try and make their poverty less pinching.

Last year, it is true, was an exceptionally bad one; but no year, no matter how well favoured, can dispense with such loans as those under your "Reproductive Fund," so long as these present circumstances continue. Every shilling earned last year in England was spent, and their last particle of credit drawn upon in an effort to stave off starvation. Their little crops were disposed of to pay the landlord and the shopkeeper, and, except that they are not starving, they are as helpless and as hopeless as on any former occasion. Many have already come inquiring about a renewal of the loans, and declaring their inability to get to England without it. I have every reason to believe them. I am sure it will be much satisfaction to those who have already subscribed to the fund, or who will do so in future, to know that they have been the means of preventing such terrible and sickening work in that [illegible] of suffering and privation, while the whole has been thoroughly free from the demoralising effects of a charity. They place the poor labourer in possession of his work without depriving him of his manly independence. They enable him to take with him his [illegible] coat, such as it is, and to leave his wife and little ones their few scanty rags, the least requisites of decency. I make no boast of the punctuality with which these loans were paid; you can vouch for that. The fund has been to this locality a blessing without any disguise. I hope you will be successful in obtaining further contributions. I know that if those who have the means of assisting could only realise the amount of good already done, and the vast [illegible] of good left undone for want of the means of doing it, they would contribute at once, and generously to this most benevolent project.

Believe me, &c.,

To Sir Thomas F. Brady, V—— C——.
Dublin.

[illegible]

The engagement of ordinary labourers is a daily one.

A ploughman has 12s. a week or 11s. and a house.

There are very few ploughmen in this country.

We have only one.

A ploughman is in regular work and employed in all weathers.

Any man is paid extra who works more than 10 hours in a day. He is paid a quarter day's wages for two hours.

Shepherds are paid in "kind," and each have to keep two [illegible].

Carters and cattle-men get 11s. a week, and have regular employment.

The men live within half a mile or a mile of their work.

At haytime and harvest we employ extra men.

They are paid 1s. 6d. to 1s. 8d. a day.

Haytime lasts a month, and harvest three or four weeks.

For mowing by piece-work we give 6s. for an Irish acre, and at that the man can make 3s. to 4s. a day of 10 hours, or we give 4s. an English acre, and a man will then cut three-fourths of an acre in a day.

The hours of work for spade labourers are:—

In summer from 6 a.m. to 6 p.m.

An hour is allowed for breakfast and an hour for dinner.

In winter from 7.45 a.m. to 4.30 p.m.

An hour is allowed for dinner.

Carters and cattle-men work in summer from 5.30 a.m. to 6.30 p.m.

In winter they work an hour longer than spade labourers.

Their Sunday work takes half an hour in the morning and half an hour in the evening.

The majority of the men do not average more than [illegible] in the year.

A few of the best could earn another 4l. by piece-work.

In 1879 and 1880 we had a little trouble with the men, but we have none now.

I think the men work as well as ever they did, though they do not work nearly as well as Englishmen.

In Wexford and Cork the men are better workmen than in the west.

They may not be stronger, but anyhow they do their work with greater efficiency.

The single men do not want half such looking after.

Those men who go to Scotland for six months or so work much better on their return here, and I believe it is mostly due to the better feeding they get there.

In 1861 the labourers were working here for 6d. a day, and women for 4d.

The rise in wages began in 1868.

You cannot now get a woman to work at any price. They all go to the American mills. It kills them quickly, but there is always a demand for more.

Boys have taken the place of women weeding and [illegible] thistles.

3. Mr. Hugh McDermott, Dingleagh.

I am a Scotchman, and have been manager to Mr. [illegible] for 30 years.

He farms 10,000 acres.

We have now about 800 head of cattle and 12,000 sheep.

We employ 30 herds and 60 labourers.

The herds are principally paid in kind.

The labourers are paid as follows:—

A house free and several acres of land.

The grass of two cows.

1s. a day when they work and 6d. a day extra if away from home.

Ordinary labourers work 10 hours a day in the summer and from light to dark in winter.

The men are not at all "stiff" about regular hours.

If there is a push they will work extra time for nothing.

Ordinary labourers get paid nothing extra in haytime and harvest.

We have divided the property into four districts, and put a Scotch shepherd in charge of each to look after the herds.

The Irishmen work under them as well as Scotchmen did, when we had more of them.

They did not do so at first, not because they were not willing, but because they had to be taught.

The work and stuff is in the people, but they want proper training.

They are willing and obedient.

There is no difficulty whatever between employer and employed.

I do not think the men's work has deteriorated.

When I came here, 30 years ago, the labourers had the grass of a cow less and 2d. a day less.

We have felt the fall in prices very much.

Five years ago sheep were selling for 10s. a head more than they are now.

The price of wool has dropped in proportion.

Cattle have come down 3l. or 4l. a head during the last three years.

3. *John Gannon, steward to Mr. Vesey Stoney, Rosturk Castle, aged 54 years.*

I have been here 18 years.

I have three sons working for Mr. Stoney. One has 9s. and two have 7s. a week.

There are six or seven labourers here engaged by the year, and are paid 9s. a week.

It is a year's notice either side, by verbal agreement.

I pay their wages weekly.

There are two or three men not engaged by the year who are paid 10s. a week, and are paid wet or dry.

These men can step away to work on their holdings if they like.

Carters are paid 9s. a week, and are engaged "wet or dry."

A steward is paid as follows:—

Seven acres of land.

A house.

Turf.

The grass of a cow and calf.

12l. in cash paid half-yearly.

I think this is worth about 15s. a week.

Boys are paid 7s. a week at first.

Women get 4s. 6d. a week. Sometimes in June, July, August, and September I have 14 or 15 women (unmarried) working.

They cut turf, spread it, and carry it. They also pick potatoes, collect seaweed, and help in harvest.

The hours of work in summer are from 6 a.m. to 6 p.m. An hour is allowed at 9 a.m. for breakfast and an hour for dinner at 2 p.m.

In winter they work from light to dark. From November to February they work from about 8 a.m. to 4.30 p.m., and an hour is given at 10 a.m. for breakfast.

A carter goes to work at 6.30 or 7 a.m. and knocks off at 6 p.m.

After that he has to clean and feed his horses. His meal hours are the same as the other men.

Ordinary labourers have no work on Sunday. Herds who look after the cattle and sheep have often as much work on Sundays as work days. Carters have to feed their horses twice a day on Sunday, and it takes them half an hour each time.

I do not think the men's work as good as it used to be.

The relations between masters and men are good.

4. Mr. Thomas Boyle, farmer, near Claggan.

I farm 200 acres, of which about seven acres is tillage. I would have tilled more, only I could not get the men, but they all went off to the relief works.

They have sometimes left 12s. a week and gone to work for 7s., because they did less work there.

At the railways they were getting 15s. at piece-work, the regular wages being 14s.

Ordinary labourers' wages are 9s. a week all the year round.

I would rather pay 1s. a day and diet, but the men with families prefer the 9s.

I pay a cattleman 12l. a year to merely look at the cattle and give them hay.

That man has plenty of time to attend to the 12 acres he gets from Lord Lucan.

My herd gets—

Two acres of land.

A house.

Feed for two head of cattle.

Grass of four sheep.

Manure for his land.

The herd and his sons help to mow at 4s. an acre. They make 3s. a day at that.

The mowing lasts from middle of July to September. All my other men are odd men.

I and my brother work at the other men.

Hours of work in summer are from 7 a.m. to 7 p.m.

B.—I. Westport.

An hour is taken for meals.

Hours of work in winter are from 8 a.m. or 9 a.m. to dark.

The men's work has got worse.

They do not try to work now.

There is not such good relationship between masters and men.

The men will desert you at a critical time.

5. Richard [illegible], Farmer, near Claggan.

I farm 30 acres, four of which are tillage, and I keep ten dry cattle, three milch cows, and 20 sheep. I work myself and employ a man, aged 60. He boards with me, and I give him 8l. a year.

I employ extra men at hay and harvest, and also in March and April. An extra man has 5s. a week and no board.

I have six acres of hay land. The wage at haytime is 10s. a week. At harvest it is the same, and lasts a month. An ordinary labourer is engaged by the day. The man I hired for the year could have any day he likes.

On a wet day a man does not come up to work, and if he did it would be no use.

I can remember 30 years ago you could get a man to work for 6s. or 7s. a week in summer and 5s. in winter, and a hired man would come for 4l. or 5l. a year.

I spend 14l. in labour, not counting my own work.

The men don't do nearly so much work per day as they used to, because they are not so inclined to work.

Masters and men don't get on so well.

The men have got to be great schemers, and if they found you in a difficulty they would raise their wages and refuse to go on working until they got it.

A man could not live on less than 15 or 20 acres, of which five or six acres was tillage.

I keep one horse, and I and another man (who keeps one too) plough by helping each other.

6. Mr. R. Kirk, farmer, Louisburgh.

I farm 3,000 acres, and have about 2,000 sheep and 300 head of cattle.

I employ 13 or 14 herds regularly.

I give them two instances of the wages I pay them:—

(1.) House rent free.
   5 acres of tillage land.
   Grass of 10 head of cattle.
   10l. in cash.

(2.) House rent free.
   5 acres of tillage land.
   Grass of 60 to 80 sheep.
   Grass of 5 or 6 head of cattle.

I employ three men in charge of cattle and horses, pay them the following wages:—

(1.) House rent free.
   3 acres of tillage.
   The grass of three head of cattle.
   The grass of 15 sheep.
   5l. a year.

(2.) 13l. in cash.
   His board and lodging.

(3.) 6l. in cash.
   His board and lodging.

The ordinary labourers are our own tenants.

They are paid 1s. 6d. a day in summer and winter, but they are not employed in wet weather, and their employment is irregular.

I employ from 15 to 20 some days.

The men one also finds here, and four or five of them go to England harvesting.

At harvest here ordinary labourers get the usual wage of 1s 6d. a day, but mowers are paid 2s 6d a day for about a fortnight.

In summer a herd has no hours, his business is to mind the stock.

He has to be out at latest by 5 a.m., and he often does not return until 8 p.m. or 9 p.m.

In winter he works from daylight to dark.

If there is snow he has a lot of work.

The hours of ordinary labourers are:—

In summer from 7 a.m. to 7 p.m.

An hour is allowed for breakfast at 9 a.m., and an hour for dinner at 2 p.m.

In winter from 8 a.m. to 4.30 p.m. (light to dark).

The meal hours in winter are the same as in the summer.

The men are not so capable of doing as much work as formerly.

I think the relations between masters and men are good.

II.—Evidence of Labourers and Herds.

1. P. Murray, labourer, aged 19. Lives near Westport.

I have been working for Lord John Browne for a year.

My wages are 9s. a week. I lost time in wet weather. Perhaps I would lose a day a week all the year round from rain.

I got 12s. a week for two weeks at harvest.

My hours of work from November 1st to St. Patrick's Day are from 7 a.m. to 5 p.m., with an hour off from 10 a.m. to 11 a.m., and from St. Patrick's Day to November 1st from 6 a.m. to 6 p.m., with an hour off at 9 a.m. and also at 2 p.m.

I walk half a mile to my work.

Relations between farmer and labourer are not very good. I think it is only a question of wages. If the farmers paid better wages the men would get on well with them.

I think 2s. to 2s. 6d. a day would be a fair wage.

We can do right enough with the hours. I live with my parents, and I "turn up" 9s. a week to them.

Besides my father and mother there are living in the house my four brothers, aged 23, 17, 14, and 12 and a sister, aged 21.

My father keeps 20 acres of bad land, some of it bog and heath.

Five or six acres are tillage land. Last year we had three acres of potatoes and oats, and about an acre of hay. We have two cows, a calf, six sheep, a donkey, and a horse, 12 or 14 hens, and five or six ducks. We have no pigs now, but often rear from two to four. The rent is 7l. 12s. It was 10l. 10s., but we got it reduced in the Land Court. Lord Sligo is the landlord.

All my brothers, with the exception of the eldest, work on my father's land. My father just supports his family. I could not support myself unless I lived at home.

The following is our daily food:—

From November to March—

Breakfast, 9 a.m.—Bread, tea, and boiled potatoes.

Dinner, 2 p.m.—Boiled potatoes, eggs and milk.

Tea, 6 p.m.—Tea and bread and butter.

Supper, 9 p.m.—Boiled potatoes and herrings.

Our meals from March to November are much the same, but if the potatoes run short, we have Indian meal bread at dinner and supper. We may have bacon sometimes for dinner, and we may eat beef or mutton once or twice a year. I am thinking of emigrating to Massachusetts, where I have uncles and friends who left these parts. They went into factories in America. If I went I would rather go to a factory. If one could make anything out of the land here I would rather stop, but you cannot make anything out of either crops or cattle here. To knock up a living you must have 20 acres, one third of which is tillage and the rest grass. My eldest brother was in a factory in America for three years. He is home now for his health, but is going back again in April. He was earning 8l. a week, and can do so again when he returns.

2. Pat and Michael Carney, labourers, aged 20 and 18 years. Live near Westport.

We are now draining for Lord John Browne. Pat has worked eight or nine years for him and Michael for three years.

Pat earns 12s. a week and Michael 9s. About 60 days are lost in the year from wet weather. Pat got his entire last year from a prize Lord John gives to the man who builds a wall best.

Our hours are the same as P. Murray's.

Our father lives on 12 acres. His rent is 10l. Father, mother, and eight others besides ourselves live at home. The eldest of the eight is 18 years and is still at school.

Last year we had three acres of our land ploughed, 1½ acres of potatoes and 1½ acres oats; we also had a rood of turnips and mangolds. Our father has two cows, four or five sheep, and two small pigs. We give all our money to our father. They could not live unless we did.

If one of us wants clothes or boots our father gives us money.

Sometimes we have as much as 3½ miles to walk to work, now we only have quarter of a mile. We never have beef or mutton. Sometimes we have bacon once a fortnight on Sunday, but never oftener.

The relations between farmers and labourers are good except on the question of wages.

We intend to go to America if we get the chance.
We have a brother there in Columbus in a saw-mill. He has been there three years.
It would not do for a man to always stop here, for he would be as poor 20 years hence as now.

3. OWEN CUNNINGHAM, labourer, aged 47. Lives at Skreen.

I am now working for Mr. Burke.
I have no land and have only my own labour to depend on.
Last summer I cut 20 acres of hay at 4s. an acre. I agreed with Mr. Burke that I was to have 1s. 6d. a day at other work if it was wet, but I lost no time.
From the middle of last November I was working on my own account, cutting rods for thatching houses and I made 10s. or 11s. a week. I was many a week making like a week, perhaps for three months.
Now I am labouring again at 8s. a week, but if Mr. Burke don't pay me 9s. after to-morrow I'll quit. I think he'll give it to me.
I can leave my employment any day I like, and Mr. Burke can put me away any day he likes.
I went harvesting to England for 9 or 10 years and I worked near Liverpool and Chester. Some years I would stay for potato lifting. A man could bring back a clear 12l. or 14l. if he worked from June to November.
I live two miles off in a house my father had. I do not know if he built it, anyhow I pay no rent for it.
My family consists of six children.
The eldest boy is 20 and is in England, the eldest girl is 22, and is in service seven miles off at 8l. a year and her board.
The eldest girl at home is 18 and the eldest boy 12.
Two years ago I was on the relief works, road-making. They paid 7s. a week. We started work at 8 a.m. and left off at 4 p.m. That was in summer time.
We did not do very much work when at that job, and to tell the truth we were not willing to do very much at those wages.
I also worked two months on the Achill Railway about this time last year, i.e., from March 1 to May 1, 1893. I then earned 12s. a week at piecework. Some times we had done our day's work, beginning at 6 a.m., by 2 p.m. or 3 p.m.

4. PAT CUNNINGHAM, labourer, aged 22. Lives near Cloghar.

I am working for Mr. Burke. I get my living by working for farmers here for about six months. For the last three years I have been harvesting in England. One year I was near Chester and two years near Liverpool.
I go in June and stay until potato lifting is over at the end of November. We make in England 15s. to 1l. at harvesting and 4s. or 5s. a day at potato lifting.
The farmer lets us the use of a barn and we feed ourselves. My food costs me 7s. a week and my return fare 25s.
The wages round here in the summer are 8s. and in winter 7s.
There is no employment in wet weather. I work for several farmers and I think they treat us right enough.
My hours in summer are from 7 a.m. to 7 p.m., with barely an hour off for meals.
I bring bread and cold tea with me to my work.
I don't work here in the winter, but work for my mother, who has four acres, half in tillage and the rest grass.
I have also a brother at home, aged 17, who works on our land, and a sister.
We pay 32s. rent, but it is bad land.
Lord Lucan is the landlord.
I am thinking of going to America when my younger brother is a little older. I have a cousin in America.

5. TOM DEVITT, labourer, aged 62. Lives at Cunnamulla[illegible].

I am a labourer employed by Mr. Kenmore and have worked 20 years for him. I chiefly build sheds and also cut hay and reap.
I get the following as wages:—

A house free.
An acre of tillage land.
The grass of two cows.
The grass of two calves until a year old.
Wages 1s. a day when employed.
When building stone sheds 9s. a week.
Harvest 9s. a week.

Employment is irregular. I only earned 3l. 18s. in cash last year, but I have earned 9l. or 10l. a year in good times.

When I began to work here at 10 years of age I was paid 4d. a day.
The labourers and farmers get on well and there is no falling out.
I have to support a wife, my old father and mother, and my eight children.
The eldest is a girl aged 18 years.

6. MICHAEL MAL[illegible], hired man, aged 25. Lives with Mr. E. King, Lanbane.

I am cattleman and herdsman to Mr. King, and I have worked for him since I was 12 years old. My wages were then 7l. a year. They are now 12l. a year, and I live and board at Mr. King's.
I had 10l. a year six or eight years ago when times were better.
12l. don't keep you in clothes and tobacco, but with these bad times we can't expect more.
In the summer time 6 a.m. is the very latest I get up in the morning. I often get up at 4 or 5 a.m., or even at 3 a.m. if cattle are sick.
Sometimes I don't go to bed at all.
I knock off work at 9 p.m.
The following are my meal hours, but I don't always get them exactly to time:—

At 9 a.m. breakfast, an hour.
2 p.m. dinner, an hour.
7 p.m. supper, 1 hour.

In winter I get up at about 7 a.m. and work until about 9 p.m. or 10 p.m.
The meal hours in winter are the same as in summer.
The farmers feed the boys in the house well. I get whatever they have in the house, what more can I expect?
That is what I get:—

Breakfast.—Potatoes and milk, bread and butter.
Dinner.—Potatoes and mutton or bacon. On Fridays, fresh fish and a cup of tea.
Supper.—Bread and tea.

On Sundays I have plenty of beef or mutton for dinner.
The herds get on well with the farmers. They are double as well off as the tenants.
I think the women who work for the farmers get on well with them.
Herds' wages have been about the same for 15 years and the people who come and work by the day have had 1s. 6d. a day for 20 years.
I have two brothers in America. They want me to go there too.
I cannot improve myself here, though I am working for the best man about here.

7. P. RALEY, herd, about 45 years old. Lives in Lord Sligo's demesne, Westport.

I am herd to Lord John Browne.
I was born under him, and my father herded for him before me.
I have a wife and six young children, and there is an old woman in the house to look after the children.
My wages are:—

A free house.
The grass of two cows.
The grass of two calves.
The grass of a brood mare.
The grass of a foal until 1½ years.
The keep of two geese, a gander and goslings.
Cash 20l.

I estimate the total value of this at about 61l.
Out of these wages I have to pay another herd.

The grass of a cow.
The grass of a calf.
Cash 12l.

Lord John Browne gives this herd a free house and half an acre of land.
Also I pay a boy (?) years old) 10l. and give him his food, worth about 12l.
I estimate that after these payments I am not worth more than 25l. a year. I include profits on cows, foals, &c. in this estimate.
I am not so well off as a herd who has no men to pay, but I have four sons, the eldest being about 19 years, and I am looking forward to the time when they can help me and I can send the other man away.
I look after 200 cattle and 40 sheep, but sometimes I have as many as 300.
I work all times and have no certain hours at all.
My Sunday work takes nearly as long as my week-day work.
Sometimes when the cattle are in the fields I throw their food down on Saturday night, but when they are in the sheds of course I have to feed them on Sunday.

B.—I. [illegible]

I believe that employers and employed are on the best of terms. I know on the five or six places round here they get on well.

There are no such things as hostile societies here. Many people would think if they insured their lives they would be hurrying on their death or an illness. That is the sort of people the Irish are.

I am always paid my wages once a quarter.

It is a good arrangement and I like it.

Many farm servants are paid no cash at all. I would rather have the keep of cows, a horse, &c. than cash.

In the first place I must keep a horse to cart my turf, a distance of six miles.

Another reason is that I prefer to keep my own cow instead of to be running about to my neighbours' houses for a drop of milk.

Besides there is the chance of gaining a little more. It is just like a lucky bag, profit or loss.

I have to buy 80 carts of turf in the year, and this costs me from 3l. 10s. to 5l.

I grow 1½ acres of potatoes, half an acre of barley, and I keep a pig.

III.—Evidence of Witnesses who work in Scotland and England.

1. [illegible], Achill.

I am 18 years of age, and am a servant at Dugort Hotel. My mother lives at Dugort. She had three children by her first marriage, of whom I was one.

By her second marriage she has five young children. My sister, aged 21, has been working in a factory in Paisley for a year.

My brother, aged 22, went to work on a farm in England a month ago.

He has gone to the neighbourhood of Southport for the last two years.

I went to work on a farm in Scotland last June to the end of September.

A good many of us girls went from Achill together. A "gaffer" goes with us from here and looks after us and tells us where to go.

I think the farmers write to him before we start and tell him how many girls will be wanted. The gaffer is paid 1l. [illegible] a week by the farmers.

He took 10 girls last year.

When I got to Paisley I took lodgings for the night.

Next day I went to a farm to ask for work and they did not employ me there, but I went on to another a mile from Paisley and they gave me work.

I only worked there for a few days.

I was hoeing potatoes at 2s. a day.

We began work at 6 a.m. and left off at 7 p.m.

An hour was allowed for dinner at 1 p.m., and we stopped at 3 or 4 o'clock for a quarter of an hour.

We took our meals into the field with us.

I slept in Paisley every night.

My lodgings cost 4d. a night, and my food cost 1s. a day.

After that I went to another farm 1½ miles from Paisley and stayed a week.

There I hoed turnips.

On this farm I was paid the same rate of wages and the hours were the same.

On both these farms several other Achill girls were working with me.

I next went by train up country. I forget which county it was, but the gaffer arranged where we were to go.

Two or three other Achill girls went too.

The gaffer sent me to a farm on my arrival, and I was employed lifting potatoes.

On this farm they gave me an outhouse to sleep in.

The other girls slept in the same room. We slept on wooden beds which had a mattress and blankets.

They also gave us as many potatoes as we wanted and milk.

We used to buy bread, tea, and oatmeal for ourselves, which cost 6d. or 7d. a day.

I was on this farm a month, and then went by train to Dumfries, where I worked on a farm for a month.

Some girls went with me and worked on neighbouring farms.

After this I went by train to Perthshire with the gaffer and eight Achill girls.

We were there five weeks potato lifting.

Irishmen were digging them up and we were picking them.

After this the gaffer took us 10 or 12 miles by train to a farm, where we were lifting potatoes two or three weeks.

Next we worked on two or three other farms in Perthshire potato lifting.

Some people gave us small dark places to sleep in, but some were good.

The work is not very hard, but we are much exposed to the wet.

Some of the girls got knocked up.

They often got colds.

On a very wet day we should not work and we should not then be paid.

If we worked half a day we should be paid for half a day.

The girls suffer very much from sea-sickness crossing over.

The voyage is worse than the whole season's work.

I would rather be in service than work in the fields. I spent 3l. on clothes in Scotland and made 6l. or 7l. clear.

I sent my mother 2l. of this by post and gave her all the rest on my return.

Some girls like going to Scotland and others would not go unless they were obliged.

2. Mary O'Donnell, Achill.

I am 18 years of age.

I have been to Scotland to work for four successive years, and my sister, aged 14, has been twice.

Last year I went in May with my father, sister, and brother (aged 16), and we all worked on the same farm.

My father was the gaffer, and looked after 22 girls and 3 boys.

We were first weeding on a farm near Paisley, and we all slept in the town.

I was paid 2s. a day.

The men paid 2s. 6d. a week for lodgings and the girls 2s.

The men's food cost them about 7s. a week.

The girls' food cost about 5s. a week.

We then went to Ayrshire potato digging on a farm for six weeks.

We slept in a barn there. The men had one and the girls another.

Sometimes when we were in Ayrshire we began work at 3 a.m. and left off at 2 p.m.

When we did this we worked as follows:—

Began work 3 a.m., stopped work at 8 a.m. for an hour to breakfast.

We stopped again at 11 a.m. for quarter of an hour, and took a piece of loaf, and we knocked off work at 2 p.m.

The rest of the day we played about and went to bed at 5 or 6 p.m.

The ordinary hours are from 7 a.m. to 6 p.m.

At 9.30 we have quarter of an hour off. At 12 o'clock an hour off, and at 4 p.m. quarter of an hour off.

For breakfast they used to give us tea, white bread, butter, and eggs.

For dinner (1 p.m.) we either had fish or meat.

The girls got 12s. 6d. a week.

My brother got 14s. a week.

Some women of more (age) got 1l. a week each.

After that we went to [illegible].

At harvest the men are paid 5s. a day and the girls 4s.

For a month's harvest a man gets about 5l. and his food and bed.

A woman gets 3l. and her food and bed.

We buy our clothes in Scotland.

3. John Carey, Ballycroy.

I have to support a wife, three young children, and my mother of 80 years.

I rent six acres of tillage from Sir Allan Bellingham. My rent is 3l.

Last year I grew one and a half acres of potatoes, two acres of oats, and a few turnips.

I have two mares.

For 30 years I have been harvesting in Lancashire. During the last 16 years I have worked for the same farmer there. Another man goes with me from here. I go at the end of April and return the end of November. I begin setting potatoes, and I do general work on the farm until haytime. Up to haytime I am paid 1l. a week, and I keep myself, which costs about 8s. a week. During haytime, which lasts eight or nine weeks, and harvest, which lasts a month, I am paid 25s. a week.

During haytime and harvest I am given "10 o'clocks and 4 o'clocks."*

Potato lifting lasts three weeks, and I can make 30s. a week by that when at piece-work.

With hard work I can clear 10l. over in England. It costs me 30s. to go to Lancashire and back. I have to walk in to Westport to get to the station, which is 17 Irish miles from here.

IV.—EVIDENCE OF WITNESSES ON CLARE AND INISHTURK ISLANDS.

1. MICHAEL FLYNN, Clare Island.

I rent 4½ acres of land, which is quarter of a mile off my house.

The house is my own.

I have living with me my father, mother, both aged about 70, an uncle of 72, a sister of 23, who is delicate, and four children of my own, the eldest being seven.

Besides working on my land I superintend county works in County Down and Dublin. I used to be the rate collector here, so I know every man here and every rood of land. I have worked in mines in Northumberland and on public works, at house building, in chemical works, and on farms in the North of England. In the winter I have earned 27s. a week. I have seen Irishmen working in England under all these conditions.

After three months, when they had sweated the water out of their body, and got good food, they worked as well as the Englishmen.

About 40 men go from here to work in England. They start in May or June, and return between September and Christmas.

They go to Lancashire, Yorkshire, and Northumberland, but of late years a great number are going to Scotland, because the journey is cheaper.

From Westport to Glasgow it costs 5s., while it would cost 1l. to Lancashire and 1l. 5s. to Northumberland. No women go to Scotland or England. All our women go to America.

There are about 30 boats here, including currachs, which are used for fishing.

They principally catch herrings and mackerel, but they have no nets, and would do much better if they had them.

The people in Clare could not live if they had the land free of rent, rates, and taxes.

They certainly could not live except for American money and their earnings in England.

The people here do not deal at Westport and Louisburgh now, as they can no longer get credit.

A great means of livelihood is exchanging eggs for goods with shop keepers.

About 170l. of seed potato was given to Clare under the Seed Supply Act, 1880.

I think they have only repaid about 30l.

The people have to row their cattle to Louisburgh from here (some miles) and then drive them 18 miles to Westport Market.

2. MRS. O'MALLEY, Clare Island.

I have my land "in co." (co-partnership).

It is about six Irish acres,† about four acres of which is fit for tillage. There is also the right of grazing on the hill.

I grew an acre of potatoes last year and half an acre of oats. The land was split up after the death of my husband's father, among my husband and his three brothers. One of them was drowned.

The land is now divided as follows:—

(1.) Myself and family.
(2.) My husband's nephew and family.
(3.) My husband's brother, who has a wife and three children.

The rent is now 10l. and it was 16l. I pay half the poor rate and the whole of the county cess. The valuation of the holding is 11l. 5s. I have two cows and a calf, seven or eight sheep and I always have a pig. I also have a mare.

I have six children, three are sons, aged 20, 17, and 15, and three are daughters, all younger than the sons.

My eldest son went to Scotland last year on the 18th June and returned December 15. He worked in a brick yard and brought back 8l. About five years ago he went to London to try and get work, but he did not get it.*

If our land here was good the rent would not kill us.

I am out of potatoes now (March 21). Last year I had them up to May 1st, as the season was good.

I eat Indian meal now.

I exchange eggs for tea, sugar, tobacco, blue, and other things, as I have about 15 hens.

I owe three years of my own share of the rent. My husband's brother owes three years and my husband's nephew four years.

It is the co-partnership that is a bad system. I could make an effort to pay and stay here, but now they will evict me if the others do not pay.†

I spin the wool from my sheep and make all my own blankets, frieze, and flannels.

OWEN O'MALLEY says:—

I held a fourth share until four years ago when the agent accepted the rent of the other three and divided the holding among them, throwing me out. I then went to Chicago, leaving my wife and seven children here.

There I earned 4s. a day [illegible]. I lost my health and came home. I get work on a road [illegible] and get a few odd jobs tailoring.

I am in receipt of outdoor relief.

3. JOHN FAHERTY, Inishturk Island.

I have five children at home.

The eldest is a boy of 18, the second is a boy of 16, and the next is a girl of 13.

I have also two girls in America, aged 19 and 21, who are with an uncle who farms there.

They have already sent me back 4l.

I have four acres of tillage land.

I grow an acre of potatoes, and half an acre of barley and rye.

I have two cows, a mare, and some hens.

My rent is 7l. 5s.

I built my house myself.

I have a boat and a currach.

There are no fishing nets here to speak of.

I only have hand lines.

No one goes harvesting to England or Scotland from Inishturk, but both men and women go to America.

---

* "10 o'clocks and 4 o'clocks" mean light refreshment at 10 a.m. and 4 p.m., usually tea, coffee, bread and cheese or [illegible]. [illegible]

† Mrs. O'Malley's portion of this is about three Irish acres.

* Mr. Lynch, Inspector to the Local Government Board, says:—"[illegible]"

† Mr. Lynch, Inspector to the Local Government Board, says:—"[illegible]"

[illegible]

Pat Joyce.*—I am [illegible] a family of 11 children. If we had the conveniences to fish we could make plenty of money. We want a trawl, long lines, and nets. Herrings and mackerel come in here, and shoals of mackerel in the summer.

John [illegible] says:—I have been to America several times. I believe I could make a better living here if we had nets. There are 40 families in the village, and we could do well if we had the conveniences to fish. The men here chiefly go harvesting to Staffordshire, Warwickshire, Lancashire, and Scotland. About 60 went from here last year to England and Scotland. They start May 1st and some return in September, others in November. We sleep in a building on [illegible]. A good many men lose their health there.

No women go harvesting from [illegible].

A Witness.—We have to carry five miles [illegible] here for our turf.

Three donkey loads, that is, six creels full, cost 2s., and last a week.

A Witness.—There is no employment here.

The Relieving[illegible].—That's it.

A Witness.—The plots of land are too small and too dear.

A Witness.—There is no man here who can live on less than 10 acres of arable land.

A Witness.—Our credit has run out.

Owen Cannon.—The men have only to live on potatoes now.

There is not a pound of meal eaten in the village from one year's end to the other.

The men here only get a fortnight on the relief works.

They are all willing to do work if they could get it.

I believe about 70 per cent. of the girls emigrate to American factories. Five girls and a boy are going from here next week.

The girls go between the ages of 15 and 22.

About [illegible] per cent. of the boys go to America, but more of them go to England and return.

The holdings here average about three acres.

Note.—Since I [illegible] that meeting the Congested Districts Board and Mr. William O'Brien, M.P., have each given [illegible] to develop the fishing industry of [illegible]. I hear from Mr. Owen [illegible] that boats and fishing gear will be purchased with the money, a committee having been formed to carry out that object.

2. Meeting at [illegible], February 15, 1893. Present, about 20 men.

Martin [illegible].—I have five acres of land at a rent of [illegible]. I used to go harvesting in Warwickshire for three months in the year from 1860 to 1891.

Thirty-five years ago they paid us 6s. a week and board. I have known [illegible] of that time offer themselves for 6d. a day. In 1891 harvest wages there were 15s. a week and beer.

We have no boats or nets here for fishing.

We could not live here without going harvesting to England, and the money our friends send from America.

Very often those in America send the passage money for others to go out there.

A Witness.—Last year we were so badly off that some could not find the money to go harvesting with. Most of the harvesters from here go to Warwickshire, Yorkshire, and Lancashire. About 10 men went harvesting from here last year.

They start between April and June, and return in September or November. Some come back in September to cut their own bit of harvest.

A Witness.—In Lancashire, harvest wages are 15s. a week, and you find your own food and lodging; [illegible] would be an average sum for a man to bring back. Some men by starving themselves could bring back 12l.

A Witness.—I saw some men in Lancashire idle for [illegible] weeks this summer.

A Witness.—About 15 years ago we could earn 20l. before the machine came into use.

We worked at piecework then, and sometimes began at 2 a.m. or 3 a.m. and worked until we could not see.

A Witness.—We have very [illegible] our land here. We have to grow potatoes and oats year after year. We must grow the oats to get straw to thatch our cottages.

A Witness.—We are starved here for manure. All the men present have been on the sea since 4 a.m. gathering it in.*

* [illegible]

A Witness.—Any good spot of land here is taken up by land grabbers. We want to get rid of land grabbers.

A Witness.—Our stock is very small. A cow averages about £9 10s.

A Witness.—Our cows are the size of goats and [illegible] show the [illegible] of [illegible].

A Witness.—What we want here is employment. We also want larger holdings.

A Witness.—If a man had 20 acres of good land he could make a decent living, but we are too congested here, and if we all had 20 acres some would have to emigrate.

A Witness.—Our credit is exhausted now and we cannot get more.

There is not a man standing here who does not owe money.

The [illegible].—Everyone owes 10l. or 20l. to the shops. Their friends in England or America sometimes pay off the debts and then they start fresh credit.

A Witness.—We are honest enough and will pay our way, if you will give us the means.

A Witness.—I have two daughters working in American factories.

They sent me 5l. in October, which I paid to the agent for rent.

A Witness.—I have two daughters in American factories. They sent me 5l. 10s. 6d. lately. I was two or three years in arrears of rent and I paid it to the agent to save the cabin.

A Witness.—The following is our usual food:—

Breakfast, 9 a.m.—Potatoes, milk, and tea.

Dinner, 2 p.m.—Potatoes, salt herrings, milk, and cabbage.

Supper.—Potatoes, milk, and herrings.

From February to August, if the potatoes are done, we eat [illegible]. There is not much bread eaten since [illegible] were bad.

3. Meeting at [illegible], February 15, 1893. Present, about 60 men.

A Witness.—Everyone who is able in [illegible] goes to the harvest in Lancashire or Warwickshire. We are obliged to go to England. We can earn 4l. a month there, but harvesting has been destroyed by machinery.

A Witness.—I go to England from March to June till November or Christmas. In Lancashire we can earn 2s. 6d. a day potato lifting, or by piece-work 3s. or 4s. a day.

A man with luck might make 10l. in England, but he might easily make less.

A Witness.—In the last five or six years a big lot of people have gone to America from here.

We would rather work on the land here than fish. We have no conveniences to fish.

There are 30 or 40 cottagers here. We grow potatoes and oats and a little hay.

A Witness.—I have between five and six acres, and pay 2l. 15s.

A Witness.—We have been at the sea all day gathering seaweed for manure.

A Witness.—A man could live on 20 acres of good land, but he could not do so here, as the land is so bad.

4. Meeting at [illegible], February 15, 1893. Present, about 60 men.

A Witness.—I was working in Lancashire as a ploughman for six years until two years ago.

My wages were as follows:—

Cash, 15s. a week.

Cottage free, and coal.

Bushel, milk twice a day.

Coffee and tea once a day.

I have an acre and a half of tillage land here, an acre and a half of meadow, and 40 acres of bog; a cow could not walk on it almost on.

We can sometimes earn a shilling or two cutting turf, but we have to take a horse over to Westport, and it means walking 16 miles.

A Witness.—I have just come back from Yorkshire. I got 15s. a week, lodging, and milk. Between 50 and 100 went harvesting from round here.

But for England and America there would not be a man left here, for there is no way of paying rent here. Most of the tenants are two or three years in arrears.

A Witness.—Most of the potatoes are finished, and some men have no seed. We are eating Indian meal now, and could do better in gaol. Every man standing here is in debt at the shop, and our credit is all up. We want employment and we cannot get it.

B.—II.

ROYAL COMMISSION ON LABOUR.

THE AGRICULTURAL LABOURER.

IRELAND.

REPORT

BY

MR. ARTHUR WILSON FOX
(ASSISTANT COMMISSIONER).

UPON THE

POOR LAW UNION OF CASTLEREAGH
(ROSCOMMON AND MAYO).

TABLE OF CONTENTS.

THE AGRICULTURAL LABOURER.

B.—III. Castlereagh.

To Geoffrey Drage, Esq., Secretary,
Royal Commission on Labour.

I.—Introductory.

Skibbereen, Co. Cork,
April 1893.

Sir,

Introduction. 1. I have the honour to present to you my report upon the condition of the agricultural labourer in the Castlereagh Union, which is situated partly in Roscommon and partly in Mayo.*

Period of inquiry. 2. My inquiries occupied me for [illegible] days, commencing on April [illegible].

Method of inquiry. 3. I obtained the information contained in this report in the following manner:—

On my arrival I at once called on the Rev. P. [illegible], P.P., and asked him to give me the names of the landowners, farmers, and others, whose experience would be the most useful to me. This he was kind enough to do, and the introductions he gave me I found of the greatest assistance.

I called on a great many farmers, both large and small, and also interviewed many herds and labourers, either at their houses or during their work.

I also inspected a good many cottages, and at the same time was able to acquire a great deal of useful information from the inmates. The results of these observations I have set out in a table (Appendix A. [illegible]).

Of those to whom I am most particularly indebted for information I would mention Lord de Freyne, the Rev. P. [illegible], P.P., Mr. Young, Mr. [illegible] [illegible], J.P., Mr. James [illegible], Mr. Michael Kelly, Mr. [illegible], Mr. [illegible], Dr. [illegible], Mr. Redding (steward to Mr. Sandford), and Mr. [illegible] (steward to The O'Conor Don).

Description of Union. 4. The Union, which is chiefly in Roscommon, though part of the western end is in Mayo, is situated about the centre of the eastern boundary of Mayo. It is bounded on the north by the Boyle Union, on the east by the Strokestown Union, on the south by the Roscommon and Glennamaddy Unions, and on the west by the [illegible] and Claremorris Unions. There are [illegible] electoral divisions in the Union, comprising [illegible] acres with a valuation of [illegible].

Description of district. 5. The district is purely an agricultural one, and of recent years a great deal of tillage land has been laid away to grass. Several farmers said to me, "There is "only one acre of tillage land now for every [illegible] there "were some years ago."

In the north, northwest, and east the land is nearly all grass, and in these districts there are some large grazing farms. In the south the land is fairly three parts grass, and there are also some large grazing farms in that part. In the west about half the land is grass and half tillage.

Cattle and sheep. 6. The principal breed of cattle in the district is a cross between the native cow and a shorthorn bull. There are also a few of the Aberdeen Angus breed. The sheep are chiefly the Roscommon breed, which are of an unusually large size, and were raised by crossing native ewes with Leicester rams.

Size of holdings. 7. The size of the holdings greatly varies. In the grass districts there are some large farms varying from [illegible] to over [illegible] acres. It is not uncommon to find one man renting two or three grass farms and putting a herd or two in charge of each, at ranging any capital.

There are [illegible] holdings not exceeding [illegible] acres, [illegible] holdings not exceeding 15 acres, and [illegible] holdings not exceeding 30 acres.

Principal landowners. 8. The principal landowners in the Union are Lord de Freyne, Lord Dillon, The O'Conor Don, Colonel French, Mr. Sandford, Major [illegible], Colonel Irwine, Mr. O'Conor, Mr. Murphy, and Captain [illegible].

Population. 9. The population in 1891 was [illegible], and of these [illegible] were in that part of the Union which is in Co. Mayo. Between 1871 and 1881 it decreased by [illegible], or [illegible] per cent., and between 1881 and 1891 by [illegible], or [illegible] per cent., notwithstanding an excess of [illegible] registered births over deaths during this latter period.

Poor Rate. 10. The poor rate averages about [illegible] in the pound, and the county cess is about [illegible] in the pound.

The following figures, showing the amount of money spent on outdoor and indoor relief in certain years, were supplied to me by the clerk of the board of guardians:—

Year	Indoor Relief.	Outdoor Relief.
[illegible]	[illegible]	[illegible]
[illegible]	[illegible]	[illegible]
[illegible]	[illegible]	[illegible]

Congested districts. 11. Out of the [illegible] electoral divisions in the Union [illegible] are congested districts.

The two electoral divisions in the county of Mayo are congested districts, and those in Roscommon are all towards the Mayo side of the Union.

Seed Loan. 12. About [illegible] was advanced to the board of guardians under the Seed Supply Act. Half of it has been collected and repaid, and the clerk informs me that there will be no difficulty in getting the remainder paid punctually.

Emigration. 13. I have no figures to show the number of emigrants from the Castlereagh Union during the past years, but there is no doubt that it is a considerable one. It is the custom to go into a [illegible] and feel that the emigrants have no near relatives in America. Most of the able bodied young women go and a large number of the young men. It is a common remark that "all our best "young men emigrate."

Mr. Redding, steward to Mr. Sandford, takes an opposite view, and says, "The emigration has affected "the quantity but not the quality of labour. Morally "it has been an advantage as the riff-raff have gone."

Early in April I interviewed a large party of young men and women about to start for America, and a young man then stated, in which a crowd of others agreed, "that those going to America would rather work in "towns there than in the country, as it gives them "more chance of rising in life." Another young man immediately added, "I would rather be a scavenger in "a town than work on the land. I have been a herd "here."

This confirms the evidence that I obtained in all the districts I visited in England and Mayo, namely, that young men turn from an agricultural life when they can get any employment which gives them a chance of rising to a better social position. In further confirmation of this view I quote the words of a most intelligent young man of [illegible] years of age, farming [illegible] acres (Irish), about [illegible] statute acres, at [illegible], whose evidence I have given in full in Appendix B. [illegible]. He says: "We "(the family) all mean to clear out to America. I do "not like the work on the land. It is very laborious "and does not lead to anything. I have met men who "have worked on it all their lives to finally [illegible] the "end as the beginning. A man employed at agriculture "is considered at the bottom of the social scale. This "is the general opinion among the young men. They "prefer a better social position."

I understand from several men who have brothers in America that it is easy to find employment there. The wages appear to be high both for men and women. A young man farming [illegible] acres told me he had three brothers, all coachmen, in Massachusetts, aged respectively [illegible], [illegible], and [illegible] years, and that their wages were from [illegible] to [illegible] dollars a month. This young man's sister, who was a cook in America, and was home for a holiday when I visited the house, but was returning to America the same week with two sisters, told me that her wages were [illegible] a week in addition to her board and lodging.

A great deal of money is sent back by those in America to help their relations at home. I could give

---

* The two electoral divisions of [illegible] and [illegible], both congested districts, containing a population of [illegible] persons, are in the county of Mayo.

[illegible]

M

many [illegible] of the [illegible] and [illegible], but I will take as an example the [illegible] of James Pryer, to whom I have previously [illegible]. "I have a sister in "America, of 19 years, who is a general servant. Her "wages are three dollars a week and her board. She "went last May and sent [illegible] 14l."

I find from the official returns that in 1892, 1,[illegible] persons emigrated from Roscommon; of whom [illegible] were males and [illegible] were females. Of the males [illegible], or [illegible] per cent., were under 20 years of age, and of the females [illegible], or [illegible] per cent., were under 20 years of age.

The emigration from Roscommon has in the last four years not varied much. In 1887 the number of emigrants were [illegible]; in 1890, [illegible]; in 1889, [illegible]; in 1888, [illegible].

The greater part of the Castlerea[illegible] Union is in Mayo, and in that county the emigration during the last five years has but slightly varied.

The number of emigrants from Mayo during the last five years has been as follows:—In 1892, 3,7[illegible]; in 1891, 3,[illegible]; in 1890, 3,[illegible]; in 1889, 3,[illegible]; in 1888, [illegible].

Classes of labourers employed.

14. In this union, as in Mayo, it is the custom for small farmers, or their sons, to go out and work for daily wages, and, although there are many more ordinary agricultural labourers than there were in the Westport Union, still a very large number of men who work for wages on the farms either have holdings of their own or live with their parents who have.

Lord de Freyne told me that all his labourers are the sons of his tenants, and The O'Conor Don also gives employment to a number of his tenants.

This district is more fortunate than the one I had just left, the Westport Union of Mayo, in that there are more owners of property who employ labour.

In the immediate neighbourhood of Castlerea, The O'Conor Don employs about 30 men regularly all the year round on the home farm ([illegible] acres, [illegible] of which are tillage), and on the late Mr. [illegible]'s property about [illegible] men were regularly employed.

The River Suck drainage scheme is also giving considerable employment at wages of between [illegible] and [illegible] a week. This has made labour scarcer on the farms, and has also raised agricultural wages to some extent. Also in consequence of these works fewer men have been to England the last two years.

The ordinary labourers are frequently small farmers at the time of work. On some farms, and particularly on the smaller ones, the ordinary labourer is expected to plough, look after cattle, and turn his hand to anything. On the larger farms ploughmen and cattlemen are separately employed. Their wages are higher than those of ordinary labourers, and they are in regular employment all the year round. Carters are usually paid the same as ordinary labourers.

The herds are [illegible], and they are the best paid set of men, as they have a great deal of responsibility. It often happens that men of the same family have been herds for several generations, and these, as a rule, they are a class who have a thorough knowledge of their business.

They are frequently put in charge of a distant farm, on which they have a house with land attached, provided for them as part of their wages. They are held responsible for the cattle and sheep under their charge, unless they die, or are injured, or lost, from unavoidable causes.

The herds sometimes have to cut and save the hay on the land of which they are in charge, but more generally they are paid at the rate of [illegible] to [illegible] an acre for cutting and saving. If a machine is used they get [illegible] an acre for saving.

On some of the larger farms the farmer sends to cut the hay, but in any event the herd has to save it unless the farmer is living on the same farm.

There are also hired men in some of the farm houses. A full-grown hired man gets from [illegible] to [illegible] and his board and lodging, and lads get from [illegible] to [illegible].

Very few women are employed.

II.—The Supply of Labour.

The supply of labour.

15. The supply of labour is sufficient in the winter, but I heard many complaints that it was scarce in the summer, and particularly at hay and harvest.* There are several reasons for this. In the first place, as many of those who work for wages are small farmers themselves, they are busy cutting their own crops at the very time the farmers would be glad of their labour. Secondly, a large number of young men have gone to America, and continue to do so,[illegible] and, thirdly, a great many go to work in England, leaving Roscommon between April and June. In consequence, wages are higher in the summer than in the winter. Mr. [illegible], steward to The O'Conor Don, says that he finds it difficult to get extra hands between spring and November owing to the migration to England, and referring to the scarcity of labour at harvest time he says, "We cannot grumble at the men if they come "to work after 7 a.m., as they have us in their "power."

It is [illegible] clear that less labour is being employed in the district than formerly, owing to so much tillage land having been turned to grass. The O'Conor Don, whose tillage land is as [illegible] as anyone's in the district, has [illegible] acres of it out of [illegible]. Mr. Stephen [illegible] rents three farms, and the following is the proportion of tillage land:—No. 1 farm, [illegible] acres, has 1 rood of tillage. No. 2 farm, [illegible] acres, has 1 acre of tillage. No. 3 farm, [illegible] acres, has [illegible] acres of tillage. Mr. Vaugh, an extensive farmer, says: "I "can remember [illegible] years ago there were [illegible] acres of "tillage for every one now. Even the little cabbage "gardens round the cabins are turned to grass, and "so much less labour is employed."

However, the emigration has more than kept pace with the decreasing demand for labour, and hence, wages are higher now than in the days when there was far more tillage land, even though less labour, as is stated, is being employed on tillage land, owing to agricultural depression.

Efficiency of labourers. [illegible]

16. On the question as to whether the men are as efficient in their work now as in former times, opinion is divided, but the majority of employers say they are not so good (Appendix B. 1).

Various reasons are given for this, among them being the emigration of the best men, the fact of there being now less opportunity for young men to learn ploughing, and an increasing disinclination on their part to work as hard as the last generation. Many of the farmers, as a proof of this, point to the growing habit of the men coming later on the morning to their work. It seems to be a very general custom for the men not to come at 7 a.m. or later, instead of at 6 a.m.

Mr. [illegible], steward to The O'Conor Don, Mr. Redding,† steward to Mr. [illegible], and Mr. Young, of [illegible], are of opinion that the men's work has not deteriorated. The two last named gentlemen consider the work has improved owing to the better food the people now eat.

[illegible]

17. One of the most difficult subjects on which to get information is the comparison of the work in one district with that in another. In this Union the stewards of both The O'Conor Don and Mr. [illegible], who have had considerable experience of labourers' work in several counties, gave the Roscommon men a good character as regards their capacity for hard work and endurance, but they do not speak very highly of their intelligence, and they also consider that they require a great deal of supervision. Mr. [illegible]'s steward, who has had experience of agricultural labourers near Belfast, in Tyrone, County Dublin, County Kildare, County Wicklow, Queen's County, and Roscommon, makes the following comparison:—"I "would not favourably compare the Roscommon men "in intelligence with any of the above classes. I "should say that hard work and ignorance are the "predominant features here" (Appendix B. 2).

III.—Conditions of Engagement.

[illegible]

18. Generally speaking, the employment of ordinary labourers is intermittent. In this district, as elsewhere, both employers and employed are responsible for this, for there are employers who do not give regular employment in the winter time, in wet weather, or at slack times, and there are men who are small holders, or the sons of such, who stay at home at certain times to see after their own land. One young man I met near Tulsk, who tills seven acres, and supports his mother, told me "that he worked between two and "three days a week for farmers, but could not spare "more time." A man in Mr. James [illegible]'s employ-

---

* [illegible] of extra labour is [illegible] at hay time on some farms. Mr. [illegible], of [illegible], who farms [illegible] acres [illegible], [illegible] labourers, [illegible], [illegible] at work during hay harvest.

[illegible] Mr. Redding says, "[illegible] in 1892 [illegible] "[illegible]."

† Mr. Redding [illegible] of [illegible] the [illegible] of the men going to England and [illegible] their work under English farmers [illegible] them.

[illegible] he earned [illegible] last year, but that he lost [illegible] time looking after his own land.

There are, however, employers in the district, both landowners and farmers, who employ their men regularly all the year round, "wet or dry," if they choose to come, and I find one or two employers who paid them even on holidays. On The O'Conor Don's property men who live entirely by working for wages are paid during sickness, but this is an exceptional case.

Living in the town of [illegible] there are about [illegible] agricultural labourers. I interviewed a good many of them, and they all told me that they did not average more than three or four days' work a week all the year round. Some of them were old men, and the rest struck me as being undersized and weakly. This may partly account for their difficulty in getting employment. In the whole course of my experience in England and Ireland I never saw such a [illegible] looking set of men, and their houses were worse than any I have seen either in England or Ireland.

An odd man in the neighbourhood of Castle [illegible], who lives entirely by working as a labourer, told me that he averaged 4½ days' work a week. He rents a cottage and half an acre of land for [illegible]. He is unmarried, but supports his mother, his sister, who is a widow, and her two children. A small holder, who employs one man, informed me that he worked [illegible] days for him in the year.

19. The engagement of ordinary labourers is usually a daily one, for it is an understood thing that there is no obligation on the part of an employer to employ them on a wet day or to pay them during sickness. Their wages are generally described as being so much a day, and not so much a week.

Herds are usually engaged by the year, with a month's notice. The terms of their engagement are often in writing (Appendix A 11). They frequently stay a long time in their situations. Sometimes several generations of herds have been with the family of the same employer.

Men in charge of horses and cattle, also ploughmen and those in charge of machinery, are frequently engaged by the week, and have regular employment. Mr [illegible] told me that Mr [illegible] always paid these men half their wages in sickness, and if a man had a large family all his wages were paid. Hired men are usually engaged by the year.

20. Very few women are employed, for the reason that they do not care to work out in the fields. A great number of the active young girls emigrate to America, and in consequence there is a scarcity of domestic servants.

The wives of small holders frequently work very hard on their own land, but they do this rather from necessity than from choice.

When women do work in the fields for hire they usually get 1s. a day, summer and winter, and their "support." Their work usually consists of [illegible], [illegible], [illegible], and [illegible]. Their hours are the same as those of men.

21. The hours of work in summer for ordinary labourers are from 6 a.m. to 6 p.m., or from 7 a.m. to 7 p.m. I have already pointed out that when men are supposed to be at their work at 6 a.m. they frequently do not come until 7 a.m. or even 8 a.m. Sometimes when this happens they stay until 7 p.m. to make up for their late arrival in the morning, but very often they leave off at the usual hour, namely 6 p.m.

The meal hours are usually half an hour for breakfast at 8 a.m., and an hour for dinner about 1 p.m. On some farms in the spring and summer a break of 10 minutes or a quarter of an hour is allowed at 4 p.m. for tea.

This brings up the total of the working hours to be nominally about 10½, but as the men are seldom punctual in starting work in the morning, they are not so long practically.

On some farms I found the working hours to be from 7 a.m. to 6 p.m., and in these cases a shorter period is allowed for dinner, or no time is given for breakfast, the men being expected to get it before they come. Again, in some cases half an hour was allowed for breakfast and half an hour for dinner, and in others I found 20 minutes was allowed for breakfast at 8 a.m., 20 minutes for dinner at 12 o'clock, and a break of 10 or 15 minutes at 4 p.m.

22. The length of the working hours in winter for ordinary labourers of course depends on the duration of the daylight. In the darkest days they do not begin work before 8 a.m. and leave off before 4.30.

On some estates and farms the meal hours are the same in winter as in summer, but in many cases the half hour for breakfast is knocked off, and the only break in the day is an hour for dinner.

23. Horsemen and ploughmen's hours in summer are from 6 a.m. to 6 p.m. They frequently have an hour for breakfast at 8.30, and also have an hour for dinner. Their total hours are, however, as long, and frequently longer, than those of the ordinary labourers, as feeding their horses occupies them during part of their meal hours, and in the evening they have to turn them out.

In the winter their hours are from 6 a.m. to 6 p.m., by which time they would usually have finished clearing their horses.

Their meal hours in winter are about the same as in summer.

24. The hours of cattlemen are frequently very long. Mr [illegible], steward to Mr [illegible], told me that cattlemen's hours in summer are from 5.30 a.m. to 8 p.m. or even to 10 p.m., with about two hours off for meals. It must, however, be borne in mind that the work of cattlemen is by no means always of an arduous nature, and their time is frequently employed in standing about in the sheds or strolling about in the fields merely looking at the animals under their charge. On the other hand, their rest and leisure are often broken into when cows are calving, or when animals are ill, and they must always be ready to attend to them, no matter what the hour of the day or night may be.

In the winter the cattlemen's hours are nominally from 5.30 a.m. to dark, and they get the same meal hours as in summer.

25. Hired men's hours are nominally the same as those of ordinary labourers, but frequently their duties are very indefinite, especially on a small farm. Such a man is ordinary labourer, cattleman, and horseman combined. His business is to do what is required on the farm, which may on some days entail very long hours, and on others much shorter ones. He practically lives on terms of social equality with his employer, and so the working hours and periods allowed for meals are not so strictly defined as on larger farms, where more hands are employed.

26. Herds have no definite hours.

Their business is to look after the animals under their charge, and this has to be done at all times. The herds in charge of grazing farms are more in the position of farmers, and they are not able, as better [illegible] of labourers are, to leave off work when the hands of the clock point to 6 o'clock. In lambing time, during sheep-washing and clipping, in haytime, or when animals are ill, their work is often very arduous, and entails long hours and broken rest. I have, however, always found the herds to be the most intelligent and the best [illegible] men, not only in this county, but in every other county I visited in Ireland and England.

Doubtless the charge of animals fosters many good qualities, and [illegible] for the herds being, as a rule, in the words of a [illegible] farmer, "a good sort."

27. No work is done on Sunday, except the feeding of animals, which usually falls to the lot of cattlemen, yardmen, horsemen, or hired men.

On Mr [illegible]'s estate, the yardmen's hours on Sunday in winter were from 5.30 a.m. to 7.30 a.m., again from 10 a.m. to 11 a.m., and again from 3 p.m. to 5.30 p.m. In the summer, from May 15th to September 1st, the work is lighter, as the cattle are turned out in the fields.

His seven horsemen took the Sunday work in turns, two being employed each Sunday to do the necessary work.

Their work in winter occupied them half an hour at 6.30 a.m., and half an hour at 5 p.m.

On Mr [illegible]'s farm, where eight men are regularly employed, summer and winter, one man looks after the stock on Sunday, and it takes him an hour in the morning and an hour in the evening, summer and winter.

I have given these two instances to show the practice on an estate and that on a farm.

IV.—Wages and Earnings

28. The current rate of cash wages is 1s. 6d. a day in summer, although a few employers pay as much as 2s. In winter it varies from 1s. 3d. to 1s. 6d.*

* [illegible]

The mode of payment varies a good deal, for on some farms the wages are 1s 6d a day in summer and 1s 3d in winter, on others they are 1s. 6d a day summer and winter, and on a few 1s 3d a day summer and winter. On many farms the labourers have 1s a day and food, that is breakfast and dinner, both summer and winter; but on one farm the wages for three months were 10d a day and food

On one property I found the wages varied, according to the man's worth, from 1s 6d to 2s a day all the year round for day men, and 10s a week summer and winter for the ordinary staff regularly employed, the married men with families getting cottages free

The lowest cash wage in winter is 7s a week, and the highest 10s. Farmers usually put the cost of a man's food per day at 1s, so a man receiving 1s a day and his food may be said to be receiving 12s. a week.

The lowest wage in summer is 9s and the highest 12s., but there are some exceptions, which I have mentioned in paragraph 32, where employers give perquisites in addition.

29 Ploughmen and men in charge of cattle often get higher wages than ordinary labourers, but even if they do not, at any rate they have the advantage of regular employment. They usually get from 10s to 12s a week.

Mr Sandford's ploughmen and yardmen, if married, are paid 10s a week, and have a cottage and turf free, and if unmarried have 12s a week, the same perquisites, but no cottage. Mr James Cheevey pays his ploughman 24l a year, and gives him a house free. The O'Conor Don gives his ploughman 12s a week, free firing, and a cottage, with a garden of a quarter of an acre (Irish) [nearly 2/5 a statute measure]. His cattlemen get from 10s to 12s a week, and the two stall-feeders 13s a week from November to May, and 9s the rest of the year.

30. Herds are frequently paid in kind, and receive no cash at all, while others are paid partly in kind and partly in cash. As the mode of payment varies considerably, and as the amount depends on the duties of the herds, I have given several instances in Appendix A 8. Their annual wages appear to be worth between 30l. and 50l.

In paragraph 15 I have alluded to the formation of a league in 1881 by the herds with the object of obtaining higher wages, and I have stated the terms of the agreement arrived at between the masters and the men. This agreement is not now strictly adhered to on some farms by the parties, as innovations have crept in regarding the mode of payment, though Mr Flanagan, of Tonroe, Tulsk, informs me that a great many employers still observe them.*

I have not attempted to estimate the herds' profits, which they make in their capacity of farmers. They depend much on the seasons, on prices, and the luck the men have with their cattle. Most of the herds keep pigs, which are a source of considerable profit to them. One of Mr Flanagan's herds told him that in 1892 he got 40l for pigs. They also keep geese and poultry. Many herds are paid extra for saving hay and for attending fairs. They grow potatoes and vegetables and they consume milk and butter the value of which is impossible to estimate. I quote the evidence of Mr Redding, steward to Mr Sandford, on the subject of herds profits and it will be seen that when these are taken into consideration in addition to the wages their position is a satisfactory one. Mr Redding says —

"Herds and their calves say (16 months), at prices varying from 6l to 8l., according to the sort of cows they breed them from, and this will depend on the quality of the land in possession of the employers. If good land they can feed good cows, and if the land is not good land it pays best to breed good cows to breed from. They manage, if possible, to have their cows calving in early spring, so as to have their calves strong when they sell in May year. The price of a calf greatly depends on the feeding it gets. In addition to feeding calves, the herds breed pigs on their land. They also make and sell butter. They buy linseed with the skim milk for feeding purposes. The herds breed better foals than small farmers having better mares. The introduction of Government grants has done good. A colt foal is worth from 12l to 20l., and a filly from 10l. to 15l."

* Mr. Flanagan informs me that a herd's wages according to the [illegible] of his herds:—

	£	s.	d.
Under 100 acres	[illegible]	[illegible]	[illegible]
Over 100 and under 150	[illegible]	[illegible]	[illegible]
Over 150 acres	[illegible]	[illegible]	[illegible]

31. Women are paid 1s a day when they work, which I have pointed out is seldom. On some farms they are employed at hay and harvest, and their wages are about 1s a day and food. A girl gets from 6d to 1s a day.

Boys' wages are about 4d to 8d a day.

32 Piece-work is seldom given, as there is so little tillage land. Mr. Redding, steward to Mr. Sandford, informed me that he found giving piece-work was not very satisfactory, as the men skimped their work. Mr Fitz Simmons, steward to The O'Conor Don, says that his men prefer piece-work to day work

The following are prices paid on Mr. Sandford's estate for piece-work —

	s.	d.
Draining (shore), opening, closing, and cleaning	2	6 per perch.
Draining (lateral drains), opening, closing, and cleaning	1	3 „ „
Draining (cutting) road drains	0	3 „ „
Turf cutting. Cutting, wheeling, saving, and putting in standard clamps—5 hands	5	0 „ „

Note.—The clamps are 12 feet long, 8 feet at the base and 6 feet high

The O'Conor Don's steward pays —

	s.	d.
Draining, cutting main drains, 3 feet deep (stony land)	0	8 „ „
Draining, cutting main drains 3 feet deep, dry soil	1	0 „ „
Making sod fences . .	4s. to 5s.	„ „
Making stone walls . .	10s.	„ „
Mowing . . .	7s	per Irish acre

Mr James Cheevey pays —

	s.	d.
Turf cutting. Cutting, wheeling, saving, and putting in standard clamps	7	0 per clamp
Dyking	2	6 per 7 yds
Breaking stones . . .	1	0 a ton.

At hay and harvest, mowing is paid for at the rate of between 7s and 10s an Irish acre (4s 4d to 6s 2d per statute acre), the price depends on the character of the crops. Several employers told me that an average man can cut half an Irish acre in a day of 12 hours. Mr James Cheevey and several others say that when they have their mowing done by day-work the men take four days to cut an Irish acre, which is just twice as long as they take at piece-work

33 At haytime and harvest a mower at day work is paid 2s. 6d a day, and is often given his food in addition. With the exception of the mowers, no extra payment is made at hay and harvest, on many of the farms

Mr. Vaugh pays his own men the same as the extra hands, that is 2s 6d. a day and their support, or else he gives them 4s a day and they find their own food. Mr. Henry Glover also pays his ordinary men 2s. 6d. a day, and gives them their food at harvest.

34. Perquisites are not given to ordinary labourers on the majority of farms. Those who are given food partly in lieu of cash, are really receiving more than the current rate of wage. For instance, a man who has his choice between 12s a week in cash or 6s a week and his food, is in the latter case allowed 12s a week, as his food equals the former 1s a day

There are, however, several exceptions. Mr Vaugh gives his married men 1s a day all the year round, a cottage, an acre of grass, and half an acre of tillage measured. He also lends them horses to plough, and to cart turf, manure, or seaweed. His unmarried men who live with their parents are paid 1s a day, given their food, and half an acre of land to sow. All his men have regular employment, and have 2s 6d a day and their food at harvest.* Mr Flanagan's men have 9s a week in summer and 7s 6d. in winter. They also have the opportunity of taking very good tillage land, well manured, at 5l an Irish acre, and they have regular

* Mr. [illegible] tenders his [illegible] to the work he does [illegible] They all have to help with the hay, the cattle, and the [illegible].

employment. Mr. Michael Kelly's men have 8s. a week all the year round, and their food, which really amounts to 12s. a week. Mr. James Cheevers makes the following arrangement with his men:—They get a cottage free, 2 Irish acres, (about 3¼ statute acres) for 5*l.* a year, and 1s. 6d. a day whenever they work for him, but they can work for anyone else they like when not working for him. Mr. Cheevers informs me that these men work about 150 days a year for him.

66. Perquisites are frequently given to cattlemen and herdsmen. They sometimes have a house rent free and an acre or so of land for nothing, or at a cheap rental, and turf free. The O'Conor Don's head cattleman, besides 12s. a week, has his house free, and also milk, vegetables, and firing. His carters get 2s. 6d. every night they are away from home. On some farms the men whose turn it is to look after the cattle on Sundays, are given their food.

The perquisites paid to herds rather come under the denomination of "payments in kind," as they are definite and regular payments, agreed upon between employer and employed, and are considered by both as part of the wages.

35. There is practically no way in which money can be earned in this district except by agricultural employment. The last two years drainage of the River Suck has given a considerable amount of work, but this is only of a temporary nature.

The wives of the small farmers make a good deal of money by selling eggs to dealers in Castlerea, which is a great centre for the egg trade, and hundreds of thousands are sent off from there in the year to the English markets. Mr. [illegible] who does a large egg trade in Castlerea, has gone into his books for me, to ascertain his purchases, and he finds they have averaged 8,000*l.* a year during the last five years. He thinks this would represent about one third of the egg trade of Castlerea. His supply of eggs is drawn from an area of about eight miles round the town.

Turf is sold in Castlerea in considerable quantities by those living in the turf districts. There are two kinds, viz., stone turf, which is the best, and brown turf, which is lighter and less valuable. Those who live out of the turf districts often burn dried cow-dung or furze.

37. A considerable amount of money is earned by the sons of small farmers who go to England to work on the farms there. They leave Castlerea between the end of April and June, and return between September and Christmas.

From a return kindly made for me by the manager of the Midland and Western Railway, it appears that 1175 harvest tickets to England were issued in 1892 from their stations in Roscommon.

I find from the official returns that in 1892, 1,[illegible] migratory labourers went from Roscommon, and of these 1,[illegible] came from the portion of the Castlerea Union in that county. The returns for the whole Castlerea Union (Roscommon and Mayo) are 1,[illegible]. Hence it would seem that about [illegible] came from the Mayo part of the Union. These figures, however, cannot be entirely relied on, for I was informed that after the returns are made up a good many men make up their minds to go who had previously said they did not intend to do so. (*See Summary Report, par. 1[illegible].*)

A great number of the migratory labourers go to Cheshire, and some to Warwickshire and Lancashire. In the Appendix to my report on the Westport Union of Mayo, I have given an account of the wages paid to Irishmen in these counties. (*See Summary Report, par. 1[illegible].*)

On April the 7th, I interviewed in the streets of Castlerea a large crowd of young men just starting for Cheshire. Some of these had been to Lancashire in previous years. They informed me that at the best they could bring back 8*l.* or 9*l.*, after paying all expenses in England (their return fare is [illegible]) and buying some clothes. I think, estimating it at [illegible] it is evident that this estimate is not an unfair one if a man returns about the end of September, but, if he stayed for potato-lifting, I think he could earn more.

The men told me that they were given "10 o'clocks and 4 o'clocks" by the farmers, which means light refreshments at 10 a.m. and 4 p.m., such as tea, milk, coffee, bread, cheese or butter. In Lancashire they frequently got what is known as a "Lancashire pie" at these times. They also told me that in Cheshire they were provided with sleeping accommodation in barns, but they found this a very rough way of living. They also said they were employed wet or dry, many farmers finding them work under cover if it rained.

They made the same complaint as some of the Mayo men said to which I referred in my report on the Westport Union, namely that they cannot always get work at once when they get to England and this happens particularly in cases of the men who go there for the first time, and who do not know the farmers.

The men told me they liked the work quite as well as Englishmen. One young man observed "we are "obliged to work as hard as the English whether we "like it or not."

38. To obtain any reliable evidence as to the annual earnings of ordinary labourers, is a matter of great difficulty, because the majority of farmers have no record of the number of days that they were work by them. Again, it must be borne in mind that many of the labourers are small tenants, at the most of such, and so if the number of the days they worked on a farm were ascertained, their earnings would not be a fair sample of that of an agricultural labourer, for the days they were absent from their employer would probably have been spent in working on their own land for their own advantage. (*See paragraph 13.*)

I have, however, obtained some information on this point.

Mr. Flanagan, of Tonrus, Tulsk, sends me the annual earnings of some of his men.

	£	s.	d.
(1.) [illegible] days, partly at 1s. 6d. and partly at 1s. 3d. - - - -	20	11	0
This man has a cottage and small patch of land rent free in return for his looking after some land of another man.			
(2.) [illegible] days, partly at 1s. 6d. and partly at 1s. 3d. - - - -	[illegible]	[illegible]	[illegible]
This man lives rent free with his mother-in-law.			
(3.) Man and son. [illegible] days, partly at 1s. 6d. and partly at 1s. 3d. - - - -	[illegible]	14	[illegible]
This man is a small tenant, rent [illegible]			
(4.) Pat Flanagan and two sons. The father works occasionally and the sons regularly - - -	[illegible]	16	[illegible]

Mr. Rushing, steward to Mr. Sandford, Castlerea, gives me the following earnings of three men. (See also App. A 1.)

	£	s.	d.
(1.) A weekly labourer with no house -	[illegible]	[illegible]	0
(2.) A weekly labourer with cottage and half an acre - - - -	[illegible]	[illegible]	[illegible]
(3.) A day man - - - -	16	10	0

Mr. Fitz [illegible], steward to The O'Conor Don, gives the annual earnings of J. W. from April 1892 to April 1893 as [illegible].

39. It is also difficult to give a correct comparison of the annual earnings of men in charge of horses and cattle, because on many of the farms no distinction is made in the mode of payment to the men, though the men whose duty it is to look after animals have the advantage of constant work throughout the year.

Such men sometimes have small privileges in addition to their ordinary pay, which vary on different farms, such as an extra meal occasionally, or, perhaps, an extra meal a day, or a meal on Sundays. Such little additions as these are difficult both to ascertain and also to value in cash. It must also be borne in mind that on large farms the herds attend to the cattle and sheep, and so it is only on the smaller farms, where no herds are kept, that the duty of looking after animals devolves on the ordinary labourer. On estates where cattlemen and carters are kept their wages are 10s. to 12s. a week, and they get regular employment. Besides this, they often get a cottage either free or at a cheap rate, and perquisites. Their annual cash earnings may be put at between [illegible] and 31*l.*

Hired men earn from 10*l.* to 16*l.* a year, and have their board and lodging, and hired boys get between [illegible] and [illegible] with board and lodging.

V.—COTTAGE ACCOMMODATION.

40. Owing to the fact that so many of the labourers are the sons of small farmers who live at home with their parents, there are not many agricultural labourers' cottages in the ordinary sense of the word. I have in Appendix A. 16 given particulars of certain cottages I examined, belonging both to labourers and small holders.

M 2

No labourers' cottages have been built under the Acts. The Clerk to the Guardians informs me that there were [illegible] applications in 18[illegible], but they were not proceeded, and there have been none since.

41. The cottages are chiefly built of stone and thatch, or slate, and the rooms are nearly always on the ground floor. Most of them have two rooms, namely, a living room, in which some of the family frequently sleep, and a bedroom opening out of it.

The living room often measures about 15 by 18 ft., with a [illegible] roof, and a usual size for the bedroom is [illegible] by 12 or [illegible] by 10 ft. If there is a third room it is generally about 10 by 10 ft. Cattle and pigs are often kept in the houses, but that practice is not so general as in the Westport Union, County Mayo. The floors are frequently clay, though they are sometimes made of [illegible] or stone. Wooden floors are never used, which [illegible] advantage, for if cattle, pigs, or both were kept in the house, the wood would become saturated with filth, and consequently would be offensive. The cottages in the Castlerea[illegible] Union are [illegible] in the country districts than in the Westport Union, but in most parts of the Castlerea[illegible] Union the people are better off than they are in the Westport Union, and so can afford to build better cottages.

Generally speaking, the men live within a reasonable distance of their work. I found several instances of odd men who had to go [illegible] or [illegible] miles, but the distance such men have to go is constantly varying. The majority of the men I saw lived within a mile of their work.

42. The agricultural labourers' cottages in Castlerea[illegible], [illegible], as they should be more correctly called, are so bad that it is difficult to give a true idea of the state of squalor in which these occupants live.

These cottages are quite the worst I saw during my inquiries in either Mayo, Cork, Roscommon, or West Meath. They are herded together in side streets or slums. [illegible] of them have only one room, in which the whole family live, sleep, and do their washing and cooking. There are no closets, and I ascertained from the inhabitants of two [illegible] that [illegible] containing [illegible] are used instead. One of these cottages has a room [illegible] by [illegible], in which a man, his wife, two grown up daughters, and a small boy sleep. Rent [illegible] a week. Another has two rooms on the ground floor, both about [illegible] by [illegible]. In the living room sleep two sons aged [illegible] and [illegible]. In the bedroom sleep, in the same bed, a man, his wife, two girls of [illegible] and [illegible], and a baby. On the [illegible] floor of the same room sleeps a female lodger with a boy of [illegible] and a baby. The rent is [illegible] a week. In another house, containing two rooms on the ground floor, there sleep in the bedroom, which is [illegible] feet by [illegible] feet, with a window [illegible] feet by [illegible] feet, a man, his wife, and two little girls. In the living room, [illegible] by [illegible], sleep two stepsons of the man, aged [illegible] and [illegible] years. Rent [illegible] a week.

In one house there are four rooms, each room being let to a different lot of tenants. A large room on the ground floor, [illegible] by [illegible], is inhabited by a man, his wife, and [illegible] children. The room is very dirty. I was unable to ascertain the rent, as the man was out. Upstairs there were three smaller rooms, all [illegible] by [illegible], and let for [illegible] a week each to different families.

I asked the Rev. P. [illegible], P.P., [illegible], where the worst cottages outside Castlerea[illegible] were to be found, and he considered that the cottages at Trien were, on the whole, worse than any others. I accordingly visited them, and certainly found some very old dilapidated ones, chiefly built of stone with straw thatch. These belonged to small holders, some of whom, or their fathers before them, had built the houses.

About the best I saw there was on a holding of [illegible] acres (Irish) [illegible] and [illegible]. The rent was [illegible], and is now reduced to [illegible]. Although the land could not be described as good, it certainly was cheap at that price. The house is stone and thatch, and has three rooms on the ground floor. The living room is [illegible] by 14, and there are two bedrooms, one 14 by 10 and the other 14 by [illegible].

Another house, inhabited by an old woman, contains one room 14 by 12. I understood she had about an Irish acre of land, and that she lives on money her sons and daughters send her from America and the produce of her poultry. A young labourer, who lives with his mother, has an old stone cottage with a bad thatch and a poor-looking open drain in front. The rent for [illegible] acres (Irish) is [illegible]. Up to recently the rent was [illegible].

Another man has a cottage, with a living room of about 14 by 18, and a small bedroom besides. He [illegible] [illegible] acres (Irish) for [illegible]. He has a [illegible], two calves, two pigs, and [illegible] hens. He has been harvesting in England for [illegible] years. I also saw a cottage at [illegible], near Trien, inhabited by a small shopkeeper. The thatch looked completely rotten. The man rents [illegible] acres (Irish) for [illegible]. He keeps a cow and grows half an acre of potatoes. He built the house a few years ago. The material and outlay in wages cost him [illegible].

43. I also saw nine comfortable-looking cottages on Mr. [illegible]'s property, about half a mile from Castlerea[illegible]. These are made of stone, plaster, and slate. The rents are [illegible] a week, including half an acre of land. The cottages have two rooms, the living room about [illegible] by [illegible], and the bedroom [illegible] by 10, and there is a loft. These cottages were built about [illegible] years ago.

About a mile from Castlerea[illegible] I saw a very neat cottage, built about [illegible] years ago by a man who was an agricultural labourer. His widow lives there now, with her son and daughter. The son is at present working on the railway for [illegible] a week, and has to walk five miles to his work. The house cost [illegible] to build. It is made of stone, with a thatched roof, and has two good-sized rooms, with good windows. Two years ago the son built a good cattle shed for [illegible]. They rent [illegible] acres of land for [illegible], of which [illegible] are tillage, and they keep two cows, three calves, a pig, and some poultry.

The cottages at Castle Plunket looked rather above the average. I examined one, now rented by a constable for [illegible] a year, which he keeps beautifully clean and neat. The house is made of stone and thatch. There are three rooms on the ground floor, the dimensions being [illegible] by [illegible] by [illegible] high, [illegible] by [illegible] by [illegible] feet [illegible] inches, and [illegible] by [illegible] by [illegible]. There is a garden of about 15 perches.

44. Owing to the rooms being usually on the ground floor, fresh air comes in whenever the front door is opened, and hence the ventilation of the houses is fairly good. Dr. [illegible], of Castlerea[illegible], strongly deprecates the habit of keeping animals in the house.

45. Mr. James [illegible] informed me that he built two [illegible] cottages [illegible] years ago at a cost of [illegible] each, and he considers that sum would be wanted to build cottages now. Mr. Michael Kelly thought that a good labourer's cottage costs [illegible], including keeping, but that it was possible to build one for [illegible]. A small holder informed me that his house of stone and thatch cost [illegible] to build three years ago, including materials and labour. Another small holder told me his house, which was a good one, cost [illegible] to build [illegible] years ago.

46. In the country districts there is no system of drainage. Closets are unknown in the houses of labourers and small holders.

It appears to be a common practice in Roscommon, as in Mayo, for people to keep their manure heap opposite the door, and in consequence in wet weather the approach to the house is frequently in a very filthy state.

Dr. [illegible] informed me that he anticipated the drainage of Castlerea[illegible] would improve when the scheme of draining the river [illegible] was completed. I saw a drain there running close to a block of labourers' cottages, which had been opened, and left in a most offensive state. The smell from it was exceedingly bad, and close to it children from the neighbouring cottages were playing. I also saw at the end of a row of labourers' cottages in the middle of the town a heap of rubbish and filth which ought never to have happened in such a place.

47. I heard but little complaint of the water supply, either as regards quantity or quality, though in a few instances I found people who had to go some distance for it. In Castle Plunket the constable informed me that the people had to go a mile to get their water in summer from a well, and in winter they used the surface water of a field.

48. There are very few labourers' cottages let with farms. With many of the great farms a herd's cottage is let, and the farmer sublets it to the herd either for the rent or for a nominal one, so long as he remains in his service.

An agreement in writing is frequently made, but, if there is none, it is always understood that notice to quit [illegible] [illegible] [illegible] the cottage ([illegible]). In Castlerea[illegible] the labourers' cottages are held on a weekly tenancy. On Mr. [illegible]'s property the [illegible]) is a monthly one, and in case of a labourer having a cottage free he enters into an agreement to quit on a week's notice.

49. The rent of cottages is usually from 1s. 6d. to 2s. 6d. a week, but the amount paid is no guide to the character of the cottages or the accommodation provided. For instance, Mr [illegible]'s cottages about half a mile from Castlerea[illegible], which are well built and comfortable, and are provided with gardens and outhouses, are let for 1s. 6d. a week, while a house with one, or perhaps two, miserable rooms in Castlerea[illegible], without a patch of garden or yard, is let for 2s. or 2s. 6d. a week.

Rents paid by small tenants compare very favourably with those paid for the Castlerea[illegible] cottages. For instance, a small holding, a mile from Castlerea[illegible], of [illegible] acres is rented at [illegible] [illegible] [illegible] small holding of [illegible] acres (Irish), some of it poor land, is rented at [illegible]. Another of 3 acres (Irish) is rented at [illegible]. A third of [illegible] acres (Irish) is rented at [illegible]. A fourth of 7 acres (Irish) is rented at [illegible].

At Castle Plunket a cottage and [illegible] acres of land is rented at [illegible].

A small farm two miles from Castlerea[illegible] of [illegible] acres (Irish), all grass, was reduced two years ago from [illegible] to [illegible].

50. When the valuation of a holding does not exceed [illegible] the landlord pays the rates, but otherwise the landlord and tenant each pay half. The tenant pays the county cess, which averages about [illegible] in the £.

The landlords of cottages which are let by the week almost invariably pay the rates.

51. The small holders always grow sufficient vegetables for home consumption on their land. They seldom have gardens round their houses with flowers. As a rule the manure heap in Ireland occupies the spot usually dedicated to the flower garden in England. [illegible] cottages occupied by labourers have a small strip of garden. The cottages in Castlerea[illegible] to which I have alluded have no garden, but a strip of back yard.

52. Those who have no land, or who require more, take "con-acre," i.e., land rented from a farmer or small holder. It is frequently rented already manured. The charge for con-acre varies from [illegible] to [illegible] for tillage land and from [illegible] to [illegible] for meadow land.

Mr James Clancy informed me that in his neighbourhood "con-acre" was let for [illegible] an acre for the first crop and for [illegible] an acre for the second crop.

A cottage tenant of Mr [illegible]'s who lives half a mile from Castlerea[illegible], and pays [illegible] for his cottage and half an acre of land, sublets the half acre for [illegible].

A few farmers give their men a plot of tillage land, but this custom is quite the exception. I found several instances of farmers letting tillage land manured to their labourers at less than the market price.

53. Most of the small holders keep a cow or two, also pigs, which of late have commanded a good price, and a considerable quantity of poultry. A good many donkeys, goats, and geese are also kept. (See note to par. [illegible])

VI.—Benefit Societies and Trade Unions.

54. Benefit societies, it is to be regretted, do not exist.

55. There are no trade unions among the labourers in the county.

In 18[illegible] a league was formed among the herds in Roscommon with the object of obtaining a higher rate of wages. The head quarters of the league was at Tulsk, and the men held several meetings there. The formation of the league resulted in the employers starting a defence fund. A certain sum of money was guaranteed, and [illegible] in the pound was called up.

The terms demanded by the men were as follows:—A herd in charge of under 100 acres to have a house, 2 acres of land, and the keep of three cows. A herd in charge of 100 acres and under 150 acres to have a house, 3 acres of land, and the keep of three cows. A herd in charge of over 150 acres to have 4 acres of land and the keep of 4 cows.*

The existence of the herd's league was of short duration. On some farms the herds struck, and the employers finding they could get no others to take their places were about to import Scotch herds when the matters in dispute were settled by the masters conceding to the men's terms. The herds' league and the masters' defence fund immediately ceased to exist, and it is satisfactory to be able to say that any feeling which existed at the time of the strike has long ago died away. A large employer of labour who took an active part in arranging the settlement said to me, "We are just as good friends as ever," and a herd who belonged to the league said, "Masters and men are very friendly now."

The terms the men demanded then are not strictly adhered to now on all farms, as since that time the mode of payment has been varied by some employers (Appendix A. [illegible]). But, at any rate, the herds do not seem dissatisfied with their present position.

I heard of one or two strikes on individual farms in more recent years. Mr. Fitz Simmons, steward to The O'Conor Don, informed me that four years ago 10 men struck on that property for higher wages. Mr Fitz Simmons was unable to accede to their demands, and sent another staff of men to do the work. The men on strike abandoned the position they had taken up in four days. "The turnout," said Mr Fitz Simmons, "left no ill feeling between us." Mr Fitz Simmons informs me that two years later six of these men struck for [illegible] a week instead of [illegible] for cutting turf. In consequence the higher rate of wage was given to them, and has been paid them ever since.

A large farmer, who lives a few miles from Castlerea[illegible], told me that a labourer in that neighbourhood tried to get up a sort of union to prevent men coming from a distance to work, as he thought by so doing the wages of the men in that locality would be improved. The proselytising ideas of this labourer appear to have been coldly received, and to have gained little or no support.

VII.—Relations between Employers and Employed.

56. The relations between employers and employed appear to be good. The only cause of complaint on the part of the men is that of low wages. I have been nevertheless told by persons not engaged in agriculture that the men look upon the farmers as their natural enemies. With this statement I am quite unable to agree, and I prefer to base my judgment on the evidence both of the masters and the men (Appendix B. [illegible])

VIII.—General Condition of the Agricultural Labourer.

57. The condition of the agricultural labourer, and in the term agricultural labourer I include all men who work for wages, whether small holders or otherwise, has improved in the last [illegible] years in many particulars. Although the prices of cattle have of late been very low, which have, of course, affected the small holders, on the other hand they have been benefited by considerable reductions in rent, made either by private arrangement or by the Land Court. Moreover, the recent high prices obtained for pigs have been of great assistance to them.

Although the population of Roscommon between 1881 and 1891 decreased by 18,[illegible] persons, the increase in the number of horses, stock, and poultry during that period is large.

Increase in number of Horses, Stock, Poultry, &c. in the County of Roscommon between 1881 and 1891.

[illegible]	[illegible]	[illegible]	[illegible]
Horses	[illegible]	[illegible]	[illegible]
Mules and asses	[illegible]	[illegible]	[illegible]
Cattle	[illegible]	[illegible]	[illegible]
Sheep	[illegible]	[illegible]	[illegible]
Goats	[illegible]	[illegible]	[illegible]
Poultry	[illegible]	[illegible]	[illegible]

Number of Live Stock in Castlerea[illegible] Union 1891.

Horses	2,[illegible]
Mules and asses	[illegible]
Cattle	[illegible]
Sheep	[illegible]
Pigs	[illegible]
Poultry	[illegible]

* [illegible] at Tulsk, informs me that before the strike [illegible] the herds in charge of [illegible] got [illegible] 4 acres of land, and the keep of [illegible] cows.

I heard from many of the older inhabitants that the diet of the present day is not nearly so strengthening as that partaken of some years ago. Some attribute the falling off in the men's capacity for work to the change of diet. Formerly porridge and milk, which used to be called "stirabout," that is, the bread of the [illegible], was the staple [illegible], but now the diet has largely disappeared, and tea and white bread have been substituted. The tea drinking is particularly [illegible] on harvest, and two doctors told me they thought it was having a prejudicial effect on the digestion of the people.

The following food is provided for the men at two farm houses each in three miles of Castlerea:—

1. For breakfast (8 a.m.), stirabout.
   For dinner (12.30 p.m.),* bread, butter, and potatoes.
   For tea (4 p.m.), bread, butter, and a can of milk.
2. For breakfast (8 a.m.), stirabout.
   At 10.30 a.m., bread and tea.
   For dinner (1 p.m. or 2 p.m.), beef and potatoes and milk three days a week, and on other days bacon, potatoes, and milk.
   At 6 p.m. [illegible], bread and tea.

A herd's wife at Castle Plunket told me that they usually eat the following food:—

1. Breakfast (8 a.m. or 7 a.m.), tea, bread, and butter.
2. Dinner (12 o'clock), potatoes, milk, and sometimes bacon.
   Supper (7 p.m.), stirabout or potatoes.

* The farmer's wife [illegible] "I would give more bacon instead of [illegible] three days a week, but they will have [illegible], and not the bacon."

In Appendix B 4, I have given the opinions both of employers and employed as to the improvement in the condition of the people during recent years, and they may be thus shortly summarised:—

1. Wages have increased and the prices of the necessaries of life have decreased, which has resulted in the people feeding and clothing themselves better, and also improving their houses.
2. Hours of work are shorter, partly because men seldom work overtime except at harvest, and partly on account of the growing practice of [illegible] work late in the evening.
3. The introduction of machinery and the use of better implements has rendered work less arduous.
4. Education has improved.
5. The fixing of judicial rents has not only relieved the small farmers pecuniarily, but has also led to the better cultivation of the holdings.[*]

I have, &c.
(Signed) ARTHUR WILSON FOX,
Assistant Commissioner.

* [illegible]

TABLE OF CONTENTS OF APPENDIX A.

STATISTICAL TABLES.

TABLE showing AREA, VALUATION, NUMBER of INHABITED HOUSES and POPULATION in 1891.

A 2.

ANNUAL EARNINGS of LABOURERS in the EMPLOYMENT of MR. [illegible] and THE O'CONOR DON.

A Mr. [illegible] writes:—"This is a good man to "whom I paid 10s. a week. He could build [illegible] "when required. He has a house and 6 or 7 acres "of land of his own, for which he pays rent."

Annual earnings of J.W., 1893, employed by The O'Conor Don:—

		£	s.	d.
Week commencing	April [illegible]	0	6	8
" "	May [illegible]	0	12	0
" "	" [illegible]	0	[illegible]	9
" "	" 16	0	[illegible]	4½
" "	" [illegible]	0	5	7½
" "	" [illegible]	0	7	[illegible]
" "	June [illegible]	0	9	10½
" "	" 13	0	7	6
" "	" [illegible]	0	8	4½
" "	" 27	0	7	7½
" "	July 4	0	9	6
" "	" 11	0	10	0
" "	" [illegible]*	0	12	0
" "	" [illegible]*	0	12	6
" "	" 1	0	8	10½
" "	" 8	0	9	0
Week commencing	Aug. 15*	0	12	0
" "	" [illegible]	0	4	9
" "	" [illegible]	0	10	6
" "	Sept. 5	0	11	6
" "	" 12	0	11	0
" "	" [illegible]	0	7	8
" "	" [illegible]	0	7	8
" "	Oct. 3	0	7	6
" "	" 10	0	9	0
" "	" 17	—		
" "	" [illegible]	—		
" "	" 31	—		
" "	Nov. 7	0	6	7
" "	" 14	0	4	8
		11	8	4½
From November 21st to April [illegible], 18[illegible], [illegible] weeks at 10s. (stall feeding)		11	0	0
		£[illegible]	8	4½

* Family earnings, at [illegible] per day.

A 2.

Herds' Wages.

Payments and Allowances.	Herd under The O'Conor Don. In charge of [illegible] acres.	Herd under Mr. [illegible], Castlereagh.	Herd under Mr Flanagan, [illegible]. In charge of [illegible] acres.	Herd under Mr. Kelly, Castlereagh. In charge of over [illegible] acres.	Herd under Mr Young, [illegible]. In charge of [illegible] acres.
House	[illegible]	House with sheds. } [illegible]	House, [illegible], and [illegible]	House } [illegible]	[illegible]
Land	[illegible]	[illegible] acres.	[illegible] acres, [illegible]	3 or 4 acres.	
Keep of cow and calf, summer and winter.	1 cow and 1 calf [illegible]	[illegible] cows and [illegible] calves, [illegible]	1 cow and 2 calves, [illegible]	[illegible] cows and [illegible] calves, [illegible]	[illegible] cows and 2 calves [illegible]
Keep of mare and foal, summer and winter.	—	—	—	1 mare and foal, [illegible]	—
Free hay	—	[illegible] worth	—	—	[illegible] worth.
Turf	Free and carted, [illegible]	[illegible]	—	—	—
Potatoes	[illegible] per week, [illegible]	—	—	—	—
Cash	[illegible] a week, [illegible]	[illegible]	—	—	—
Geese and pigs	—	—	—	[illegible]	—
Total amount in wages and allowances.	[illegible]	[illegible]	[illegible]	[illegible]	[illegible]
Remarks	The O'Conor Don's steward informs me that the wages of another herd on [illegible] acres are worth [illegible]	This herd is assisted by a grown up son; if he had not his son's help he would have to pay an assistant [illegible] a year and keep him. Calves [illegible] months old sell for from [illegible] to [illegible]. A [illegible] foal is worth from [illegible] to [illegible], and a filly from [illegible] to [illegible]	Mr Flanagan says that for two years a yearling calf has been worth [illegible], but this year ([illegible]) only [illegible]. The herds also sell butter. As a rule they keep pigs. One of Mr Flanagan's herds told him that up [illegible] he got wool and hay [illegible]. Mr Flanagan has [illegible] herds, and pays them according to the agreement made between the employers and the "Herds' League" in [illegible]. Mr Flanagan reckons that the wages of a herd on land [illegible] under [illegible] acres are worth [illegible], and those of a herd on over [illegible] acres are worth [illegible].	Mr. Kelly says that this is a low estimate. He considers that a herd on [illegible] acres may [illegible] a year, and a herd on [illegible] acres or upwards, [illegible] a year. Mr Kelly says most herds are almost [illegible] paid for saving hay, and going to fairs.	Mr Young gives a herd on [illegible] [illegible] the same as [illegible], with the addition of the keep of a mare and foal, which is worth [illegible]

A. 4.

Wages paid in cash from [illegible] to [illegible] on Mr. Flanagan's Farms. 2,47[illegible] acres 3 roods 24 perches (Irish). All grass except 40 acres tillage.

([illegible] acres statute measure.)

Year.	Total amount paid in Cash Wages.	Ordinary Rate of Weekly Wages.	
		Summer.	Winter.
	£ s. d.	s. d.	s. d.
[illegible]	[illegible]	[illegible]	[illegible]
[illegible]	[illegible]	[illegible]	[illegible]
[illegible]	[illegible]	[illegible]	[illegible]
[illegible]	[illegible]	[illegible]	[illegible]
[illegible]	[illegible]	[illegible]	[illegible]
[illegible]	[illegible]	[illegible]	[illegible]
[illegible]	[illegible]	[illegible]	[illegible]
[illegible]	[illegible]	[illegible]	[illegible]
[illegible]	[illegible]	[illegible]	[illegible]
[illegible]	[illegible]	[illegible]	[illegible]
[illegible]	[illegible]	[illegible]	[illegible]

The average cost yearly is [illegible].

This is less than [illegible] per statute acre, but the value of grazings and perquisites is not included. This amounts to a considerable sum, as Mr. Flanagan has [illegible] herds, whom he pays chiefly in kind, and whose earnings vary from [illegible] to [illegible] a year.

A. 5.

Prices of Food in 1873 and 1893, taken from Mr. [illegible]'s books, Castlerea.

Food.	Amount.	1873.	1893.
Flour (best class)	Per sack ([illegible] stones)	[illegible]	[illegible]*
Indian meal	Per [illegible] cwt.	[illegible]	[illegible]
Oatmeal	Per stone	[illegible]	[illegible]
Tea	Per lb.	[illegible]	[illegible]
Sugar (loaf)	"	[illegible]	[illegible]
Soap	"	[illegible]	[illegible]

[illegible]

A. 6.

Number of Persons engaged in Agriculture in the Castlerea Union.

Occupation.	Males.	Females.
Farmers, graziers	[illegible]	[illegible]
Farmers', grazier's sons, grandsons, brothers, nephews	[illegible]	—
Farm bailiff	[illegible]	—
Agricultural labourer, cottager	[illegible]	[illegible]
Shepherd, herdsman	[illegible]	[illegible]
Farm servant (indoor)	[illegible]	[illegible]
Others engaged in or connected with agriculture	[illegible]	—
General labourer*	[illegible]	[illegible]

* Probably many returned under this head are agricultural labourers.

A. 7.

Number of Holdings and their Size in Statute Acres in Castlerea Union.

Not exceeding—

1 Acre.	5 Acres.	15 Acres.	30 Acres.	50 Acres.	100 Acres.	200 Acres.	500 Acres.	Over 500 Acres.	Total.
[illegible]	[illegible]	[illegible]	[illegible]	[illegible]	[illegible]	[illegible]	[illegible]	7	[illegible]

A. 8.

Occupation of Castlerea Union in 1891, and proportion per cent. under Crops, Grass, Woods, Marsh, &c.

Crops, including Meadow and Clover.	Grass.	Fallow.	Woods and Plantations.	Turf bog.	Marsh.	Barren Mountain Land.	Water, Roads, Fences, &c.	Total.
Acres.	Acres.	Acres.	Acres.	Acres.	Acres.	Acres.	Acres.	Acres.
[illegible]	[illegible]	[illegible]	[illegible]	[illegible]	[illegible]	[illegible]	[illegible]	[illegible]

Proportion per cent. under—

[illegible]	[illegible]	·1	[illegible]	[illegible]	[illegible]	[illegible]	[illegible]	

A. 9.

Extent under Crops in Castlerea Union, in Statute Acres, and estimated produce in 1891.

—	Extent.	Estimated Produce.
	Acres.	Cwts. of 112 lbs.
Wheat	2	[illegible]
Oats	[illegible]	[illegible]
Barley	4	[illegible]
Rye	[illegible]	[illegible]
		Tons.
Potatoes	[illegible]	[illegible]
Turnips	[illegible]	[illegible]
Mangold wurzel and beetroot	[illegible]	[illegible]
Carrots and parsnips	[illegible]	[illegible]
Cabbage	[illegible]	[illegible]
Vetches	[illegible]	[illegible]
Rape	[illegible]	[illegible]
Other green crops	[illegible]	—
Clover, sainfoin, and grasses under rotation	[illegible]	[illegible]
Permanent pasture	[illegible]	[illegible]
Total under crops	[illegible]	

A. 18.

[illegible]

[illegible]

Name.	Number of Persons.	[illegible]	[illegible]	Rent.	Remarks.
[illegible]	[illegible]	[illegible]	[illegible]	[illegible]	[illegible]
[illegible]	[illegible]	[illegible]	[illegible]	[illegible]	[illegible]
[illegible]	[illegible]	[illegible]	[illegible]	[illegible]	[illegible]
[illegible]	[illegible]	—	—	[illegible]	[illegible]
[illegible]	[illegible]	[illegible]	[illegible]	[illegible]	[illegible]

[illegible]

[illegible]	[illegible]	[illegible]	[illegible]	[illegible]	[illegible]
[illegible]	[illegible]	[illegible]	[illegible]	[illegible]	[illegible]
[illegible]	[illegible]	[illegible]	[illegible]	[illegible]	—
[illegible]	[illegible]	[illegible]	[illegible]	[illegible]	—

[illegible]

[illegible]	[illegible]	[illegible]	[illegible]	[illegible]	[illegible]
[illegible]	[illegible]	[illegible]	[illegible]	[illegible]	[illegible]
[illegible]	[illegible]	[illegible]	[illegible]	[illegible]	[illegible]

Town.

[illegible]	[illegible]	[illegible]	[illegible]	[illegible]	[illegible]

[illegible]

[illegible]	[illegible]	[illegible]	[illegible]	[illegible]	[illegible]
[illegible]	[illegible]	[illegible]	[illegible]	[illegible]	[illegible]

[illegible]

[illegible]	[illegible]	[illegible]	[illegible]	[illegible]	[illegible]

A. 11.

Herd's Agreement.

I, M. G., do hereby promise and agree to take and become herd to J. B. at the yearly pay of grass for three cows with calves till yearlings. Cottage, 2 acres of land for tillage, and an additional acre for hay. The said cottage to be kept in repair by the said J. B. In consideration of which allowances I do hereby agree to become responsible in health and otherwise for all stock committed to my charge, and should any be lost, and should be proved to my neglect, I hold myself responsible.

I further agree to give up possession of cottage by one month's notice on either side. Should it be when my crop is in the ground I shall leave the value of same to arbitration.

Given under my hand this day of 1893.

(Signed) M. G.

Witness, P. G.

A. 12.

Agreement for Cottage at nominal Rent as part of Wages.

I, A. B., do hereby promise and agree to take and become weekly tenant to J. B. of all that the cottage in the town land of K., parish of N., and Barony of Castlereagh, now occupied by me at the nominal rent of one penny, to commence from the first day of February 1894, the said cottage to be kept in tenantable order and repair by the said J. B. I further undertake that I will not commit nor permit any dilapidation to the said cottage while the same is in my occupation, and I agree to keep the said cottage clean and neat.

Given under my hand this 1st day of April 1894.

his
A. B.
mark.

Witness present,
P. G.

APPENDIX B.

TABLE OF CONTENTS.

B. 1.

Efficiency of Labourers' Work as compared with the Past.

Name.	District.	Evidence.
Lord de Freyne	Frenchpark	The men do not work as well as they used to, as they do not care so much about it.
Mr. Fitz Stephen, steward to The O'Conor Don.	Clonalis	The work has not deteriorated. [illegible]
Mr. [illegible], steward to Mr. Sandford.	Castlereagh	[illegible]
Mr. Kenny, land steward.	Castlereagh	The men are better fed than they were, and so work better.
Mr. [illegible]	[illegible]	One of the men [illegible]
Mr. Henry Glynn, [illegible]	[illegible]	I think the men are [illegible]
Mr. [illegible], farmer	[illegible]	[illegible]
Mr. James [illegible], farmer	French Lawn	The men are [illegible]
A shopkeeper and farmer	Castlereagh	I do not think the men work as well as they did formerly.
A shopkeeper with farm.	Castlereagh	The men are not so skilled, and [illegible]
Mr. [illegible]	[illegible]	The men's work has deteriorated. [illegible]
Mr. John [illegible]	Near Castlereagh	I do not think the men are as able [illegible]
Mr. [illegible]	[illegible]	The men do not work as well as they used to [illegible]
Michael [illegible], labourer	Castlereagh	The [illegible]
Edward [illegible]	Castle Plunket	I do not think the men work [illegible]
Pat [illegible], labourer.	Castle Plunket	I think the young men of the present day [illegible]
Michael Leonard, herd	Castlereagh	I do not think the work [illegible]

B 2.

[illegible] of Labourers in [illegible] as compared with other [illegible]

Name	District	Evidence
[illegible]	[illegible]	[illegible]
[illegible]	[illegible]	[illegible]
[illegible]	[illegible]	[illegible]
[illegible]	[illegible]	[illegible]
[illegible]	[illegible]	[illegible]
[illegible]	[illegible]	[illegible]
[illegible]	[illegible]	[illegible]
[illegible]	[illegible]	[illegible]
[illegible]	[illegible]	[illegible]
[illegible]	[illegible]	[illegible]
[illegible]	[illegible]	[illegible]
[illegible]	[illegible]	[illegible]
[illegible]	[illegible]	[illegible]

B 3.

Relations between Employers and Employed.

Employers' Evidence.

Name	District	Evidence

Relations between Employers and Employed

Evidence of Employed.

Name	District	Evidence
[illegible]	[illegible]	[illegible]
[illegible]	[illegible]	[illegible]
[illegible]	[illegible]	[illegible]
[illegible]	[illegible]	[illegible]
[illegible]	[illegible]	[illegible]
[illegible]	[illegible]	[illegible]
[illegible]	[illegible]	[illegible]
[illegible]	[illegible]	[illegible]
[illegible]	[illegible]	[illegible]
[illegible]	[illegible]	[illegible]

B. 4.

The General Condition of the Agricultural Labourer.

Name.	District.	Evidence.
[illegible]	[illegible]	[illegible]
[illegible]	[illegible]	[illegible]
[illegible]	[illegible]	[illegible]
[illegible]	[illegible]	[illegible]
[illegible]	[illegible]	[illegible]
[illegible]	[illegible]	[illegible]
[illegible]	[illegible]	[illegible]
[illegible]	[illegible]	[illegible]
[illegible]	[illegible]	[illegible]
[illegible]	[illegible]	[illegible]
[illegible]	[illegible]	[illegible]
[illegible]	[illegible]	[illegible]
[illegible]	[illegible]	[illegible]
[illegible]	[illegible]	[illegible]

Name.	District.	Evidence.
[illegible]	[illegible]	[illegible]
[illegible]	[illegible]	[illegible]
[illegible]	[illegible]	[illegible]
[illegible]	[illegible]	[illegible]
[illegible]	[illegible]	[illegible]
[illegible]	[illegible]	[illegible]
[illegible]	[illegible]	[illegible]

B. 5.

Evidence of James P. [illegible], Small Holder, [illegible].

I am 23 years of age. I live here with my mother and two sisters aged 17 and 15. The holding is 4½ acres Irish (about 7½ statute acres). The rent is 2l. 15s. It was reduced from 4l. by the Land Commissioners. The present valuation is [illegible].

My father is in America, and sends us back money nearly every month.

We have an acre and a half of tillage. I work the land with the help of my sisters, and occasionally we employ an odd man. I pay him 1s. a day and his support, summer and winter. He is generally employed here in spring, at haytime and at harvest.

I am sure one man could work this holding. My father used to do it, but I expected to do something better than work on the land, and I do not like it.

My father left Ireland for Yorkshire about 1858. He was at Dewsbury for 15 or 16 years as a [illegible], and left in August 1873. My mother worked in a mill there. He then came here and settled us and left for America at once, and there worked in a foundry in Jersey City. He stayed six years, and sent money home every month.

I went out to him in 1884 because I heard he had his legs taken off, which turned out to be untrue. I was only [illegible] years old then. We both came back after three months and stayed here two years.

My father then went out again, and has now been almost seven years in America in a foundry. We all want to clear out to America and join him.

I have a sister in America aged 19 years, who is a general servant. She went last May. Her wages are 3 dollars a week and her board. Since May last she has sent home 14l. She writes regularly, and says she likes it. Before she went to America she had never left her own house. On her arrival she stayed with friends a short time, and they treated her [illegible]. Most of the girls here are only too anxious to go.

I do not like the work on the land; it is very laborious and does not lead to anything. I have seen men who have worked on it all their lives as badly off at the end of it as at the beginning.

The agricultural labourer.

A man employed at agriculture is considered at the bottom of the social scale.

This is the general opinion among the young men. They prefer a better social position. We who work on the land here have no margin in a bad year. A cow dies, or there is a mishap, and it does for a man.

In trade there is not much risk. The income is steady, though low.

If I got this place rent free I could not support myself out of it.

The people here are mostly in debt at the shops. A good many men have to borrow the money for the journey when they go harvesting in England.

We paid 35l. fine for this house, and also a year and a half's rent to the former tenant, as he was in arrears.

I might get 60l. or 70l. now as tenant right, as we have improved the place wonderfully, drained it, and built a place for pigs. I was educated at the national school. I read the newspapers regularly, and also Irish history. I am also fond of books, and chiefly read Dickens, Thackeray, and Shakespeare.

LETTER FROM JAMES P. FRIEL.

DEAR MR. WILSON FOX, September 8th, 1893.

As regards the query your letter contains, in my humble opinion I consider that small farmers in this country work much harder, and more perseveringly than agricultural labourers. For, whereas a labourer, be they agricultural or otherwise, has no interest in the work at which he is engaged, beyond looking for the usual number of hours in the day, and receiving his hire, the farmer has a vested interest in his holding, and naturally expects that the longer and harder he works the larger will be his reward.

I have known farmers at harvest time to commence cutting corn for hours after the hired men have gone home, and this as a general rule. Again, I know others, or perhaps I should say examples, of holdings [illegible] to make, to have three hours work of meadow cut, before going to work at 7 a.m. in the river drainage works, and after 6 p.m. to start again at the same work, and continue while they had light. They did this so that their children might attend to it in their absence during the day.

No matter what your hurry is, when 6 p.m. arrives, your labourer puts on his coat, and goes home. I think you will see it is quite different with the small farmers. Moreover, the labourers, or at any rate most of them, try to "kill the time" as best they can, while the small holder works perseveringly, and on wet days he finds something to do around his yard while the labourer sits down.

I think I have said enough to show that, as a general rule, small farmers in this country work harder and longer hours than agricultural labourers, that they are industrious and persevering, and I am sure that if they are not as successful, financially speaking, as an impartial observer of their efforts [illegible] would expect them to be, it is not due to their laziness and negligence, as their enemies would fain make out, but to the very trying circumstances in which they are placed.

Yours very truly,
JAMES P. FRIEL.

THE AGRICULTURAL LABOURER.

IRELAND.

REPORT

BY

MR. ARTHUR WILSON FOX
(ASSISTANT COMMISSIONER).

UPON THE

POOR LAW UNION OF SKIBBEREEN
(COUNTY CORK).

TABLE OF CONTENTS.

THE AGRICULTURAL LABOURER.

To Geoffrey Drage, Esq., Secretary,
Royal Commission on Labour,
6, Crown Office Row,
Temple, E.C.

Sir,

The Agricultural Labourer.

I.—Introduction.

Scope of inquiry.

1. I have the honour to present to you my report upon the condition of the agricultural labourers in the Skibbereen Union of County Cork, where I was pursuing my enquiries for about three weeks in April last.

Sources of information.

2. I obtained the information contained in this report by driving to all parts of the Union, and visiting many employers of labour and labourers. I also inspected a number of cottages in the town of Skibbereen, and in various other districts, and, whilst so engaged, I had ample opportunities of gaining information from the labourers.

Of those to whom I am specially indebted for assistance I would mention Canon Goodman, Colonel Somerville, the Rev. Dan O'[illegible], P.P., Baltimore, the Rev. J. O'Sullivan, C.C., Sherkin Island, the Rev. John Murphy, P.P., Drimoleague, the Rev. Thomas Palmer, P.P., Kilmacabea, Captain Morgan, Captain Townsend, Mr. Welply, Mr. Swanton, Mr. Owen Sweeny, Mr. [illegible], Mr. Barry, steward to The O'Donovan, and Mr. Donovan, the superintendent of the Baltimore School of Fishery.

Situation of Union.

3. The Union is situated on the south coast of the County of Cork. It is bounded on the north by the Bantry and Dunmanway Unions, on the east by the Clonakilty Union, and on the west by the Skull Union.

The principal town is Skibbereen, about three hours' journey by rail from Cork.

Size of Union.

4. The size of the Union is 1[illegible] acres, and it contains [illegible] electoral divisions, of which six are congested districts.

The population of the Union is [illegible], of whom 15,[illegible] are males and 13,[illegible] are females. Between 1871 and 1881 the population increased by [illegible], or [illegible] per cent., and between 1881 and 1891 it decreased by 3,[illegible], or 11.[illegible] per cent., notwithstanding an excess of registered births over deaths of [illegible].

Expenditure on relief.

5. For the year commencing September 29th, 1891, the amount spent in indoor relief was [illegible] [illegible]s. [illegible]d., and on out-door relief 1,[illegible]l. [illegible]s. [illegible]d. The rates vary from [illegible]s. [illegible]d. to [illegible]s. in the £. The valuation of the Union in 1891 was [illegible].

Seed Supply Act.

6. In the Spring of 1891 the guardians borrowed [illegible] [illegible]s., under the Seed Supply Act. Of this sum they spent 7,[illegible]l. [illegible]s. [illegible]d., and returned the balance. The guardians have repaid the first instalment, that is, [illegible] [illegible]s. [illegible]d., but the clerk to the union informs me that he does not think they will be able to repay the second instalment, which becomes due in August next.

Relief works in 1891.

7. In 1891, consequent on the partial failure of the potato crop, various relief works were undertaken in the union. These works comprised making, repairing, and fencing roads, building walls, making boat slips, and repairing quays.

For a period of [illegible] weeks, commencing February [illegible] 1891, [illegible] persons were employed on an average every week, involving an expenditure in wages of [illegible].

Size of farms.

8. In the northern part of the district the land is chiefly rough mountain, and there many of the farms are large ones.[*]

In the southern part there is both arable and pasture. In the east the land is chiefly pasture. In the west there is a great deal of rough [illegible] land, and in the centre of the union there is more arable land.[†] (Appendix A. 4 and A. 9)

Breeds of live stock.

9. The breeds of sheep in the district are Border Leicesters and Southdowns. The cattle are chiefly Shorthorns, Ayrshires, and a few Kerrys.

Markets and fairs.

10. A market is held in Skibbereen on Saturdays, and a fair every month in the year.

Principal landowners.

11. The principal landowners in the district are Lord Carbery, The O'Donovan, Sir Henry Becher, Captain R. H. Townsend, and Mrs. Munday.

Labourers' cottages built by guardians.

12. The guardians have built 153 labourers' cottages, under the Labourers Acts, and [illegible] more are in the course of erection. Those with three rooms built on the ground floor are let for [illegible]d. a week, and a two-storied house with two rooms on the ground floor, and two bedrooms on the upper floor, measuring about 11 ft. 3 in. × [illegible] ft. is let for 1s. a week. Each cottage of [illegible] has a half a statute acre of land.

Emigration.

13. I have no figures bearing upon the emigration from the Skibbereen union, but, judging from the census returns, it must have been considerable.[‡] They show an decrease during the last ten years of 3,[illegible] persons notwithstanding an excess of registered births over deaths of 2,4[illegible] persons.

During the year 1892, 7,[illegible] persons emigrated from the county of Cork, 3,7[illegible] being males and 3,[illegible] being females. Of the total number of 7,[illegible] persons, [illegible], or [illegible] per cent., were under 25 years of age.

In 1891, 10,[illegible] persons emigrated from the county of Cork, and in 1890, 9,150 persons.

The fishing industry.

14. Fishing is extensively carried on as an industry on the coast, which gives a great deal of employment. The census returns for 1891 state that there are 1,1[illegible] fishermen in the union, but as so many small farmers and their sons take part in the fishing, and also the work of labourers during part of the year, it is very difficult to determine whom to describe as fishermen.

The spring fishing begins the first week in April and ends the first week in July, and the autumn fishing begins the first week in September and lasts until about the 20th of October.

There is no doubt that the development of this industry has been a great boon to the neighbourhood, by providing employment. Possibly it has been the means of entirely stopping the migration to English or Scotch farms from this union, and, although the emigration to America is still considerable, it has been of late checked at Baltimore, the chief centre for fishing.

Moreover, the fishing industry brings indirect advantages to the neighbourhood, for it forces up agricultural wages, while the presence of fishing boats and

---

[*] A large farm in this district is one of [illegible] acres and upwards. [illegible] [illegible] [illegible] [illegible]

[illegible] [illegible] [illegible]

[illegible] [illegible] [illegible]

[illegible] [illegible] [illegible]

[illegible] [illegible] [illegible]

[†] The following is the proportion of tillage land on various farms:—

No.	Total Acreage.	No. of Acres of Tillage.	No.	Total Acreage.	No. of Acres of Tillage.
1	[illegible]	13	6	[illegible]	[illegible]
2	[illegible]	[illegible]	7	[illegible]	21
3	[illegible]	[illegible]	8	[illegible]	6
4	[illegible]	15	9	[illegible]	[illegible]
5	[illegible]	[illegible]	10	[illegible]	7

[‡] The O'Donovan's [illegible] informed me that two out of [illegible] young men [illegible] to America [illegible].

crews create a demand for vegetables and other farm produce.

The small farmers on the coast get their farm work over as early as possible in the year, in order to be free when the fishing season commences. Some of them get employment by carting fish to Skibbereen from Baltimore at 3s. a load, though the railway, which was opened in May last, will soon do away with the necessity for this work. Employment is also found in curing and packing fish in ice. A number of men are employed in what is known as "hambling," that is, rowing the fish buyers out to the fishing boats when they come in at night. These men are paid from 1l. to 2l. a week for this work, which is a large wage when compared with 8s. a week earned on the land. They are engaged by the week, and their employment lasts from March to July. No doubt the work is arduous when they are at it, as there is considerable competition to reach the fishing boats after they have come in at night. It is an interesting and picturesque sight to see these crews racing out from Baltimore across the harbour to the fishing boats as they come in view.

It is difficult to say what the crews of the fishing boats earn, as so much depends on the season; but I was told by a gentleman in Baltimore of great experience that the average earnings during the spring fishing, of each man in a crew, for three months in an average year, are about 15l. to 20l., and during the autumn fishing 4l. or 5l.

As a rule seven men and a boy form a crew,* and the owner and the crew share the fish between them, after deducting the cost of the men's food, which costs about 2l. 10s. a week. A vessel properly equipped costs 350l. to 600l., and a train of mackerel nets with spring backs, about 150l. If well cared for by barking frequently, they will last four or five years.

The boats are usually made in the Isle of Man, Kinsale, and Arklow.

A considerable number of Manx boats, with fully equipped crews, come to fish off the coast.

The fish caught in these are mackerel, by trawling, soles, plaice, turbot, and other flat fish; and by long lines cod, ling, and conger, haddock and halibut. Large quantities of lobsters are caught by the fishermen on the adjacent islands.

The fish are either sent by rail, packed in ice for the Liverpool and London markets, or else are taken by steamers employed by buyers in Milford, Fleetwood, Liverpool, and Bristol. A quantity of mackerel are now cured for the American markets.

Before leaving the subject of fishing, I must refer to the Baltimore Industrial Fishing School, which was opened in 1887, for the purpose of training young lads to be fishermen. The existence of this excellent institution will always be connected with the energy and generosity of the late Father Davis, the Baroness Burdett Coutts, and Sir Thomas Brady, Inspector of Irish Fisheries.

At the present time there are about 150 boys in the institution, recruited from the ranks of those whose destitution brings within the scope of the Industrial Schools Act. The Government pays 5s. a week to the school towards the maintenance of each boy, and the grand juries of the counties from which the boys are sent subscribe 2s. a week per head. Boys are admissible from the age of 6 to that of 16 years. The superintendent is of opinion that they should be allowed to remain until 18 years of age. He considers that at the age of 16 a boy's mind is not sufficiently formed to enable him to choose the best career for himself, and that instead of following the fishing industry he would probably "take up any occupation he first chanced to "meet with, or tramp the country nothing meanwhile if "he couldn't happened to be doing it."

Moreover, the superintendent is of opinion that it would be an advantage to the school to keep the lads until the age of 18 years, as they could pull an oar and do heavy work, which is now performed by men at a considerable cost in wages.

The boys learn everything connected with fishing. They work nine hours a day, six hours of which are devoted to technical education.

They are taught to knit, to mend, and to make nets, to splice ropes, to mend sails, and to cure fish. Last year the school cured 333 barrels. They are also taught to fish with nets, trawls, and lines, and are instructed in navigation. Some of the bigger boys are employed in the four fishing boats which belong to the school. The crews of these boats are chiefly grown-up men, who make the usual arrangement that they are to receive half the fish caught, it being understood that a man's share is to be double that of a boy's. The superintendent informs me that in a few years the school makes a profit by the fishing, after paying all expenses in connection with gear, and wear and tear.

The following figures show the division of profits between the men and the school, made by the four boats in the autumn fishing between September 7th and October 22nd, 1892:—

School.	Men.	Proceeds.
[illegible]	[illegible]	[illegible]

There were seven men and two boys in each boat. Thus each man earned about 9l. 17s. 6d. in six weeks, and had his food in addition.

The following food is provided for men and boys on the school boats:—

Breakfast	Bread, butter, tea.
Dinner	Meat and potatoes.
Tea	Bread, butter, and tea.
Midnight	Coffee and perhaps bread.

Besides the six hours technical education in fishing the boys have three hours of schooling, and are taught up to the 6th Standard of National Education.

Some of the boys learn shoemaking and tailoring, and all the clothes, boots, shoes, &c. worn by the boys in the establishment are made and repaired by them.

A small farm of 10 acres is attached to the school, on which all the vegetables are grown. Four cows and a horse are kept. The boys do all the work necessary on the farm, and thus have the advantage of technical education in farm work.†

15. A dairy company, formed for the purpose of making butter on a large scale, started operations in Skibbereen on April 18th last. The undertaking was assisted in its inception by the Congested Districts Board, who advanced on mortgage the sum of 800l. at 3¼ per cent. repayable by instalments, in order that farmers who are too poor to become shareholders in the usual way may obtain the benefits of the dairy.

The dairy promises to become a great success, and if it does, both the farmers who sell milk, and the poor people who buy skim and butter-milk, will greatly benefit.

* 10 vessels at work, the crew consists of six men and a boy.

† The following is an extract from the first annual report of the Congested Districts Board, 1892: [illegible]

During the month of April (commencing on the 10th last) the company bought 78,879 gallons of milk, and made [illegible] tons of butter, and during the month of May they bought 88,[illegible] gallons of milk and made 6½ tons of butter.

Several small farmers told me that they thought the dairy would prove a great boon for them, because it would give them a certain market for their milk at a good profit. The manager informed me that several farmers had told him that since the dairy was started their profits on milk had been doubled.

The company give the farmers 4d. a gallon for fresh milk* and return them 75 per cent. of the skim milk, which is given to calves and pigs. Before the dairy came into existence, the farmers made butter and sold it for 8d. a pound, and it took three gallons of milk to make a pound. But now they get 1s. from the dairy for three gallons, and can sell as much as ever they want to. Moreover, they have not the trouble of making butter, or the risk of not selling it, and they receive besides 75 per cent. of the skim milk back for their animals and other purposes.

The company sell butter-milk at ½d. a gallon to the poor people in Skibbereen, who are, as the manager informed me, very glad of the opportunity of getting it. While I was inspecting some labourers' cottages there, I saw a cart coming round with this milk, and it seemed to be greatly in demand.

Apart from these advantages of the dairy, the fact that large quantities of good butter of uniform quality can be turned out from a district, is likely to create a demand for it in the market, as I understand it is the difference of quality in English and Irish butter which frequently induces dealers to prefer foreign butter. I was told, when making inquiries for the Royal Commission in Suffolk in the summer of 1892, that the lack of uniformity in the Suffolk butter was the chief reason for dealers preferring Danish butter.

16. The principal islands off the coast are Cape Clear Island (1,[illegible] acres) with a population of 3[illegible] persons, Sherkin Island (1,[illegible] acres), with a population of 1[illegible] persons, Hare Island ([illegible] acres), with a population of [illegible] persons, Ringarogy Island ([illegible] acres), with a population of 3[illegible] persons, and Inishbeg Island ([illegible] acres), with a population of [illegible] persons.

Cape Clear Island, about 3 miles in length, is situated about a mile from Sherkin Island, and its nearest point is about four miles from Baltimore. Some of the land is very good for grazing. Generally speaking, the holdings are about 10 to 20 acres of good land, and some of them have in addition from 10 to [illegible] acres of rough mountain land. There are a few larger farmers with 30 or 40 acres of good land, and rough land besides.

Most of the people are engaged in fishing as well as agriculture. The markets are very inconveniently situated for them. To get to Skibbereen they have to row from four to seven miles according to where they live on the island, and then to walk seven or eight miles by road, and to get to Skull they have to row six miles. I am informed that years ago the people used to swim their cattle over to Skull tied behind their boats.

The people on this island are a fine race, which is, perhaps, surprising, as it is customary for them to intermarry. I am informed it is unusual for an islander to marry anyone on the mainland. Possibly the sea air, the healthy occupations of agriculture and fishing, and the nutritious diet of potatoes, fish, and milk,† all tend to develop their muscles and sinews.

Furze is frequently burnt for fuel. The people spin their wool and make frieze and flannels.

Mr. [illegible], a farmer of 40 acres, informed me that labour is very scarce there in the fishing season, and that during that time wages are 8s. to 12s. a week with food, whereas in the winter they are 6s. without food. There are very few agricultural labourers in the ordinary sense of the word. Three labourers' cottages have been built by the guardians. Some of the people emigrate to Boston, America.

The conditions existing in Sherkin Island are very similar to those on Cape Clear Island, but the latter has the advantage of being only a mile from Baltimore. There are six or seven men there who live entirely as agricultural labourers. There are others who are small tenants, keeping, perhaps, one cow. These men fish in the season and are willing at other times to work on the land for wages. There is no emigration from Sherkin, but those who cannot make a living on the island either join the trading schooners between Baltimore and South Wales, or go to sea on steamships or merchant vessels. The people on this island, as also on Cape Clear Island, are able to procure manure for their land, as most of them keep a cow or two and a few pigs, while they can always obtain sea-weed.

The condition of the people on Hare Island, which is close to Sherkin, was described to me by the Reverend J. O'[illegible] of [illegible] as one of chronic destitution. The holdings are very small. The people eke out a living by rowing fish buyers out to the fishing boats in the season, and they also catch lobsters.

On Ringarogy Island there are 37 or 40 small farmers. Most of the men go fishing from there. Mr. Jerry [illegible], who farms 20 acres, informed me that labour was very scarce in [illegible]. He [illegible] wanted a man and could not get one anywhere. There is only one man who lives exclusively by employment as a labourer. I looked at his cottage, which was very old. He pays no rent and [illegible] it belongs to him.

Inishbeg Island belongs to Mr. McCarthy Morrogh. There are three or four tenant farmers on the island. Mr. McCarthy Morrogh lives there and gives employment. There are about eight agricultural labourers. Labour is scarce on account of the fishing. I met a man there who was paid 12s. a week, wet or dry, and a farm servant who was paid [illegible] a year and given his board and the grass of a sheep.

17. In this district there are no herds or caretakers engaged on the farms, because there are no large grazing farms. The great majority of farms are under 100 acres. There are only 11[illegible] between 100 and 300 acres, and only 27 over 300 acres. The charge of horses and cattle usually falls to the lot of the farm servant, or else to the regular man, both of whom have in addition the ordinary work of the farm to attend to.

On many farms there are a certain number of labourers who live entirely by agricultural employment for wages, and these men are usually employed regularly wet or dry. The odd men are usually small farmers and their sons, who are working on their own land when not working for wages, or else fishermen, who are quite ready to work as labourers out of the fishing season. In the town of Skibbereen there are men who are solely agricultural labourers, and whose employment, unfortunately, is irregular. There are few ploughmen in the Union but, owing to the scarcity of tillage land, they can hardly be said to exist as a class.

Very few women are employed. In some districts a few do a little weeding, and they are sometimes employed during harvest. It is said that women now look down on agricultural employment, and prefer to emigrate or to seek work in towns. Domestic servants are difficult to get on account of the emigration.

Boys begin to work as soon as they leave school, and they are sometimes hired on the farm houses as young as 11 years of age.

II.—The Supply of Labour.

18. The supply of labour is frequently very insufficient in the districts near the coast during the fishing season, that is from the beginning of April to the middle of July, and again in the autumn. This cannot be wondered at as the men who form the crews of the boats are, during the fishing season, able to earn a considerable sum compared with what they could earn at agricultural employment, while those who are employed "[illegible]," that is, rowing fish-buyers out to the large fishing boats, are paid from 1l. to 1l. 5s. a week. Moreover the small farmers are able to earn a good deal of money by curing fish (see paragraph 16).

The effect of the fishing is that agricultural wages near the coast are sometimes driven up to 2s. a week more than are paid some 7 or 8 miles inland.

Particularly in the neighbourhood of Baltimore, where mackerel fishing is extensively carried on, labour has of late been very scarce, owing to the construction of the railway from Skibbereen to Baltimore.

The men there were paid 15s. a week, with the result that sometimes agricultural wages in the neighbourhood rose nearly as high.

In the inland districts, not near enough to the coast to be affected by the fishing, the supply of labour appears to be just sufficient in summer.

* The company pay for milk according to quality. [illegible]
† [illegible]

‡ In some of the [illegible] in the neighbourhood, [illegible]

During the winter there seems plenty of labour everywhere, in fact the great complaint in many places is the want of employment, as those who fish in the summer and autumn are out of work and only too ready to get employment on the land in the winter.

Possibly the fishery industry has been the means of scarcely checking the emigration to England or Scotch farms from this Union,* certainly without it there would be no abundance of labour in the winter. I was told that in recent years it has been the means of preventing much emigration in the neighbourhood of Baltimore.

There is no doubt that less labour is being employed in this district than formerly, chiefly owing to the converting of arable land into grass. A large farmer on 250 acres said to me, "In the last few years I have "reduced my permanent staff from five to three owing "to my giving up tillage land." I heard several complaints that the land was not so well farmed in some places owing to reduction of labour on economical grounds.

19. In this district, as in every other I visited in England and Ireland, I heard complaints from employers that the men do not do so much work now as formerly, and several of the older labourers corroborated this view.

Opinion is divided as to the cause of this. A great many say that the best young men have emigrated, and so only the old and inefficient are left behind. Others say that the men now do not care for agricultural employment and so do not exert themselves. One farmer thought that since the fishing had taken the men off farm work they were lacking in experience as labourers. Another thought that the irregularity of the fishing life made them acquire habits of idleness. Some were of opinion that the scarcity of labour enabled the labourer to do less work than formerly, as there was little or no competition. It was also urged that the men were less skilled now as there is so much less arable land, and in consequence they were unable to gain the same experience in ploughing and other farming operations.

On the other hand some men of experience say that better men are now to be obtained than 20 years ago, while others are of opinion that the poor work comes generally of experience. Such contradictory evidence makes it extremely difficult to arrive at any definite conclusion on this subject, but certainly the majority of witnesses agree in thinking that the labourer does not do so good a day's work as he used to. (Appendix B 2.)

20. With regard to the still more difficult question as to how the work of the Cork men compares with that in other districts, I was not able to get much information. Mr. A. Beed, engineer and contractor, agreed, a gentleman who has had great experience of labour in various parts of the world, and who has been employed on a light railway in Mayo, and is at present employed on the Baltimore Railway in the Skibbereen Union, is of opinion that the Mayo men are finer physically and harder workers than the Cork men.

Mr. Beamish, a large farmer in the north of the Union, is of opinion that the Cork men are more skilled and work harder than the Kerry men. Mr. Bryan, The O'Donovan's steward, a Lancashire man, thinks the Irishmen work well under supervision, but he considers that Lancashire men work far better. Of course the standard of Lancashire work is a very high one, and perhaps a comparison between a set of men who get 11 a week and are meat-fed, with others who receive less than half that sum and have no meat, is hardly a fair one?

Mr. Bryan has also had experience of Queen's County and Waterford men, and he considers the Cork men "quite as good, if not better and heartier."

A great many farmers employ their ordinary staff "wet or dry," and thus many of the agricultural labourers have continuous employment.

There are many small farmers, or their sons, who sometimes work as labourers, but these men have also to attend to their own land, and so do not work regularly for wages.

22 It is not easy to determine what are the actual terms of engagement of ordinary labourers. Generally speaking, the men who are regularly attached to the staff of a farm have a weekly engagement, and many are paid wet or dry. Frequently if either master or man desire to part company in the middle of the week neither raises any objection as to notice.

But the mode of payment adopted on some farms to the regular man practically renders their term of service a long one, unless anything unusual occurs. For instance some farmers give them land, the grass of sheep and a bank of turf as part of their wages, and they are thus not in the position of men who can move away at a week's notice and put the whole of their worldly goods on to a cart.

I could not get a few statements of ordinary labourers who were engaged by the year.

The small holders who work for farmers do so by the day, and stay at home to till their own land when they want to.

Odd-men are always engaged by the day.

23 Cattlemen are generally engaged by the week, but often are engaged for longer periods, or sometimes by the year. They often stay in their places a long time. In this Union there is frequently, on the demesnes, I may almost say a necessity, for them to do so, as part payment of their wages in kind, the grass of sheep or a cow, and a turf bank is not uncommon.

24 Ploughmen are usually engaged by the week, and are employed wet or dry, but as there is now so little tillage land, there are but few of them. On several farms I found that the farmers did their own ploughing, as they say they can do it better than any men they can get. Ploughmen usually stay in their places a considerable time.

25. Hired men are generally engaged by the year, though seven years to a eleven's notice, but frequently no legal obligation is observed. Mr. Connell at Castle Townsend says—"I give a month's notice. They "give the same. I believe legally it is a yearly agreement."

26. The hours of work for ordinary labourers and hired men in summer are usually from 6 a.m. to 6 p.m., or else from 7 a.m. to 7 p.m. I did not, however, visit farms where the hours were from 6 a.m. to 7 p.m.

The ordinary meal times in summer are an hour, or half an hour, for breakfast, and an hour for dinner. Thus the usual number of working hours on most farms are 10 to 10½ hours.

On one farm of 82 acres I ascertained that the hours are from 6 a.m. to 7 p.m., with only an hour off for meals, thus making a working day of 12 hours.

27. The hours in winter are always difficult to state, as they vary according to the daylight, but some farmers have fixed dates for their winter and summer hours. Thus Mr. Beamish's summer hours are from March to September, during which time the men's actual working hours are ten and a half. The winter hours are from September to March. They commence at 7 or 8 a.m. and end at 6 p.m. and an hour and a half is allowed for meals. Thus these men's winter work occupies them for 8½ or 9½ hours a day.

Mr. Crowe Beamey's winter hours are from 8 a.m. to 5 p.m. with two hours off for meals. This makes a working day of seven hours.

Mr. M. Kingston's winter hours are 7 to 7 with two hours off for meals, thus making a working day of ten hours.

are kept, but little employment can be found for the men after dark.

The meal hours in winter vary from one to two hours. When work begins as late as 8 a.m. the men invariably breakfast before they commence work, and in that case only one hour is allowed for dinner.

28. The length of time occupied in Sunday work varies according to the stock kept.

Mr. Owen Sweeny, who farms 150 acres, and employs three or four regular men, tells me that two lads who live in his house, attend to the cattle on Sundays, and their work occupies them an hour in the morning and an hour in the evening.

On The O'Donovan's estate, where 25 regular men are employed, and a quantity of stock kept, two yardmen are employed half the day, but this includes milking. Two horsemen out of four attend to the horses on alternate Sundays. In the summer the horses are turned out so that there is practically no Sunday work for horsemen during that season.

Mr. B. O'Connell, who farms 140 acres, and employs three regular men, apportions his Sunday work as follows:—One man milks, one man feeds cattle, and one man feeds the horses. This work occupies each man two hours both morning and evening, summer and winter, except in the case of the man who feeds horses, and he has no Sunday work during the summer, when they are turned out to grass. These men have their breakfast and tea given them on Sundays.

Mr. Walsh's six regular men take the Sunday work in turns, one man doing all the work every sixth Sunday. This occupies him six hours.

IV.—Wages and Earnings.

29. The mode of paying ordinary labourers varies considerably, as part payments in kind in lieu of cash are frequent. Moreover, the rate of wages in summer depends on whether the farms are near the coast or not and thereby affected by the scarcity of labour consequent on the fishing industry.

Generally speaking the cash wages for regular hands in summer is 8s. a week, or, if food is supplied, 4s. If a man is paid according to the latter scale he is in reality better off than if paid 8s. a week, as the farmer certainly does not feed him for 4s. a week.

I found instances where the cash wages were 10s. a week, and one farmer who lived near the fishing and the railway was paying 6s. a week and giving food, while in the country districts away from the coast, I found wages of regular men 5s. with no food.

In the fishing season farmers near the coast have sometimes to pay 2s. a day for extra hands, but inland they are frequently paid the same as the regular men. Mr. Sharpley, who farms 60 acres in Cape Clear Island, told me that, sometimes in May and June he has to pay from 8s. to 12s. a week and give food as well.

Owing to the custom of paying regular men partly in kind, their actual position is not easy to arrive at. I have given several instances of these payments in Appendix A 2. It will be seen that these men are often much better off than those who are paid entirely in cash.

30. On many farms the winter wages are the same as those paid in summer, but along the coast fishermen who are then out of employment are willing to work for less. 5s. a week is usually the lowest cash wage paid (Appendix A 2).

31. The wages of ploughmen are frequently higher than those of ordinary labourers. On small farms there is a very small proportion of tillage land and the ploughing is done by one of the ordinary labourers, or also by the farmer himself.

The O'Donovan's ploughman is paid 10s. a week, wet or dry, and also in sickness. He is also given a suit of clothes a year.

A farmer near Clonakilty gives his ploughman 10s. a week and their food. This represents a wage of over 15s. a week.

Captain Morgan's ploughman has 9s. a week, wet or dry, and when sick. He also has a house value 3l., turf (3l.), half an acre of potatoes (2l. 10s.), grass of cow (3l. 10s.). This represents a weekly wage of about 13s. 6d.

32. On a few large farms or estates where sufficient stock is kept to necessitate the employment of a cattleman, his wages are usually a little higher than those of the ordinary labourers. But, on the smaller farms, as I have pointed out, it is often the case that no distinction is made in respect of the work the men have to perform, and a uniform rate of wage is paid to all. On farms where hired men are kept the charge of animals usually falls to their lot.

Captain Morgan pays his yardman 9s. a week, wet or dry, and during sickness. He also gives the following perquisites:—A house (3l.), turf (3l.), half an acre of potatoes (2l. 10s.), grass of a cow (3l. 10s.). This represents a weekly wage of 13s. 6d. The yardman's wife is also employed by Captain Morgan as dairy or hen woman. Thus their united earnings are 18s. 6d. a week.

33. Hired men are usually paid from 10l. to 12l. a year, and they are fed and lodged in the farmhouse. I found no instance where their cash wages exceeded 12l. Two men I met were paid 12l. and given the grass of a sheep.

A farmer informed me that the lowest wage paid to a young hired boy who had just left school would be from 1l. 10s. to 2l. a year. I saw two lads of 16 who were paid 6l. and 5l. respectively, and two lads of 16 and 18 who were paid 9l. and 12l. respectively.

34. Boys and lads employed as ordinary day labourers are of course paid less than men. The O'Donovan employs two boys aged 14 and a lad aged 17. Their respective wages are 3s. 6d., 5s., and 7s., per week.

Captain Morgan gives a boy, aged 16, 6s. a week, and a cowboy, aged 13, 3s. a week. In the neighbourhood of Baltimore, boys work at 1s. a day.

35. Women are seldom employed. Father O'Brien informed me that at Baltimore they are paid 1s. a day for weeding, but that during the railway works their wages rose to 2s. a day, because the boys, who generally do weeding, were getting employment on the railway. The hours are exactly the same as those of men. During harvest women are employed in some districts. The small holders' wives and daughters frequently work very hard on their own land.

36. In some cases several members of a family, who have land of their own, work partly on their own land and partly for wages on neighbouring farms. It is a matter of great difficulty to ascertain their united weekly earnings, as they frequently work for several farmers during the year.

The Dean of Ross gives regular employment to a family at the following rate of wages per week:—The father, 8s.; son, aged 21, 8s.; son, aged 18, 7s.; son, aged 15, 5s.; son, aged 13, 3s. 6d. This amounts to a weekly wage of 1l. 11s. 6d. between them.

In addition they have a house free, and as much ground for potatoes as they can manage, and a horse and cart lent them when required. Moreover, they have the use of one of the Dean's best shorthorn cows (a show cow) at 2s. a week. The dean provides all hay, grass, and straw. The man has the calf. He sells the butter, and says he pays for the cow's keep out of it, and gets the skim milk free. He also has the advantage of the dairy.

37. Very little piecework, "task-work" as it is called in Ireland, is done. This is partly because there is so little tillage land, and partly because neither masters nor men care about it. Several employers told me they found the men scamped their work when employed by the piece unless they had constant supervision. The work usually undertaken by task-work is cutting drains and turf and making fences.

38. It is often the case that the men on the ordinary staff of a farm are paid nothing extra in haytime and harvest, though some farmers give something to eat or drink. I was told that before machines were brought into use the ordinary staff of men were paid 1s. a day extra for mowing.[*] On most farms harvest is of short duration, as so very little corn is now grown, but there are farms where the harvest lasts many weeks.

Extra men at haytime are, however, paid considerably more than the ordinary rate of wages. There are several reasons which render extra help very difficult to obtain at this time. One is that everyone requires it, another that most of the available men are fishing, another that the small farmers are getting in their own hay and so cannot get away to work, and, lastly, of recent years, the construction of the railway has drained the districts of spare men.

For extra men harvest wages are 2s. to 2s. 6d. a day. A farmer's wife in Inisbeg Island told me they paid 3s.

---

[*] Mr. Owen Sweeny says that the introduction of machinery has not decreased the labour on his farm, except at haytime and harvest. At these times he now does with fewer men than he [illegible].

Wages of hired men.

Wages of boys and lads.

Wages of women.

Family earnings.

Piecework.

Payment of extra men at hay and harvest.

a week and food. Mr Walpin gives 6s 6d. a day and no food, but to those who come from a distance he gives dinner, consisting of corned beef, potatoes, [illegible], or milk.

39. As a rule ordinary labourers do not receive perquisites. There is, however, this exception to be noted, and that is where men are paid 6s a week and food in lieu of 9s a week, they are getting more than 3s. worth of food.*

The following are instances of ordinary labourers receiving perquisites.

Mr [illegible] gives his men as much milk as they want, ploughs their land and carts their manure. He sometimes gives them wool to make clothes of.

Servants or employees of The O'Conor's[illegible] estate, who are also sons of tenants, are always paid half wages in sickness. One man has been ill three years and has had half pay all the time, and [illegible] pints of new milk a week. Another man has only worked half time through illness in three years and has received half pay when absent. One man has two tons of coal in the year. All the men on this estate receive little kindnesses such as are often known on English estates, namely, a dinner at Christmas and also 8 to 11 pounds of beef each, with other small presents, and a Christmas tree for the children. At harvest time they also have a dinner and a dance.

Mr. Walpin, who pays 7s. a week wet or dry, gives in addition a house, as much tillage land as they like up to half an acre, the milk of a cow, or the grass of two sheep, and a bank of turf which lasts a year.

40. Some ordinary labourers, regularly attached to the staff of a farm, receive part of their wages in kind, such as a cottage, or some land or the grass of a sheep (Appendix A [illegible]). Also ploughmen and cattlemen not unfrequently are paid partly in kind, to which matters I have alluded in paragraphs 31 and 32.

41. There are practically no other industries but agriculture and fishing (paragraph 19). A little money is made by selling seaweed and turf. Eggs are sold by the people in considerable quantities to large buyers, who send them to English markets.

42. In this union I have not succeeded in getting the annual earnings of labourers from books, but a fairly accurate estimate can be made of the regular men's earnings, who are engaged "wet or dry," as is not uncommon.† If a man is paid 9s. a week all the year round, his annual earnings, deducting 16 days for Catholic holidays, come to [illegible]. If he is paid 9s. a week for half a year and 8s. for the other half, his annual earnings, deducting 16 days for Catholic holidays, come to [illegible], and if he is paid 10s. a week for six months and 8s. a week for the rest of the year, his annual earnings, deducting 16 days for Catholic holidays, come to [illegible]. A regular man on 6s. a week and his food, summer and winter, deducting 16 Catholic holidays, gets [illegible] in cash and his food as well, which may fairly be estimated at another [illegible] (1s. a day).‡

Some men may earn more than the sums I have mentioned, as on some farms there are perquisites in addition to wages, examples of which I have given in Appendix A [illegible].

On the other hand, ordinary men who are not regularly employed earn less than I have stated; but it must be borne in mind that many of them have land of their own, and absent themselves from work for the purpose of cultivating it while others seek employment at other occupations connected with the seaboard fishery.

43. The annual cash earnings of hired men are between [illegible] and [illegible], without board and lodging, for which at least 7s. a week must be added. This brings their total earnings to between [illegible] and [illegible].

44. Ploughmen's annual cash earnings may be put at between [illegible] and [illegible], but they frequently get perquisites in addition. (See paragraph 31.)

V.—Cottage Accommodation.

45. Accommodation for labourers has greatly improved in the country districts, owing to the recent building of 151 Union cottages. Another [illegible] are now in the course of construction. Some of these cottages have all the rooms on the ground floor, while others have two stories. The former are rented at 9d. a week, and the latter at 1s. Both classes of houses have half an acre of land, and it is proposed to give some an acre.

They are built either in pairs or singly, and are made of stone, lime, and slate. The houses constructed on the ground floor have three rooms and a scullery. The living-rooms are about 16 feet by 16 feet, and the other two rooms about [illegible] feet by [illegible] feet each. The roofs are unceiled and sloping, but of a sufficient height. In the two-storied houses there are two rooms on the ground floor and two bedrooms upstairs, measuring [illegible] feet [illegible] inches by [illegible] feet [illegible] inches each.

The advantages of the Union cottages built by the sanitary authorities are obvious. Decent dwellings planned and built by professional hands are far superior to houses run up by the people themselves. The rooms are of sufficient size and height; the roofs are of slate instead of rotten thatch, the repairs are done by the landlord, the tenants have half an acre of land close to their houses, and, apart from that, their erection must tend to raise the standard of cottage building throughout the country.

46. I have heard several objections to the building of Union cottages. Perhaps naturally enough some farmers dislike having men planted compulsorily on their farms, who never have done and never will do a day's work for them.

Again, the depredations of the labourers' animals are frequently a sore thing, and certainly a great temptation. The donkey, the cow, the pig, the geese and hens by no means recognise the limits of their owner's half acre, and it appears that they frequently wander at night time to better pastures.

A parish priest expressed himself strongly on this point as follows:—

"Half an acre is worse than nothing to a labouring man, for he grows the same crops year after year and the land becomes valueless. Moreover, there is no room to keep a cow. The people drive their cow on the farmer's land at night, and so the scheme makes thieves of the labourers. The hens and geese stray too. Sometimes when the farmer goes to town they put the cow and donkey on to his best land. They also steal hay and turnips at night. The farmers are justified in grumbling. If a man keeps a cow under this scheme, he must keep her by theft.

"I am a Nationalist and a Home Ruler, but I think this was a most ill-considered scheme, brought forward by a few people who wished to get a little cheap popularity at other people's expense.

"Now, I would build no labourers' cottages on the good land of the farmers, but I would take [illegible] acres of bad land for each and fence it in. I should have a community of them.

"The man could start building up new land, and they could keep a cow, which is everything for a family, and it also means manure for the land and milk for the pig. By degrees they would make good land of the [illegible]."

47. Speaking about the other cottages in the rural districts, among which I include the houses of the small tenants, who earn their livelihood by farming, fishing, and working for wages, there are some very bad ones; but, on the whole, they are considerably better than those in Mayo. The existence of well-built houses can hardly be expected in a country where the majority of them are erected by small farmers, who have no knowledge of building or sanitary matters, and whose one object when erecting a dwelling is to run it up as cheaply as possible.

At Myross I saw some wretched hovels, chiefly inhabited by fishermen. They consisted of two rooms on the ground floor opening into each other, the bedroom being often without light and air, unless the door was open into the living-room. The thatch appeared in many instances to be rotten. On the whole, these cottages were the worst I saw in the country districts. In Appendix A [illegible] I have given in detail particulars of certain cottages I visited, both in the town of Skibbereen and in the country districts.

48. Some of the labourers' cottages in Skibbereen are very bad indeed. It seems difficult to understand how a sanitary authority can allow such a state of things to exist. In Appendix A [illegible] I have given several examples of them. The rents usually are 1s. a week, but some are as much as [illegible]. The people

* Mr [illegible], a farmer in [illegible], considered that his men were [illegible] a week worth of food. He however gives his men [illegible] food dinner [illegible] days a week, and [illegible] with the other days.

† [illegible] out of [illegible] Mr. [illegible] work [illegible] days between [illegible] [illegible] [illegible] of these were [illegible] Catholic, and [illegible] holidays [illegible] [illegible] [illegible] [illegible]

‡ Although a farmer must have some work on Catholic holidays, as he has to attend to the animals, he forbids his men on these days, on which very little work is done.

[illegible] living in these hovels are much to be pitied. They have in this small country town all the disadvantages of those who live in a big city, being without gardens or spaces round their houses, and are thus too much cramped for room to be able to keep a pig or grow potatoes and vegetables. At the same time they have not the advantage of efficient sanitary supervision such as is usually exercised in a big city.

The roofs of one row of five houses are in the most disgraceful condition. Some of them have practically fallen in. In one there is a hole under the thatch through which a man could crawl. At the back of this row there are small yards where pigs are kept. These are covered with several inches of mud and filth, and the back doors open immediately upon them.

I visited a row of cottages built up a steep hill. An open drain was trickling against the main wall outside. This has percolated through the wall of an old man's house, and consequently the floor of one of his rooms was sloppy with sewage. In the same row lives an old woman in two miserable rooms with clay floors. The living-room is 12 ft. by 9 and the window 18 inches by 18. Opening out of this room is the bedroom, 10 ft. by 6. The window frame is 12 inches square. There is no glass, and the space is stuffed with rags. The bed consists of rags and straw. The furniture is a broken table, one old wine barrel, a broken travelling chest, a [illegible], a milk jug, a tin pot, a jam pot, and a picture of his Holiness the Pope. There is no back door and no yard or garden. The rent is 1s. a week.

Of late years some new cottages have been built in Skibbereen which are in all respects superior to the older ones.

Over-crowded. 49. It is simple to assume that in two-roomed houses there must be, not unfrequently, cases of overcrowding, but I met with an instance on Cape Clear Island which exceeded anything I had seen elsewhere in England or Ireland. The house contains a living room, two bedrooms, and two lofts. The inhabitants number 16, and consist of two brothers, their wives, sons and daughters, and also the old grandmother, who was primarily responsible for their numerous human beings.

In one bedroom on the ground floor, 15 feet by 13 by 7½ high, sleep the grandmother and two young children. In another bedroom on the ground floor, 15 by 7 by 8½, sleep a man, his wife, and young child. In a loft approached by a ladder sleep a man, his wife, and two young children. This place is very stuffy; the bed is a wooden one, and the bedclothes rags and straw.

In a long low loft, about 20 by 14, with a sloping roof, a very hot stuffy place, full of lumber, three sisters, aged 19, 16, and 9, and three brothers, aged 22, 18, and 16, sleep. There are two beds; the girls all sleep in one, and the boys in the other.

Ventilation. 50. The ventilation of the old class of houses is pretty good, as the rooms are all on the ground floor, and hence fresh air comes into the house every time the door is open. In the Union cottages good windows are provided, and if the rooms are not properly ventilated, the tenants are themselves to blame. Animals are not so frequently kept in the houses in this Union as in the Westport Union, co. Mayo; still, it is not uncommon to find them there. In a two-roomed house in Skibbereen, inhabited by a man, his wife, and six children, two of whom are grown up, I found a horse kept in the living-room.

Sanitation and water supply. 51. There is no system of drainage in the country districts. The people in this Union, as in the other two Unions I had previously visited, choose the front of their houses for the manure heaps or pits. In many instances where the manure has just been carted away to put on the land, there were pools of filthy and foul-smelling manure water raised only opposite the front door, to which the natives appeared perfectly indifferent. In the town of Skibbereen I saw quite enough bad drains outside cottages to demonstrate that there can be no sanitary inspection worth mentioning.

Closets in the ordinary houses of the country are unknown. Outside the Union cottages they have been erected, but I never found one used for the purpose intended, and I am told most people consider such usage an unnecessary and absurd innovation.

In the cottages I visited I found the closets used either as henhouses or lumber-sheds, and in some cases locked.

The water in the district seems to be good as regards quantity and quality.

Rent. 52. The rents of cottages are usually about 1s. a week, though there are instances where they are as much as 2s. 6d.

* 7832. [illegible]

I have already stated that the Union cottages are rented at 9d. a week for the one-storied houses, and at 1s. a week for two-storied ones, a very cheap rental considering that an acre of land is attached to each house. It must, however, be borne in mind that the ratepayers are contributing somewhat liberally towards the rent, as each house costs 130l. to build, including price of land, besides which rates, repairs, insurance, and cost of collection of rent, have to be taken into consideration. [illegible]

Cost of erection. 53. The cost of actually building the Union cottages is 70l. each, but the total cost, which includes purchase of the land and other expenses, brings the sum up to 130l.

Captain Morgan, who has built several excellent cottages on his estate, tells me they cost him between [illegible] and [illegible].

On Cape Clear Island I saw a new house recently built by a tenant on a holding of 40 or 50 acres. It was made of stone, mortar, and slates. It contained a big living-room on the ground floor, with large windows, and three nice bedrooms upstairs. The tenant helped a builder to make it, and it cost him between [illegible] and [illegible].

The rent of this holding is 10l. 10s., but has recently been reduced by the Land Court to 8l. 10s.

Rates. 54. If the valuation is under 4l. the landlord pays the rates, but if it is 4l. or upwards the landlord and tenant each pay half. The tenant pays the county cess.

Distance from work. 55. As a general rule the men work for farmers who live near their houses. I met no labourer who lived more than two miles from the farm on which he was working.

VI.—Gardens, Potato Grounds, and Con-acre.

Gardens and potato grounds. 56. There are practically no gardens to the cottages such as are known in an English village, that is a garden surrounding the house and filled with flowers and vegetables. In Ireland the space round the house is usually given up to the animals and the manure heap.

Many labourers, however, have a bit of land, about half an acre or more, which they have given them as part of or in addition to their wages, or which they rent. (See Appendix A 11.)

It is not uncommon to find farmers who plough their men's land for them, or lend them their ploughs, and cart their manure.

In the town of Skibbereen many of the cottages have no gardens, which obliges the tenants to buy their potatoes and vegetables, besides which a pig cannot be kept. The want of a garden also adds to the discomfort of a small dwelling, as the cooking has to be done in the living-room, and the inmates are altogether more cramped for space.

The labourers in the Union cottages, as I have already pointed out, have the great advantage of half an acre of land surrounding each house.

Con-acre. 57. It is not very common to find men taking con-acre in this district. The price is about 2l. an acre. The tenant finds the manure and the landlord ploughs it.

VII.—Benefit Societies and Trade Unions.

Benefit societies and trade unions. 58. There are no benefit societies of any description, neither are there trade unions, or any form of organisation among the labourers.

Strikes. 59. About 10 or 14 years ago there were strikes on some of the small farms for higher wages, which resulted in their being slightly raised in some cases. I heard of no recent instance of strikes. Mrs. [illegible] informed me that at [illegible] they saw some signs of striking for higher wages.

VIII.—Relations between Employers and Employed.

Relations between employers and employed. 60. Masters and men seem to get on well in this district (Appendix B 5). Some of the farmers say the men are not so easy to deal with as they used to be. Perhaps this may be partly attributed to the spread of education among the men and partly to the great scarcity of workers during the summer season, which enables the labourers to demand better terms for themselves. The farmers seldom complain of the men being unwilling to work, though a good many say the young men do not take such an interest in their work as formerly. The evidence is conflicting on the subject of the efficiency of the men's work now as compared with the past, as I have previously pointed out (par. 27 and Appendix B 3).

[illegible] The labourers themselves usually say that they get on quite well with the farmers, and that their only grievance is on the question of wages (Appendix B [illegible]).

IX.—The General Condition of the Agricultural Labourer.

General condition of the agricultural labourer. 41. The general condition of the agricultural labourer has certainly improved in the last 20 years, and this is due to a great extent to the development of the fishing industry. Sir Thomas Brady, who for years has been actively interested in the improvement of the fishing, referring to its beneficial result on the agricultural population, says "The advantages of a "prosperous fishing industry to a locality are mani-"fested in the case of Baltimore, Co. Cork, in the increase "in the value of ordinary labour."

But apart from the effect of the fishing industry on the value of agricultural labour, wages in the districts which are not affected by other employments, have been slowly rising. At Drumsleague I was told that wages had increased during the last 20 years from [illegible] [illegible], and [illegible] with food, to [illegible] with food per week. (Summary, Appendix [illegible].)

There is no doubt that some men who live solely by agricultural labour have a struggle to exist. In the town of Skibbereen there are men who are not attached to the staff of a farm, and work anywhere they can. Irregular employment at [illegible] a week, with [illegible] a week or more to pay for rent, makes a desperate position for a man to be in who has a family to support. It must be remembered that an odd man can earn from [illegible] to [illegible] a week at haytime and harvest, and that the hay harvest lasts a considerable time; still the difficulty of living to the regular man often be very great.

About six miles north of Skibbereen I met two men who were paid at a very low rate of wages, and the condition of our two particulars did not appear to place them in such a good position as a man on [illegible] of [illegible] a week. One is a ploughman and the other an ordinary labourer. Their cash wages [illegible] a week. They both have cottages free, and pay [illegible] a year each for the grass keep of their sheep. The labourer pays [illegible] a year for half an acre of land, and the ploughman gets his free. They have breakfast and dinner provided, and turf free. The labourer has a wife and two daughters to support, the eldest being [illegible] years old. The ploughman has his mother, his wife, and two little children to support. Although these men are given two meals a day, they each want tea or supper on their return home in the evening, and they both have to be fed on Sundays. How, as in the case of the labourer, on [illegible] a week, a woman and two children can be fed entirely, and a man given one meal every night, and all his meals on Sundays, and in addition the family clothed and shod, is a problem which few would care to solve. Of course the family live chiefly on the potatoes grown on their land, but still they have to pay a rent of [illegible] an acre for it, which I understand is the usual sum paid for con-acre. They also keep a pig, from which they doubtless make a profit, especially at the present time, and [illegible] hens, whose eggs they sell in Skibbereen to egg merchants. The wife spins the wool of the sheep to make clothing, and sometimes makes a little money by spinning for neighbours. To a man in such a position a bad potato year, or ill-luck with his sheep or the pig, means something akin to starvation. The ploughman is in much the same position, except that he has not to pay [illegible] for his land, but he has his mother to support, and his two children are older than those of the labourer. He keeps a pig and [illegible] hens. This man, in discussing his position, said that he would prefer [illegible] a week, and to "look out for ourselves." "Here we are," he said, "working for [illegible] a day, and if the bit of land don't "grow we are lost entirely."

It will be noticed by referring to Appendix A [illegible] that the position of these two men is exceptionally bad.

I think there is no doubt that many of the small tenants are considerably better off than formerly, unless, indeed, the present low prices of stock and sheep have entirely swamped the benefits which have of late years accrued to them. For instance, rents have in many cases been reduced by the Land Court, or by private arrangements. Wages have risen, and so the sons of these small tenants have been able to earn more, and as they practically employ no outside labour themselves, their farming operations are not more expensive in consequence. Those near the coast are able to readily sell produce during the fishing season, while they or their sons are able to earn money at some branch of that industry. Although, as I have mentioned, the prices of stock and sheep are very low, the price of pigs is unusually high.

As far as actual hard work is concerned, I was told by small holders that their work is more arduous than that of labourers. This is also the experience of those in Northumberland, Cumberland, and [illegible].

One man about 5 miles from Skibbereen on a holding of [illegible] acres, which he works with his son aged [illegible], stated he worked all hours every day. This year he has [illegible] acres of corn, [illegible] acre of potatoes, [illegible] acre of meadow, and the rest pasture. He has three cows and three calves. The rent is [illegible] and was lately reduced by the Land Court from [illegible]. He has 10 children to support. His father had the same holding. The man considers no one could live on less than [illegible] acres.

With the question of housing I have dealt at length elsewhere, but it is clear that many of the labourers in the country districts have greatly benefited by the Labourers Acts, for there are now [illegible] families in good houses with half an acre of land for [illegible] or [illegible] a week, and [illegible] more families will soon be in a similar position.

The hours of work, which are usually from [illegible] to [illegible] in the summer, are stated to be shorter than formerly. Mr Matthew [illegible] of [illegible] says that he can remember working from [illegible] a.m. to [illegible] p.m. during his father's lifetime.

In consequence of the higher wages and the lowering of prices of articles of consumption and clothing, the people eat better food and dress better than formerly.* The food of the people used chiefly to consist of potatoes, stirabout, and milk, and now they have potatoes, fish, and tea, and also bread and bacon.

In Appendix A [illegible] I have given a list of the class of food supplied at six farmhouses to the labourers. It will be seen that all these farmers supply fish for dinner, and in two cases bacon or beef.

In this district the same complaint is made about the tea drinking as in the others I visited; namely, that men, women, and children take it to excess and that it is having a harmful effect on the stomachs of the people. They take it at all meals, and the tea-pot seems to be always on the hearth brewing tea which looks nearly black when poured out from having stood so long. The Skibbereen Dairy Company are now sending round the towns butter-milk for sale at [illegible] a gallon, which I saw being eagerly bought, so it is to be hoped that the children will benefit thereby.

There appears to be very little drunkenness amongst the rural population. I was told several times that the young men engaged in fishing are rather apt to get into drinking habits as they have a good deal of spare time on their hands, and during the fishing season some ready money.

No doubt education is improving, though many labourers and small farmers can neither read nor write. Referring to this subject, the Rev. John Murphy, P.P., of Drumsleague, says:—"The young people in America "and Australia are constantly writing home advising "the parents to keep the children at school as much as "possible as they see how difficult it is to get employ-"ment abroad without education."

The morality of the people in this district, as in the others I visited, is unimpeachable.

No doubt considerable sums of money are sent home annually from relations or friends in America, a fact which must be remembered when considering the pecuniary position of the people.

I have, &c.
(Signed) Arthur Wilson Fox,
Assistant Commissioner.

Note.—Increase in the number of live stock and poultry in the county of Cork between [illegible] and [illegible]:—

	[illegible]	[illegible]	Increase.
Horses	[illegible]	[illegible]	[illegible]
Mules and asses	[illegible]	[illegible]	[illegible]
Cattle	[illegible]	[illegible]	[illegible]
Sheep	[illegible]	[illegible]	[illegible]
Poultry	[illegible]	[illegible]	[illegible]

* Many women possess very good black cloaks which reach to the feet, and have hoods which they can pull over their heads if wet. They are made of the best English cloth, and are usually black or dark blue, and sometimes lined with silk. They cost between [illegible] and [illegible], and last many years.

APPENDIX A.

TABLE OF CONTENTS

A 1.

Area, Population, Number of Inhabited Houses and Rateable Value of the Union.

Electoral Divisions	Area in Statute Acres (A.)	(R.)	(P.)	Population 1891.	Inhabited Houses.	Rateable Value. (£)	Rates in the £ (s.)	(d.)
Aughadown North	[illegible]	[illegible]	[illegible]	[illegible]	[illegible]	[illegible]	[illegible]	[illegible]
*Aughadown South	[illegible]	[illegible]	[illegible]	[illegible]	[illegible]	[illegible]	[illegible]	[illegible]
*[illegible]	[illegible]	[illegible]	[illegible]	[illegible]	[illegible]	[illegible]	[illegible]	[illegible]
Caheragh	[illegible]	[illegible]	[illegible]	[illegible]	[illegible]	[illegible]	[illegible]	[illegible]
*Cape Clear	[illegible]	[illegible]	[illegible]	[illegible]	[illegible]	[illegible]	[illegible]	[illegible]
[illegible]	[illegible]	[illegible]	[illegible]	[illegible]	[illegible]	[illegible]	[illegible]	[illegible]
Castle Haven North	[illegible]	[illegible]	[illegible]	[illegible]	[illegible]	[illegible]	[illegible]	[illegible]
*Castle Haven South	[illegible]	[illegible]	[illegible]	[illegible]	[illegible]	[illegible]	[illegible]	[illegible]
[illegible]	[illegible]	[illegible]	19	[illegible]	[illegible]	[illegible]	[illegible]	[illegible]
[illegible]	[illegible]	[illegible]	[illegible]	[illegible]	[illegible]	[illegible]	[illegible]	[illegible]
[illegible]	[illegible]	[illegible]	[illegible]	[illegible]	[illegible]	[illegible]	[illegible]	[illegible]
*[illegible] North	[illegible]	[illegible]	[illegible]	[illegible]	[illegible]	[illegible]	[illegible]	[illegible]
[illegible] South	[illegible]	[illegible]	[illegible]	[illegible]	[illegible]	[illegible]	[illegible]	[illegible]
[illegible]	[illegible]	[illegible]	[illegible]	[illegible]	[illegible]	[illegible]	[illegible]	[illegible]
[illegible]	[illegible]	[illegible]	[illegible]	[illegible]	[illegible]	[illegible]	[illegible]	[illegible]
[illegible]	[illegible]	[illegible]	[illegible]	[illegible]	[illegible]	[illegible]	[illegible]	[illegible]
[illegible]	[illegible]	[illegible]	[illegible]	[illegible]	[illegible]	[illegible]	[illegible]	[illegible]
[illegible]	[illegible]	[illegible]	[illegible]	[illegible]	[illegible]	[illegible]	[illegible]	[illegible]
[illegible]	[illegible]	[illegible]	[illegible]	[illegible]	[illegible]	[illegible]	[illegible]	[illegible]
[illegible]	[illegible]	[illegible]	[illegible]	[illegible]	[illegible]	[illegible]	[illegible]	[illegible]
[illegible]	[illegible]	[illegible]	[illegible]	[illegible]	[illegible]	[illegible]	[illegible]	[illegible]
*[illegible]	[illegible]	[illegible]	11	[illegible]	[illegible]	[illegible]	[illegible]	[illegible]
[illegible]	[illegible]	[illegible]	[illegible]	[illegible]	[illegible]	[illegible]	1	[illegible]
Total	[illegible]	[illegible]	[illegible]	[illegible]	[illegible]	[illegible]	—	

The electoral divisions marked thus * are congested districts.

A 2.

Wages paid by certain Employers, Summer and Winter, to Ordinary Labourers on the Regular Staff of Farm

	Cash.	Food.	House and Land.	Milk.	Keep for Animals.	Turf.
1	[illegible] a week, wet or dry.	Supplied.				
2	[illegible] and food, or [illegible], no food.					
3	[illegible] a week, wet or dry.	Supplied	Cottage, and ½ acre of land manured.			
4	[illegible] a week, wet or dry.	—	Cottage and land up to 1½ acre if they like.	Milk of a cow	Grass of two sheep.	Supplied.
5	[illegible] a week, wet or dry.	Supplied	Cottage	—	—	Supplied.
6	[illegible], and food, or [illegible], no food.	—	Cottage, and ½ acre of land at [illegible] a week.			
7	do., wet or dry.					
8	do., wet or dry	—	House, and ½ acre of [illegible]			
9	do., wet or dry	Supplied	House, ½ to 1 acre of land			
10	do., wet or dry	Supplied	Employer ploughs land and carts manure	As much as they want.		
11	[illegible], wet or dry	—	House, a [illegible] of garden. As much land as they want for potatoes, unmanured. Employer ploughs land and gives [illegible] manure.			
12	do., wet or dry	—	House, as much land as they like if they manure it.			
13	do., wet or dry	—	½ acre potato ground	A pint a day.		

A 4.

Food supplied to Labourers on certain Farms.

Size of Farm.	Breakfast.	Dinner.	Supper.
[illegible] acres	[illegible] bread, milk, and [illegible]	Potatoes, [illegible], fish, and [illegible]	Milk and tea.
[illegible] acres	Bread, tea, and butter	Fish, beef or bacon, potatoes	—
[illegible] acres	Bread and [illegible]	Potatoes and fish	Bread, milk, and tea.
[illegible] acres	Bread, butter, tea	Potatoes, milk, [illegible]	Bread, butter, tea.
[illegible] acres	Bread and milk	Potatoes, fish, and milk, [illegible]	Tea, bread, and [illegible]
[illegible] acres	Bread, tea, [illegible]	[illegible]	

Note.—The day labourers who live in their own houses and who receive food at the farmhouse as part of their wages are given breakfast and dinner. The hired men who live in the farmhouses get supper as well.

Note.—A young labourer who lives with his parents and goes home to his meals gave me the following account of his diet:

Breakfast.—Milk and bread.
Dinner.—Potatoes and fish.
Supper.—Bread, milk, tea.

A [illegible].

Contract Prices for certain Articles in the Skibbereen Workhouse, April 1893.

	£	s.	d.	
Bread (white)	0	0	3	per 4 lbs.
Indian meal	5	15	0	per ton.
Oatmeal	11	10	0	per ton.
Beef	0	0	1	per lb.
Tea	0	1	10	per lb.
White (moist) sugar	0	19	0	per cwt.
New milk	0	0	4	per gallon.
Sweet skim milk	0	0	2	per gallon.

A 5.

Persons engaged in Agriculture in Skibbereen Union in 1891. (Extracted from the Census Returns.)

	Male.	Female.
Farmer, grazier	2,261	304
Farmer's, grazier's son, grandson, brother, nephew	1,267	—
Farm bailiff	8	—
Agricultural labourer, cottager	744	—
Farm servant (indoor)	974	80
Others engaged in or connected with agriculture	9	1
General labourer*	443	16

* Probably some of those returned under this heading are agricultural labourers.

A 6.

Extent of Land under Crops in Statute Acres, and Estimated Produce in 1891.

This and Tables A 7, A 8, and A 9 are extracted from the Agricultural Returns for 1891.

Crops.	Extent.	Estimated Produce.
Wheat	1,185 acres	17,070 cwts. of 112 lbs.
Oats	4,239 "	66,711 "
Barley	61 "	924 "
Bere	1 "	73 "
Rye	116 "	1,430 "
Potatoes	1,893 "	22,897 tons.
Turnips	1,789 "	32,479 "
Mangold Wurzel and beetroot	603 "	12,824 "
Carrots and parsnips	4 "	30 "
Cabbage	150 "	1,980 "
Vetches	117 "	447 "
Rape	35 "	140 "
Other green crops	150 "	
Clover, sainfoin, and grasses under rotation	3,385 "	6,776 "
Permanent pasture	1,880 "	2,451 "
Total extent under crops	23,116 "	—

A 7.

Poor Law Union.	Number of Holdings and their Size in Statute Acres.									Total Number of Holdings.
Not exceeding—	1 acre.	5 acres.	15 acres.	30 acres.	50 acres.	100 acres.	200 acres.	500 acres.	Above 500 acres.	
Skibbereen	163	136	536	531	746	604	114	20	—	3,160

A 8.

Live Stock in Skibbereen Union in 1891.

Horses	2,463
Mules	83
Asses	813
Cattle	20,250
Sheep	17,889
Pigs	10,211
Goats	1,203
Poultry (ordinary fowls)	46,103
Ducks	17,094
Turkeys	5,273
Geese	14,810

A 9.

Cultivation of Skibbereen Union, 1891, and proportion per cent. under Crops, Grass, Fallow, Turf, Marsh, &c.

[illegible]	[illegible]	[illegible]	[illegible]	[illegible]	[illegible]	[illegible]	[illegible]	[illegible]
Acres.	Acres.	Acres.	Acres.	Acres.	Acres.	Acres.	Acres.	Acres.
23,116	40,713	80	1,577	2,063	3,035	16,420	4,257	113,970
Proportion per cent. under—								
19.8	35.7	·1	1.4	1.8	2.7	14.5	3.6	

A 11.

PARTICULARS of certain COTTAGES in the [illegible] UNION.

Cottages in [illegible].

Number in family.	Living-room.	Bedroom.	Rent.	Remarks.
Man, wife, and one son and daughter. Eldest son, [illegible]. Second son, 16. Eldest girl, 14.	Ground floor, 14 x 13. Sleeping [illegible] [illegible].	Ground floor, 14 x 10 x 7.	[illegible] a year, paid monthly	This man does carting work at [illegible] a day with his horse and cart. Employed on an average five days a week. He keeps the horse in the living-room. Eldest son [illegible]. Second son [illegible] a week as [illegible] boy. The house is stone. The [illegible] of roof bad. The floor earth. There are no [illegible] garden. No closet. Water good.
Man, wife, and five children. Eldest 12.	Ground floor, 18 x 13. High sleeping [illegible].	Ground floor, 13 x 10, also a loft above.	1s. a week	The man is a labourer. House [illegible] and roof thatch. Floor clay. There is no garden. At the back of the house and the [illegible] door a [illegible] drain [illegible] enough to [illegible] any amount of fever. No closet.
Man, wife, and four children. Eldest boy, 15. Eldest girl, [illegible].	Ground floor, 18 x 13. Half the room covered by a loft. The height [illegible] loft is 7 feet. [illegible] of [illegible] [illegible].	Ground floor, 15 x 10 x 7. A bed also in the loft.	1s. a week	There are [illegible] yards of potatoes at the back. Outside back door [illegible] are kept in a [illegible] which is full of [illegible] and filth. The [illegible] in and out of the house. No closet.
Man, wife, and five children. Eldest girl, [illegible] years. Eldest boy, 10 years.	Ground floor, 18 x 16.	Ground floor, 10 x 12.	1s. a week	Man is a labourer in very irregular employment in winter. At [illegible] with father and son [illegible] [illegible] [illegible]. The house is stone. Roof thatched. Floor clay. No closet.
Man and wife	Ground floor, 11 x 16. Sleeping [illegible].	Ground floor, 10 x 9 x 7.	Free	Man is an agricultural labourer, [illegible] a week and food. Regular employment. The house is very old. It is built of stone, the roof is thatch. There is no garden or closet. House and floor is [illegible].
Man, wife, one young children.	Ground floor, 15 x 10. Sleeping loft.	Ground floor, 10 x 9. Sleeping loft. Window 1½ ft. x 1 ft.		Man is an agricultural labourer in irregular employment. House is stone, roof thatched.
A widow	Ground floor, 12 by 8. Sleeping loft. Window 1½ ft. x 1 ft.	Ground floor, 12 x 6. Window, 1 ft. x 1 ft. No glass and stuffed with rags.	1s. a week	The house is made of stone and the roof [illegible]. This is one of a [illegible] built on a steep hill. Outside the house runs a filthy open drain. The occupant's bed is on the floor and consists of rags and straw. The only articles of furniture in the house are a [illegible] table, two old [illegible], a broken travelling chest, a [illegible], a tin pot, a milk jug, a [illegible] pot, and a picture of his Holiness the Pope.

P 2

B.—III. [illegible]

Number in Family.	Livingroom.	Bedroom.	Rent.	Remarks.
A labourer	Ground floor 15 × [illegible] sloping roof	Ground floor 9 × 6 (bed room).	1s. a week	House is damp, a stone roof. [illegible] the clay floor [illegible] a bed of rags and [illegible]. The floor in bedroom is saturated with sewage which has percolated through the wall from drain outside. This house [illegible] the land-[illegible] [illegible]
Man, wife, two boys aged 1[illegible] and 1[illegible]	Ground floor 15 × [illegible], sloping roof.	Ground floor 15 × 9	1s. a week	This man is a labourer in regular employment at [illegible] a week. The boy of 1[illegible] earns [illegible] a week, and is given two meals. The house is [illegible]. The roof clean. The floors are clay. They have four rows of potatoes. Man, wife, and boy sleep in the only bed. By the side of bed, on rags laid on floor, sleeps the other boy.
Man and wife	Ground floor 17 × 16 × 8.	Loft over living-room approached by a ladder.	1s. 6d. a week	Man in regular employment as labourer at [illegible] a week. House is clean, almost, and clean. Damp comes in through roof. Four rows of potatoes.
Man, wife, and four children. Eldest girl [illegible]. Eldest boy 1[illegible].	Ground floor 15 × [illegible]	Ground floor 16 × 9 × 7½	1s. 6d. a week	Man is an agricultural labourer in [illegible] employment. House is [illegible] and [illegible]. Four rows of potatoes on bad land.

Cottages on Captain Morgan's Property.

Number in Family.	Livingroom.	Bedroom.	Rent.	Remarks.
Man, wife, grandmother, [illegible] children. Eldest boy 1[illegible]. Eldest girl 1[illegible].	Ground floor 27 × 11 × 7½, clay floor	Ground floor (1) [illegible] × 9 × 7½. (2) Big loft where children sleep, approached by a ladder.	Free	This man is a ploughman in regular employment, he keeps a [illegible] and a donkey. He also keeps [illegible] and geese. Has a portion of potato land with house. In front of house [illegible] heap and a lot of drainage water. Plenty of space to put heap elsewhere. A well close to house. No closet.
Man, wife, three children. Boy aged [illegible]. Girls [illegible] and 1[illegible].	Ground floor 16 × 16 × 15	Ground floor 16 × 16 × 12.	Free	This man is herdsman in regular employment. [illegible] to [illegible] Carmarthen, [illegible] full [illegible]. Daughter comes [illegible] a week [illegible] at [illegible], but stays with parents from Saturday to Monday.

[illegible]

Cottages on Mr. T. [illegible]'s Farm, [illegible].

Number in Family.	Living-room.	Bedroom.	Rent.	Remarks.
Man, wife, [illegible], and two little children.	Ground floor 16 × 15, sleeping roof.	Ground floor 15 × 15	Free - -	Man in regular work for Mr. [illegible] as ploughman. Has a pig, two sheep, and [illegible]. Wages [illegible], house free, [illegible], [illegible], free [illegible], [illegible] and [illegible] a day.
Man, wife, two girls about 1[illegible].	Ground floor 19 × 12, sleeping roof.	Ground floor 12 × 9 × 7	Free, pays 1l. for [illegible] acre land.	Man in regular employment. Wages [illegible]. Has a pig, [illegible], two sheep. The [illegible] [illegible].

Cottages at Castle Townsend.

Number in Family.	Living-room.	Bedroom.	Rent.	Remarks.
Man, wife, and four young children	Ground floor 13 × 12 × 7½	Upstairs 14 × 12. Very bad repair, rain [illegible] in through roof.	1s. a week - -	The house is made of stone and plaster. The roof slate. The house is very old, and in very bad repair.
Man, wife, and two young children. Also a daughter of 20.	Ground floor 16 × 12 × 8.	Upstairs 15 × 10. Sleeping roof and bad repair.	1s. a week -	This man is in regular employ as a labourer. House is stone [illegible] roof, slate. Bedroom in bad repair. [illegible], pigs and water. Man is given ¼ acre of land by his employer.

Cottages in [illegible] Island.

Number in Family.	Living-room.	Bedroom.	Rent.	Remarks.
Man, wife, three children. Eldest son 20. Eldest girl 16.	Ground floor 11 × 10 × 7½.	Upstairs 1[illegible] × 10, sleeping roof.	10l. for 10 acres good land, and also grazing on hill	To get to living-room you must go through a very dirty cattle shed. Opposite entrance is a big pool of drainage water, caused by keeping [illegible] there.
Man, wife, nine children, an old woman. Eldest son 22. Eldest girl 16	Ground floor 15 × 14 × 7	Ground floor (1) 10 × 6 × 7½, (2) 11 × 10 × 6½	7l. for about 15 acres, three or four of which is tilled.	House stone, roof thatch; pig and hens kept in house.
Man, wife, and six children, eldest 9.	Ground floor 13 × 11 × 7½	Ground floor 10 × 7 × 7. Also a loft where [illegible] [illegible]. Woman says children will have to sleep there when older.	4l. for 5 or 6 acres good land	Husband [illegible]. Has been away two weeks. Wife looks after land. Has two cows and a heifer.
A widow, son of 18, and two young children	Ground floor 13 × 15 × 8½	Ground floor 10 × 9 × 6.	1l. [illegible], 5 or 6 acres of tillage, and about 15 acres of mountain land	Rent [illegible] years in arrears. Woman has three cows, two pigs, six [illegible]. [illegible]. Has another son in California and another in West Indies. A big pool of [illegible] water in front of door. Woman believes she is the [illegible] generation of her family who have had this house.

Cottages on Cape Clear Island.

Number of Family.	Living room.	Bedroom.	Rent.	Remarks.
Man, wife, [illegible] children. Also the man's father, mother, and [illegible] brother	Ground floor [illegible]	Ground floor [illegible] feet high. Also a dark loft.	[illegible] acre.	[illegible]
Man ([illegible] years), wife, [illegible] about [illegible].	Ground floor [illegible]	Ground floor [illegible] No [illegible]	[illegible] Holding, [illegible] acres.	[illegible] years old.

APPENDIX B.

TABLE OF CONTENTS.

Efficiency of Work as compared with the Past.

Evidence of Employers.

Employer.	District.	Evidence.
[illegible]	[illegible]	[illegible]
[illegible]	[illegible]	[illegible]
[illegible]	[illegible]	[illegible]
[illegible]	[illegible]	[illegible]
[illegible]	[illegible]	[illegible]
[illegible]	[illegible]	[illegible]
[illegible]	[illegible]	[illegible]
[illegible]	[illegible]	[illegible]

Employer.	District.	Evidence.
[illegible]	[illegible]	[illegible]
[illegible]	[illegible]	[illegible]
[illegible]	[illegible]	[illegible]
[illegible]	[illegible]	[illegible]
[illegible]	[illegible]	[illegible]
[illegible]	[illegible]	[illegible]
[illegible]	[illegible]	[illegible]
[illegible]	[illegible]	[illegible]

Evidence of Employed

Name.	District.	Evidence.
[illegible]	[illegible]	[illegible]

B 2

Regularity of Work as compared with other Districts

Name.	District.	Evidence.
[illegible]	[illegible]	[illegible]

B 3

Relations between Employers and Employed.

Evidence of Employers

Name.	District.	Evidence.
[illegible]	[illegible]	[illegible]

Evidence of Employed.

Name.	District.	Evidence.
[illegible]	[illegible]	[illegible]

GENERAL CONDITION OF THE LABOURERS.

Evidence of Clergy and Employers.

Name.	District.	Evidence.
[illegible]	[illegible]	[illegible]

Evidence of Employers.

Name.	District.	Evidence.
[illegible]	[illegible]	[illegible]

B.—IV.

ROYAL COMMISSION ON LABOUR.

THE AGRICULTURAL LABOURER.

IRELAND.

REPORT

BY

MR. ARTHUR WILSON FOX

UPON THE

POOR LAW UNION OF DELVIN (WESTMEATH).

TABLE OF CONTENTS.

THE AGRICULTURAL LABOURER.

To Geoffrey Drage, Esq., Secretary,
Royal Commission on Labour.

6, Crown Office Row, Temple, E.C.,
July 1st, 1893.

I.—Introductory.

Sir,

1. I have the honour to present to you my report on the condition of the agricultural labourers in the Delvin Union of Westmeath, where I was making inquiries in May last.

2. The union is about 50 miles from Dublin. It is bounded on the north by the Oldcastle and Kells Unions, on the south by the Mullingar Union, on the west by the Granard Union, and on the east by the Trim Union.

3. I obtained the information contained in this report by driving to all parts of the union and interviewing landowners, land-agents, stewards, farmers, and labourers. I also inspected cottages in various districts, and was able to gain from the inmates a considerable knowledge of the conditions under which they lived.

Among those to whom I am especially indebted for assistance I would mention Mr. Fetherstonhaugh, Mr. G. D. Cochrane, agent to the Earl of Longford, Colonel Clarke, agent to the Earl of Longford (Kilbrena estate), the Rev. P. Tuite, P.P., Delvin, Dr. Carleton, Delvin, Mr. L. Ramage, J.P., Crookedwood, Mr. Talbot, Collinstown, Mr. Michael Mulligan, Delvin, Mr. Jack, steward to the Earl of Longford, and Mr. Patterson, steward to Major Pollard Urquhart.

4. The area of the union is 73,080 acres, and it is divided into 19 electoral divisions. It is chiefly grass, and contains miles of rich looking pastures, which form a strange contrast to the barren and poverty stricken district I visited in Mayo. The country in outward appearance, looks prosperous, and being well wooded, is picturesque.

The soil is a fairly good loam, with a gravel subsoil, but it varies a good deal in quality. I was informed that in past days the cottiers tilled some parts deep with spades and that the land in those places shows the good result of this still.

5. The cattle in this district are mostly shorthorns, Kerry cattle, and a few Herefords. Of late years the Aberdeen Angus breed, and their crosses, have been extensively introduced.

The sheep are chiefly Roscommons, which are a cross between Roscommons and Leicesters, but there are also many of the Shropshire breed.

6. There are 1,[illegible] holdings in the union. Of these [illegible] do not exceed 1 acre, [illegible] do not exceed 5 acres, [illegible] do not exceed 15 acres, [illegible] do not exceed 50 acres, and [illegible] do not exceed 50 acres.*

7. The principal landowners are the Earl of Longford, Lord Greville, Major Pollard Urquhart, Mr. M. Chapman, and Mr. Fetherstonhaugh.

9. The population of the union is 9,[illegible] persons, of whom 4,[illegible] are males, and 4,[illegible] are females. Between 1871 and 1881 the population decreased by 1,[illegible] or [illegible] per cent., and between 1881 and 1891 it decreased by 1,377, or 12.[illegible] per cent., notwithstanding an increase of [illegible] registered births over deaths during the latter period.

8. The poor rates vary from 1s. to 2s. [illegible]d. in the pound. The county cess is [illegible]d. in the pound. The valuation of the union in 1891 was 53,[illegible]l.

* Number of holdings on the Earl of Longford's Pakenham Hall Estate:—

Under 25 acres (tillage)	[illegible]
" [illegible] "	[illegible]
" [illegible] "	[illegible]
Over [illegible] "	[illegible]

Note.—[illegible] to labourers.

Number of holdings on the Earl of Longford's Kilbrena Estate:—

Under 15 acres (tillage)	[illegible]
" [illegible] "	[illegible]
" [illegible] "	[illegible]
Over [illegible] "	17

Note.—[illegible] Irish acres equal [illegible] English acres.

10. In 1892 the number of persons who emigrated from Westmeath was [illegible]. Of these 204 were males and [illegible] were females. The number of persons who emigrated in 1891 was 752, in 1890 [illegible], in 1889 [illegible], and in 1888 1,1[illegible]. Thus the emigration has been steadily decreasing during the last five years in this county.

11. There is no migration to English or Scotch farms, which is a practical proof that, apart from the question of emigration, which is decreasing in Westmeath, the district can support its resident population.

12. Agriculture is practically the only industry in the union.

A large trade is carried on in eggs and fowls from which the small holders and labourers, who have space to keep poultry, derive considerable profit. Those living on the turf districts are able to make money by selling turf. On the Earl of Longford's Kilbrena estate there are 1,[illegible] acres of turf, and on the borders of it many small holders live. These men are allowed to cut it at [illegible]d. to 1s. [illegible]d. a perch and they sell it in Mullingar at a considerable profit. The black coal turf realises [illegible]s. a perch.

13. A market is held in Castle Pollard every Wednesday, and fairs in January, March, April, May, August, October, November and December. A fair is also held in Collinstown in May and October.

Mullingar, which is outside the Union, has a market every Thursday, to which a great many people in the Delvin Union go, and fairs are held there in January, April, May, July, August, November and December. Also fairs are held at Edgeworthstown in February, April, May, July, September and November.

14. In this union the men usually employed on the farms are ordinary labourers regularly attached to the staff, herd men, herds or cattlemen, and occasionally ploughmen. Girlsmen are of course employed if necessary.

On many of the smaller farms no distinction is made in the duties of the men, and the care of horses and animals falls to the lot of some or all of the ordinary staff in addition to their usual work. Where hired men are kept, the charge of animals is frequently their duty. On some of the large farms herds or cattlemen are employed, who look after the stock and sheep, and, if there is a ploughman, it is often his business to attend to the horses.

On estates, where there is usually a larger proportion of tillage land, and also more stock and sheep kept, than on farms, definite duties are assigned to the labourers. One or two ploughmen are frequently employed, and the ordinary labourers have nothing to do with animals, as shepherds, herds, cattlemen and carters are kept for that purpose.

15. Women are very seldom employed in agriculture. Formerly they were extensively, but now they look down on that class of employment, and the young women either emigrate or go to shops or service in Dublin.

They are also difficult to get for domestic servants in the country. Mr. Talbot, of Crookedwood, tells me that if his servant were to go he does not know where he could get another.

Some of the farmers complain that this scarcity of women workers is a great drawback to them. Mr. Ramage, of Crookedwood, says: "Very few women will "work now. They were the chief number of the farmer "in harvest, but now they go off to America."

Mr. Jack, steward to the Earl of Longford, says: "Women are very seldom employed in the fields, as "they won't work there. At 18 years of age they quit "above working on the land and they try and do better "for themselves. They are even difficult to get for "domestic servants, as they emigrate."

B.—IV. [illegible]

In one instance only I found girls who preferred a country life to a town one. Two of Lord Longford's dairy maids told me that they would much rather remain where they were, than go into a town. However, being a dairymaid at Pakenham Hall and living in a comfortable cottage with their parents, is a different thing to working out in the fields, at ordinary farm work.

Some women are still employed at certain work, though they get scarcer every year.

At Pakenham a few girls of 12 and 13 years of age are employed weeding at from 2s. 6d. to 4s. a week.

In the neighbourhood of Castle Pollard women are employed at 1s. a day in hand after the reaping machine, to dig and pick potatoes and at weed, and a few work at harvest at Crookedwood and elsewhere for 1s. 6d. or 1s. 8d. a day.

In the bog districts some women are employed at 2s. a day putting turf into barrows after men have cut it.

Girls are sometimes employed hoeing turnips and dropping potatoes for about 10d. a day.

II.—THE SUPPLY OF LABOUR.

Supply of labour.

16. In many parts there is a scarcity of labour in the summer, while in the winter it seems to be so plentiful that odd men are then frequently out of work.

As few labourers go to work on English farms from this union, the greater scarcity of labour at the summer times is not due to that cause, as it is in some counties, but is chiefly in consequence of the great demand for men at hay-time in this grass country, and also to the fact that the small tenants, who at certain seasons are willing to work as labourers, are busy with cutting and saving their own hay.

With reference to this subject, Mr. Cochrane, agent to the Earl of Longford, writes: "There are two disadvantages employers of agricultural labour have to meet.

"(1.) In the hay season the militia are called up, which often causes great inconvenience to employers. It is also a disadvantage to the men themselves, as employers avoid engaging as permanent men those who are in the militia. They are thus out of employment in the winter. If the militia could be trained in the winter there would be the double advantage of no interference with farm work, and the men would have employment in the idle season.

"(2.) Roman Catholic holidays, or Holy days, are also a great inconvenience, as some of them occur in the very busiest season. Generally in the North of Ireland these holidays are not kept by farm labourers, but in the rest of the country they are strictly observed. Practically these holidays appear only to exist for the agricultural classes. Shopkeepers and trade labourers do not keep them."

All employers agree that, in recent years, a great deal of tillage land has been turned into grass, and no doubt this must have displaced labour.

With reference to the question as to whether the use of machinery diminishes the necessity of employing so many men, Mr. Jack, steward to the Earl of Longford, is of opinion that it has not had that effect. "On the Pakenham Hall home farm there are about 116 acres (Irish) of tillage, which has not been decreased of recent years. Considerable purchases of modern machinery have been made from time to time, but no reduction in the staff of men have taken place in consequence."

I have shown in paragraph 10 that the emigration from this union has been steadily decreasing during the last five years, but how far this affects the supply of agricultural labour in this particular union it is impossible to say.

In the "Emigration Statistics of Ireland, 1892," the Registrar-General states that of the 25,571 males who emigrated from Ireland in 1892 19,[illegible], or 76·6 per cent. were returned as "labourers." Of these 8,[illegible] came from Leinster, 7,[illegible] from Munster, 4,[illegible] from Ulster, and 3,916 from Connaught.

Efficiency of labourers' work compared with the past.

17. As to the question of the efficiency of the men's work as compared with the past, the evidence in this Union confirms that which I obtained in Mayo, Cork, and Roscommon, namely, that the men are not so skilled as they were twenty or thirty years ago, neither do they accomplish so much in the day. (Appendix B. 1.)

* English farmers in the Midlands and [illegible] [illegible] [illegible] [illegible] of this opinion.

It is quite clear that some years ago the men worked longer hours, and had to perform more arduous work, as they had not the assistance of machinery, and the implements they then used were much heavier. But, apart from these considerations, it is stated that the work of the present day compares unfavourably with that of the past.

The Absence Work lessening.

Several reasons for this state of things are advanced. In the first place many say that emigration is draining the country of the best men. It is also said that education has made the men dislike the monotony and drudgery of agricultural life, and in consequence they take but little interest in their work. The Rev. F. Tuite, P.P., of Delvin, thinks that the men do not purposely exert themselves so much as formerly. He says, "The men are more enlightened, and won't kill themselves with work now," though he adds, "they are not unreasonable at a pinch, and will always do extra work at harvest."

Mr. Jack, steward to the Earl of Longford, advocates the principle of paying the men according to merit, as he considers it calculated to make the good men work better.

Some people say that since tillage land was given up the labourers have less opportunity of learning ploughing, and other work, and that this accounts to a great extent for their lack of skill.

But there is another reason, which possibly may be as good a one as any I have mentioned. I refer to the people's diet having changed from stirabout and milk to white bread and tea, which is admitted by both employers and employed to be producing a harmful effect on the health and strength of the labouring classes. Referring to this subject, Dr. Carleton, medical officer of health to the union, says: "The people's strength has deteriorated because they will take bad tea, bad tobacco, and bad whiskey. They did thrive on stirabout and butter milk, but now they won't touch it. They don't work so well as 20 years ago, when wages were less, and I think this is due to their present diet, and to the fact that they drink more."

There are plenty of people who corroborate Dr. Carleton's view. (Appendix B. 4.) Among others, M. Lynch, a labourer, says: "The children are spoilt in their youth from not having milk. The people are killing themselves with tea. The men don't work so well in consequence. Stirabout and milk used to be a great thing for them."

Efficiency of [illegible] [illegible]

18. Such evidence as I was able to obtain as to how the work of the Westmeath men compared with that of men in other districts was not to their advantage. (Appendix B. 8.) A steward, who has travelled considerably in England and Ireland, told me that in his opinion the Westmeath and Meath men are the worst class of labourers he had ever met. Comparing the men in these two counties, a large farmer told me that the Meath men were the better workers of the two.

Lord Longford's steward expressed himself very satisfied with the men who work on that estate, but as many of them have been born on the property, and their fathers before them, a friendly feeling exists between the owner and his labourers, which has to be considered when discussing the willingness of the men to do their best. The steward informed me that, in his opinion, the West Meath men are better than the Limerick men, because the latter country, being a dairy farming one, gives but little opportunity for the men to become experienced in tillage farming.

An agent to a large property expressed the opinion that the Mayo men are better than the West Meath men.

III.—CONDITIONS OF ENGAGEMENT.

Duration of employment.

19. Employment is regular and continuous on all the larger farms, as far as the ordinary staff are concerned. In the winter, however, odd men, for whom there is plenty of occupation in the summer, are frequently out of work.

In this union there are several properties where large staffs of regular men are given constant employment.

On the Earl of Longford's Pakenham Hall estate, 1[illegible] regular farm hands are kept, [illegible] of whom receive men's wages, and on the Killucan estate there are 40 regular men, [illegible] of whom are employed to keep watercourses open, and generally improve the land for the benefit of the tenants. During the summer six of these men are taken off this work, but they are then paid 2s. 6d. a day at turf cutting. The number of men employed on this estate is sometimes as many as 70 or 80, but these are not all regular hands.

Sir M. Chapman and Major Pollard Urquhart each employ 20 regular men summer and winter, and there are several farmers whose regular staff consists of 8 or 10 labourers.

I have already alluded to the fact of oddmen often finding work hard to get in the winter, but it is very difficult to obtain any definite information as to the proportion of men unemployed, and the extent of their non-employment.

In and around the town of Delvin, where there are about 80 resident agricultural labourers, the Rev. F. Tuite, P.P., says that in the winter "there is a [illegible] want of employment," and the Relieving Officer is of opinion that the oddmen there are out of work for three months in the year, chiefly in the winter, through scarcity of work or bad weather.

At Ballymore, the police sergeant informed me that there were about 14 resident agricultural labourers, of whom three or four were out of work in the winter months.

A great many men would be out of employment in the winter in Castle Pollard, Coole, and Rathowen, if it were not for the kindness and generosity of Lord Longford, who extensively employs men in want of work on both his Pakenham Hall and Killucan estates. Major Pollard Urquhart at Kinturk pursues a similar course as regards Castle Pollard men.

Referring to this subject, Mr. Jack, steward to the Earl of Longford, says: "In the winter we employ "every man out of work, almost to an unlimited extent. "When the winter time comes on, Lord Longford asks "if there are any men out of employment, and if he "finds there are, he says 'take them on.'"*

20. It is difficult to say definitely what is the actual period of engagement of an ordinary labourer, who is attached to the regular staff of a farm. A steward on a large property described it as "a daily engagement paid by the week." But generally speaking the engagement is steadily speaking a daily one, though in some cases they are definitely engaged by the week. But it does not matter very much how the terms of engagement are expressed as regards the regular men, for they are almost invariably employed, wet and dry, and remain in their places in many cases a long time.

21. Oddmen are always engaged by the day.

22. The engagement of ploughmen, cattlemen, and carters, is usually a weekly one. These men are employed wet and dry, and usually remain in their places a considerable time.

23. Shepherds and herds are frequently engaged by the year, sometimes they have a half-yearly one and sometimes a quarterly one. Mr. Fetherstonhaugh's five herds have a six months' notice and they have remained in his service for 40 years. The Earl of Longford's shepherds have a three months' notice.

24. Hired men are engaged by the year, but the length of notice given to them varies according to agreement. Some leave on a month's notice, and others on a longer one. Mr. Tuite informs me that as a rule the employer and man agree to part at once if there is a difference.

25. The hours of work in summer for ordinary labourers are from 7 a.m. to 6 p.m. Employers say they frequently do not begin work until 7.30 or even 8 o'clock. They usually breakfast before they come, and have an hour off for dinner. Assuming they commence punctually, their actual working day is 10 hours.

26. The winter hours are always difficult to ascertain, as they depend on the duration of the daylight. In the county of Cork many employers fix a definite date where summer and winter hours begin, but I found but few cases where this was done in West Meath.

Sir M. Chapman's steward informed me that they considered winter began on October 1st and ended on April 1st.

On Lord Longford's property at Pakenham Hall the steward gave me the winter hours as from 7.30 a.m. to 4.15 p.m. with an hour off for meals, and on the property at Killucan the agent there informed me they were from 8 a.m. to 5 p.m. with an hour off.

The steward on Major Pollard Urquhart's property stated the winter hours there were from 8 a.m. to 5 p.m. with an hour off for meals.

A great many farmers told me their winter hours are from light to dark. No doubt those who attend to milking and looking after cattle have to stay later than those whose work is out of doors and which of necessity ceases with the daylight.

27. As I have already stated, carters and cattlemen are only employed on large estates. On farms, either the herds or shepherds, and on small farms the hired men, attend to the animals. Carters' hours are usually the same as those of ordinary labourers, but those of cattlemen are rather longer, as they have to begin earlier in the morning and sometimes leave off later in the evening. However, when cattle are ill they have to attend to them, no matter what the hour may be.

Lord Longford's cattlemen work from 6 a.m. to 6 p.m. in the summer, but they have two rests in the day. One at about 9 a.m. for an hour and a half, and another of an hour, later. This makes their actual working hours in summer to be between 9½ and 10½ hours. In winter they work from 6 a.m. to 5.30 p.m., and have 2½ hours off. Thus their actual working hours are nine.

28. As so many of the farms are small, and the country is chiefly a grass one, ploughmen can hardly be said to exist as a class.* Their hours are usually longer than those of ordinary labourers, as they have their horses to attend to before they start work, and after they return in the evening.

On Lord Longford's estate their hours in summer are from 7 a.m. to 6 p.m. They have no extra work in connection with their horses, either before or after work, except to harness and unharness them, as they are turned out in the field and it is the duty of two men, who receive extra pay, to have the horses in the stable and to give them a feed of corn, before 7 a.m. The men have a clear hour for dinner in the middle of the day, as they stop work in time to be in the yard at 12 o'clock and return there at 1 p.m. In the winter their hours are from 7.30 a.m. to 4.15 p.m. with a clear hour off for dinner. A stableman feeds and cleans the horses and also cleans out the stables.

29. Herds and shepherds have no definite hours. In lambing time, during sheep-shearing, or when animals are sick, they frequently have very long hours and arduous work. None of those I interviewed complained of their hours, and they recognised the impossibility of having definite hours when in charge of animals.

30. The hours of hired men are usually the same as those of ordinary labourers, but living as they do with the farmer it is only natural that at times they are called upon to do a job before or after the usual hours, such as attending to sick animals.

31. Very few women are employed, but when they are their hours are the same as those of ordinary labourers. The working hours of boys are also similar to the men's.

32. No work is done on Sunday except by those who have to feed and attend to horses, cattle and sheep. When there are hired men living in the farmhouse, the work usually falls on them, and the time they are thus occupied depends on the number of animals kept. On a farm where no hired man is kept, a ploughman, cattleman, or a labourer often comes to attend to the animals, or, if the farm is a small one, the farmer does it himself. The arrangements made on farms and estates for the performance of Sunday work vary so much that it is impossible to state any general rule. There is of course much less work to do on Sunday in the summer time when the horses and cattle are out in the fields.

On the Earl of Longford's estate at Pakenham Hall, a great number of stock are kept of every description. There are two regular cattlemen, and of these one attends to the cattle on Sundays. Their work occupies them for three hours in the morning, and four hours in the afternoon, for which they receive a full day's pay.

In the winter two ploughmen out of four, and two carters out of five, attend to the horses.

Their work takes them 2½ hours in the morning and 2½ hours in the evening, and they receive a full day's pay.

Margin notes: [illegible] — Hours of work of carters and cattlemen. — Hours of work of ploughmen. — Hours of work of herds. — Hours of work of hired men. — Hours of work of women and boys. — Sunday work.

* The Earl of Longford's ordinary labourers are engaged by the week. [illegible]

* Many employers say that ploughmen are difficult to get.

In the summer the horses are turned out and during this time only the two carters come to see after them, and they are paid a half day, as in the winter.

On Major Pollard Urquhart's estate, near Castle Pollard, one ploughman attends to all the horses (six), and this occupies him for three-quarters of an hour in the morning and three-quarters of an hour in the afternoon. The herd looks after the cattle and sheep, and he informed me that his fencing work sometimes took him two or three hours and sometimes all day.

IV.—Wages and Earnings

33. The weekly wages in summer for ordinary labourers, regularly employed, vary between 8s and 9s. In winter they are usually between 7s and 8s. In some cases food is given as part payment of wages. One farmer pays 7s a week all the year round and gives breakfast and dinner. The men who form the ordinary staff of the farm are almost invariably paid wet or dry.

In Appendix A. 6 I have given the rate of wages paid on certain estates and farms in summer and winter.

On several estates the wages are higher than those paid on the farms. The Earl of Longford's men get between 9s and 10s summer and winter according to merit, and Major Pollard Urquhart's men get 10s. from March 1 to November 1, and 9s from November 1 to March 1.

34. The wages of oddmen in summer are usually [illegible] a day, and in winter from 1s 2d. to 1s 4d. During hay and harvest they get 2s 6d a day.

Extra men employed to shear sheep are paid about 3s a day and given food and drink.

35. Ploughmen's wages are about 9s a week summer and winter, and they have regular employment. On some properties, however, they are paid more than this.

On Lord Longford's estate they get from 10s. to 10s 6d. a week. They have excellent houses, with from one to six statute acres of land, at a cheap rent, the grass of one cow free, which is worth about 3l a year, the right of grazing a heifer for 2l 10s. (value 3l) and also a turf bank. (Appendix A. 4).

Major Pollard Urquhart's ploughman is paid 11s in the summer and 10s. in winter. He pays 2l 5s a year for 1½ acres of land (Irish). This land is ploughed for him and his potatoes planted. He also has a turf bank free, value 1l.

36. Herds are usually paid partly in cash and partly in kind. Their wages vary considerably according to their charge. In Appendix A. 3 I have given examples of herds' wages on both estates and farms. It will be seen that they vary from 15l to 40l a year. The actual financial position of those who receive part of their wages in kind is impossible to ascertain, but no doubt considerable profit is made on calves and pigs. They also have the advantage of potatoes and vegetables from their land, butter, milk, eggs, &c.

37. Cattlemen and yardmen are only kept on estates or large farms. Their wages are between 9s and 11s a week, and they sometimes get perquisites in addition. (Appendix A. 4.)

38. The Earl of Longford's estate at Pakenham Hall was the only one I visited where carters are kept, and on that property there are two. They are paid 9s a week, and some have a house free and a certain quantity of turf supplied. They also receive 6d extra a day when they are sent outside the property. (Appendix A. 4.)

39. Hired men get 10l or 12l a year, with food and lodging, and are engaged either by the year or half year. Mr. Lumsden informed me that in the neighbourhood of [illegible] six out of seven farmers have a hired man who ploughs, looks after horses, does carting and other farm work.

Hired lads between the ages of 14 and 18 years get 7l to 10l, with board and lodging.

40. As previously [illegible] women are very seldom employed.

For weeding, dropping potatoes, and binding after harvest they are paid about 1s a day. When picking turf into barrows after the men have cut it, they get 2s a day. During harvest they are paid 1s 6d to 1s 9d a day.

Girls, for dropping potatoes and hoeing turnips, are paid about 10d a day. A few little girls of 12 to 13 years are occasionally employed on Lord Longford's Pakenham Hall estate at wages from 2s. 6d to 3s a week.

41. Boys are paid 6d or 8d a day when they first begin to work after leaving school. The boys employed on the Earl of Longford's estate earn from 2s 6d to 7s a week according to merit.

42. Very little work is done by the piece. As the county is chiefly grass there is but little opportunity for farmers to give out piecework, but apart from this I am informed that masters and men prefer the day-work system.

At hay harvest oddmen are paid 3s 6d. a statute acre for mowing (see paragraph 43).

Mr. Fetherstonhaugh has ditches made by contract, and pays 6s for an Irish perch. Three men in the short days of winter can cut a ditch of 20 perches in two weeks, thus they can earn 13s 4d each a week.

Some farmers have drains made by piecework by oddmen.

43. The ordinary staff of a farm are, as a rule, paid nothing extra during haytime and harvest, though they are sometimes given porter to drink.

The Earl of Longford's men are given 1s 6d. for two hours overtime, and Major Pollard Urquhart's men have two pints of porter a day.

Oddmen are paid 2s 6d for day-work at harvest, or about 3s 6d for mowing a statute acre at piecework. At this an average man can earn about 5s a day. Between the hay and corn harvest an oddman can get about 10 weeks' mowing.

44. Perquisites and allowances are very seldom given to ordinary labourers employed by farmers, though some get turf and others are given the grass of a cow cheap.

On large estates perquisites are given to ordinary labourers and ploughmen, such as either free or cheap cottages with land, turf, and milk, or the keep of a cow under cost price. (Perquisites given on Lord Longford's property, see paragraph 35.)

45. Herds are generally paid part of their wages in kind. They usually have a house with some land free, and frequently the grass of cows and calves, and turf, free. (Appendix A. 3.)

In some cases labourers are given their breakfast and dinner as part payment of their wages, but this system is not nearly so prevalent as in the Castlerea Union of Roscommon or the Skibbereen Union of Cork. Men with families usually prefer to be paid entirely in cash, as they desire to take as much money home as possible.

There seems little doubt that an employer who provides his men with food (breakfast and dinner) in part payment of wages is really giving them more than if he paid entirely in cash. For instance Mr. [illegible] of Delvin, who gives his man 7s. a week, summer and winter, and provides breakfast and dinner, is only paying 1s to 2s a week less than the current rate of wages in summer, and 6d a week less than the current rate of wages in winter. It is evident that he cannot provide two meals a day during six days for these sums.

46. I have not been successful, except in the case of the Earl of Longford's men, in ascertaining the annual earnings of ordinary labourers from books, but men attached to the staff of a farm are nearly always in regular employment, and so their earnings can be roughly estimated. Thus taking a man at 9s. and 7s 6d a week for 26 weeks respectively and deducting two weeks for Catholic holidays, his annual earnings come to 20l 12s 6d.

It will be seen that their weekly wages vary between [illegible] and [illegible] and their total annual earnings between [illegible] and [illegible]. The man who earned the lowest sum was absent from work for [illegible] days on his own business (not through illness) and the man who earned the latter sum was absent eight days on his own business (not through illness).

In addition to cash wages the [illegible] families, which include [illegible] workmen, who live on the Pakenham Hall estate have exceptional advantages.

The rent charged for cottages and land is far below the real value.* The houses are most excellent in all respects. They are provided with cow sheds, pigstyes, outhouses and closets, with gardens of about half-a-rood and meadow land ranging between 1 acre 3 roods and [illegible] acres. (Appendix A. [illegible] and A. [illegible].)

Any man can have the grass of a cow for [illegible] months (value [illegible]) for [illegible], the grass of a two-year-old (for six months (value [illegible]) for [illegible], the grass of a yearling for six months (value [illegible]) for [illegible], and the grass of calves [illegible] each. Also every man gets his turf free.

Mr. [illegible], the steward, informs me that [illegible] of these families keep a cow, two yearlings, and a calf, and the other [illegible] a cow and calf, all paying for their grass at the above rates, except the ploughmen and a few others who get the grass of a cow free.

From this it will be seen that these men, besides the advantages of a comfortable house and cheap land, have the possibility of making a considerable addition to their incomes by the sale of stock, pigs, fowls and eggs. They also have potatoes, vegetables, milk, eggs, butter and bacon for their own consumption.

47. I have found it impossible to get the annual earnings of oddmen from books. They cannot be obtained from a farmer, as such men work for several employers during the year, and themselves keep no record. As already stated they, as a rule, get regular employment in summer, but find work scarce in the winter. The difference in the demand for labour in summer and winter can be measured by the different rate of wage paid, for in the summer they can command [illegible] a day, that is [illegible] or [illegible] a week more than the ordinary staff of a farm, while in winter they have to be content with a wage varying from [illegible] to [illegible] a day.

In reply to my inquiries the oddmen usually said that they "worked regularly in summer and irregularly in winter." Some said they were out of work one day a week in winter, others two, and others three days. But taking the statement of the relieving officer that the oddmen in Delvin town are out of employment for three months in the year, chiefly in the winter, then their annual earnings, assuming their wages are [illegible] a day for [illegible] weeks, [illegible] a day for [illegible] weeks hay and corn harvest (day work) and [illegible] a day for [illegible] weeks, would amount to [illegible]. The estimate is, however, a low one, as no allowance is made for money earned by mowing at piece-work which comes to [illegible] a day, or by turf cutting, at which [illegible] to [illegible] can be earned. If a man got [illegible] a day at piece-work for [illegible] weeks during hay and corn harvest, he would earn [illegible] more than the sum stated above. As to the earnings of the oddmen in Castle Pollard, Mr. [illegible], steward to the Earl of Longford, writes:—

"An oddman of average ability in Castle Pollard will earn, as an agricultural labourer, from [illegible] to [illegible] a year. Their wages run from [illegible] to [illegible], [illegible], or even more per day. The latter sum is earned during turf cutting, mowing and harvest, which is mostly piece-work. They may be idle for six or eight weeks in the year. Men in the neighbourhood of Castle Pollard get more employment than those in the neighbourhood of Delvin."

48. The annual earnings of ploughmen may be put at [illegible] to [illegible]. Two of the Earl of Longford's ploughmen got [illegible] and [illegible] respectively last year. The former pays [illegible] for his cottage with 1 acre and [illegible] roods of land, and the latter pays [illegible] for his cottage with [illegible] acres [illegible] roods of land. Both these men have the grass of a cow (worth [illegible]) free (Appendix A. [illegible]). They also get [illegible] every year.

Major Pollard Urquhart's ploughman earned [illegible] last year. He also has a turf bank free, value [illegible], and rents [illegible] acres (Irish) (about [illegible] statute), which are ploughed for him, for [illegible].

49. In Appendix A. [illegible] I have given examples of herds' wages, which vary in value from [illegible] to [illegible], according to their responsibilities. I have not been able to estimate the profits they make from their payments in kind, namely grazing for cattle, calves, or pigs, so much depends on prices and luck, but no doubt many of them are in a comfortable position in a good year.

50. Hired boys are paid [illegible] or [illegible] and get their board and lodging in the farmhouse. If the cost of their food is estimated at [illegible] a week they are receiving in cash and food [illegible] or [illegible]. Lads between 7 and [illegible] years of age are paid between [illegible] and [illegible] in cash and get board and lodging in the farmhouse.

51. I have already stated that carters and cattlemen are only employed on large estates. Two of the Earl of Longford's carters earned respectively last year [illegible] and [illegible], and both have a house and milk free (Appendix A. [illegible]).

Two of the cattlemen earned respectively [illegible] and [illegible]. The former pays [illegible] for a house and [illegible] acres of land, and [illegible] (value [illegible]) for the grass of a cow, the latter lives in [illegible] village, where the rents are between [illegible] and [illegible] a year. The Earl of Longford's cattlemen and carters are given waterproof coats and leggings once a year (Appendix A. [illegible]).

52. Mr. [illegible], agent to the Earl of Longford, has supplied me with the total earnings of two families who work on the Pakenham Hall estate for last year (Appendix A. [illegible]). One man, James [illegible], and three sons, between the ages of [illegible] and [illegible], earned [illegible]. James [illegible] and two of his sons were absent for [illegible] days during the year on their own business, and not on account of sickness. Had they worked as often as they might have done they would have earned [illegible].

Another man, James [illegible], and his two sons aged [illegible] and [illegible], earned last year [illegible]. They were absent for [illegible] days during the year on their own business, and not on account of sickness. If they had not been thus absent they might have earned [illegible]. Both these families have cottages on Lord Longford's property, for which they pay [illegible] a year rent, which includes 1 acre and [illegible] roods of land, and they each have the grass of a cow for [illegible] (value [illegible]) and turf free.

V.—Cottage Accommodation.

53. This union has some good cottages in it, because there are several large estates belonging to landlords, who do not expect a direct return on the money they spend on building and repairs, and also because there are [illegible] labourers' cottages.

There are, however, some old cottages, both in the country districts and also in the villages, which are ill constructed, cramped for room, and in very bad repair.

54. The Earl of Longford has, in his Pakenham Hall estate, [illegible] labourers' cottages, and on his [illegible] estate about [illegible]. Some of those on the Pakenham Hall estate are old, but nevertheless comfortable and, considering their age, in good repair. They are, [illegible], however, about to be pulled down, and new ones built in their place. These old ones are made of brick, stone, and thatch. They have two living rooms on the ground floor, about [illegible] by [illegible] and [illegible] by [illegible] respectively, and two bedrooms upstairs [illegible] by [illegible] and [illegible] by [illegible] respectively. The only faults to be found with these cottages are that the rooms are not very high, the living rooms being [illegible] feet and bedrooms [illegible] feet, and also that there are no [illegible]. Nevertheless, such cottages are [illegible] compared with those in [illegible], and also when compared with a number in Delvin Union itself.* The outhouses are particularly good and convenient. They each have a good stone shed, with a corrugated iron roof for cows, a thatched shed where pigs can be kept, and a lean-to shed for a cart or where lumber can be stored. The rents are, especially considering the land is good meadow, very low. They vary from [illegible] to [illegible] according to the amount of land, which varies from 1 acre [illegible] roods to [illegible] acres [illegible] roods (statute measure).

The new houses are built in blocks of two, and in all respects can be described as model cottages. They are made of brick and slate, and have a rood of garden each and good meadow land of the same description and size as that attached to the old ones previously mentioned.

* [illegible]

* [illegible]

There are three rooms and a larder on the ground floor, the measurements being 16 by 15, 9 by 8, 8 by 8 respectively, and the height of all three rooms 9 feet. The floors are concrete. Upstairs there are three bedrooms, the measurements being 14 by 12, 10 by 9, 10 by 9, and the height of all three rooms 7 feet. The windows in all the rooms are large.

Each pair of houses is provided with a block of outhouses, situated at a convenient distance from the houses. These consist of two good cow sheds, made of brick and slate, two piggeries, two hen houses, and two closets.

The rent of these new cottages is the same as that charged for the old ones, that is, from 2*l.* 5*s.* to 3*l.* according to the amount of land.

On the [illegible] estate there are about 70 labourers' cottages. Each has four rooms, a piggery, a closet, and in some cases a shed. The average amount of land let with each cottage is half an acre (Irish). The rents average about 2*l.* 10*s.*

55. Major Pollard Urquhart has six good labourers' cottages on his estate. Three of these have recently been built. These are made of stone, plaster and slate, and have three rooms on the ground floor and two upstairs. Outhouses are provided for cows and styes for pigs. Each cottage has an acre and a half (Irish) of land (about 1½ to 2½ acres statute). The rents for the cottages and land are 3*l.* The tenants can have the grass of a cow and calf in summer for 3*l.* [illegible] and their keep in winter for 2*l.* 10*s.* if they have not sufficient hay of their own. All the men have a turf bank free.

Sir M. Chapman's men (about 20) live in [illegible] village. They have good cottages, with quarter of an acre of garden, for 30*s.* a year, and all keep pigs.

Mr. Fetherstonhaugh has some good cottages with nice gardens which he lets free to his men. Mr. Peter Gaily, who is agent to Hon. G. Greville Nugent, informs me that there are 50 labourers' cottages in that property, with half an Irish acre (over three-quarters of an acre statute), of land let for a yearly rent of 2*l.*

56. The guardians have built 134 Union cottages, and 17 are now in course of construction. Of those already built 111 have half a statute acre of land with a piggery and closet. Of the 17 houses now building 15 have a statute acre with cow houses and closets.

Some of the houses are built in pairs, but most of them are now built singly, which the people prefer because they object to be overheard talking by neighbours, and to have them trespassing on their land. There are three rooms on the ground floor, the living room or kitchen being 14 by 12 by 7½ and the other two 8½ by 7 by 7½. Upstairs there are two rooms, one being 14 by 12 and the other 11 by 8½. The ceilings of the bedrooms are sloping and so vary in height.

The rents of the labourers' cottages are 1*s.* a week, whether they have half an acre or an acre of land. They are collected every month by the poor rate collectors, who get a commission of 1*s.* 6*d.* a pound, they having to lodge all rents due. Two collectors informed me that some of the tenants get from eight to twelve months into arrear, and in a few cases two years. The guardians have had to evict some for non-payment of rent.

57. In Delvin there are some very old houses, ill-constructed and in bad repair, with thatch roofs and clay floors. Two I inspected there have no windows at all, so that when the front door is shut the houses are in total darkness. These houses, like many of the old ones, have two rooms on the ground floor, divided by a partition, one being used as a bedroom, and the other as a living room.

At Raharney there are some cottages very much of the same stamp, which frequently let in both rain and wind. Most of them have small gardens.

At Castle Pollard there are a number of cottages, some of which are very small, in bad repair, and without any land. Two houses I saw there, owned by a gamekeeper, one let to a widow at 1*s.* 3*d.* a week, and the other to a labourer at 1*s.* a week, were very old and in bad repair. The former house had one-eighth of an acre of land and the latter half a rood.

One row of 13 old houses made of brick, stone, and slate, have no gardens and no back doors. Some have three rooms, some two, and some only one. I measured the rooms of one of these, a two-roomed house. The living room was 14 by 9 and the bedroom above the same size. The rent is 1*s.* a week.

There are, however, some new cottages in Castle Pollard. One belonging to Major Pollard Urquhart, built of stone and slate, has three airy rooms on the ground floor, and half a rood of land is let for a rent of 3*s.* 4*d.* a month. A pair belonging to the same owner are made of stone and slate, each have two good rooms on the ground floor and two above, and with 15 perches of garden are let for 6*s.* 8*d.* a month. [illegible]

There are also some very fine cottages in Collinstown. A row of five or six made of stone and tile have two rooms on the ground floor, 15 by 12 and 9 by 9, and two bedrooms upstairs of about the same size. There are gardens of half a rood. The rent is 1*l.* 12*s.* 6*d.* a year.

58. On the whole the ventilation of the cottages is fairly good. The rooms in the old class of houses are on the ground floor, and though many of the windows are very small they are kept ventilated by the draughts of fresh air which comes into the houses when the doors are opened. Ventilation.

The union cottages, and the more modern cottages, erected by private individuals, are usually supplied with good windows and ceilings of sufficient height. Consequently if they are not properly ventilated the tenants are to blame for not opening the windows.

59. In the country districts there is no system of drainage, and but little in the villages. Dr. Carleton, the medical officer for health, informs me that no cattle are kept in any of the houses in the union. This is an advantage to health, and also when that manure is not thrown out opposite the front door, as is the case in the other three unions I visited. Dr Carleton also informs me that the drainage in the town of Delvin is good. Drainage.

Generally speaking there are no closets provided to the cottages throughout the union, except in the case of those built by the guardians, and by one or two large landowners.

People who have them do not always use them for the purpose for which they are intended, but keep their hens or pigs in them. This, however, is not so frequent as in the Kilkenny Union, where the closets provided with the union cottages are never used for the proper purpose.

60. Dr Carleton, medical officer of health, informs me that the water supply is good throughout the union. I, personally heard of no complaints on this score when visiting cottages, and I usually found there was an ample supply of good water close to them. Water supply.

61. Generally speaking cottages are not let with farms. The majority of farms are too small to require them. Many of the small farmers work their land with the help of their sons, or they have a hired man or two boarding in the house with them. I did, however, meet with farmers on 150 acres and upwards, with cottages on their farms. Mr. Ramage, near Crookedwood, has [illegible] with his. Cottages [illegible] with farms.

Estate owners let their cottages direct to the labourers they employ. Men employed on large properties told me they had not the least objection to renting their cottages from their employer, both because the cottages were good ones and kept in good repair, and also because they were not unduly pressed for rent.

In the towns and villages many of the cottages belong to independent owners, some of whom have very little money to spend on repairs. Such cottages are not infrequently in a bad state, and have little or no gardens, while the rent is often as much or more than that asked for excellent cottages with several acres of land on large properties.

62. A labourer who works on an estate, or a farm, and rents a cottage either from the estate owner or the farmer would have to leave his cottage if he left his employment, as of course his employer would desire to have it vacant for his successor, but would at most yield to the latter if this were not the case. The regular staff on an estate or a farm usually stay in their situations a long time, and I heard no complaints on that subject whatever. Conditions of tenure.

63. The notice given for the termination of tenancies varies considerably. In the towns of Castle Pollard, Delvin, Raharney and Collinstown many are held by the month, but some by the week, and a few by the quarter and the year. In Castle they are mostly let with a six months' notice. Rules as to termination of tenancy.

The union cottages are held by the month.

The Earl of Longford's cottages are let by the year, the rent being paid half yearly. It, however, matters very little to these men what the tenancy is, as they never appear to leave their employment. Mr. Cochrane, agent to the Earl of Longford, informs me that no man has been discharged during the last 10 years, while many of them have lived for years on the property, as did their ancestors before them.

Sir M. Chapman's men who live at Killucan have a weekly tenancy, while Mr Ramage lets the six cottages on his farm with a six months' notice.

Herds who are engaged by the year or the half year have to quit their cottages when they leave their employment.

64. Rents greatly vary, and are no guide to the accommodation provided, to the state of repair, or to the amount of land let with the cottages.

In Appendix A. 4. the rents of some of Lord Longford's cottages on the Pakenham Hall estate are given, together with the descriptions of the houses, and the amount of land provided. It will be there seen that the rents range from 3l. 1s. to 5l., the land varying from 1 acre 2 roods to 6 acres 0 roods. These cottages are excellent in every respect, and are provided with good cattle sheds, piggeries, henhouses and outhouses.

The cottages on Lord Longford's Killucan estate, which contain four rooms, are provided with out-houses and half an acre of land (Irish), and are let for about 2l. 10s.

Sir M. Chapman's cottages, with half an acre of land, are let for 3l. a year; the Hon. G. Greville Nugent's cottages, which also have half an acre of land, for 2l. a year; and Major Pollard Urquhart's cottages on his estate (not in Castle Pollard) with five rooms, outhouses for cows and pigs, from one acre to an acre and a half (Irish—about 1½ to 2½ acres statute) of land, and a turf bank, are let for 3l. a year.

A farmer near Killucan who employs two regular men, lets his cottages and half an acre of land for 1l. and 1l. 10s.

At Coole the rents vary from 1l. to 3l. 10s. A good many of them have half a statute acre, and some as much as three acres, part of which the men have reclaimed from the moor.

The rents of the worst cottages are 1s. a week.

In the towns and villages I saw cottages of a bad description let at rents from 1l. to 4l. a year. Some of these had little or no garden and no outhouses.

Mr. Patterson, steward to Major Pollard Urquhart, informs me that labourers' cottages in Castle Pollard are let from 2l. to 5l. a year, and that many have no garden.

65. The Rates vary from 1s. to 2s. 6d. in a pound. The county cess is 6½d. in the pound.

When the valuation is 4l. and under, the landlord pays the rates, but where it is over 4l. the landlord and tenant each pay half. The tenant pays the county cess.

66. The Earl of Longford's new cottages on his Pakenham Hall estate, including outhouses, cost 256l. a pair.

Colonel Clarke, agent to Lord Longford's Killucan estate, informs me that a pair of good cottages made of stone, brick and slate, with four rooms, can be built for 150l.

Mr Patterson, steward to Major Pollard Urquhart, says that the cottages they built last year made of bricks, plaster and slate cost 75l. each, and that a pair costs 150l.

The same cottages cost 100l. to build, and the land costs about 22l. 11s. This money is borrowed, repayable in 35 years at 3½ per cent.*

67. I met with no regular men who had to walk far to their work. Oddmen living in Delvin, Castle Pollard, Rathowen, Collinstown, or other villages, have sometimes to walk nearly four miles.

Out of the 50 labourers receiving men's wages on Lord Longford's Pakenham Hall estate, 41 live within a quarter of a mile of their work, while of the remaining 9 some walk a mile and others a mile and a half.

Sir M. Chapman's men walk a quarter of a mile, and Major Pollard Urquhart's not more than half a mile, while many live close to their work.

VI.—Land, Gardens, Cow-grass.

Land and garden. — Gardens.

68. In some previous paragraphs (54, 64, 66,) I have dealt with the subject of gardens. Generally speaking, cottages on country domains are supplied with them, while in the towns and villages they are frequently without. As I have pointed out, the rents for the houses with no gardens are often as high or higher than for those with them.

One hundred and fourteen of the estate cottages have half a statute acre of land and 40 have half an acre [illegible] perches. There are 25 others now in course of erection, which will have a statute acre of land each.

Cottages without gardens have great drawbacks. All potatoes and vegetables have to be bought, pigs or fowls cannot be kept, the washing has to be done in the living room, and besides, turf, and firing have to be carried into the house.

I have already alluded to the fact that the owners of estates usually provide good gardens with their cottages. The Earl of Longford's cottages on the Pakenham Hall estate have from a rood to a rood and a half of garden, and also from one acre 2 roods to about 6 acres of meadow land in addition, and the cottages on the Killucan estate have half an acre (Irish). Sir M. Chapman's cottages have a quarter of an acre. The Hon. G. Greville Nugent's cottages have half an Irish acre (over three-quarter statute). Major Pollard Urquhart's cottages on his estate (not in the town of Castle Pollard) have 1 to 1½ acres (Irish) (about 1½ to 2½ acres statute). Mr Fetherstonhaugh's cottages have about 1 acre statute.

Cow-grass.

69. Several employers give their men meadow land at a very cheap rent. In the previous paragraph I have alluded to the land let by the Earl of Longford with the 50 cottages on his Pakenham Hall estate. In Appendix A. will be found some examples of the size of these plots and the rents charged for them.

Mr Patterson, steward to Major Pollard Urquhart, informs me that a good many farmers give their men a rood of land free, on the condition that they keep it properly manured.

It is also not infrequent to find estate owners and farmers who let their men have the grass of a cow considerably below the market price.

The Earl of Longford allows any of his men to have the grass of a cow for 12 months at 2l. 12s. (value 5l.), the grass of a two-year-old at 2l. (value 3l. 10s.), the grass of a yearling at 1l. 4s. (value 2l. 10s.), and the grass of calves at 1s. each.*

Major Pollard Urquhart's men can have the grass of a cow and calf in summer for 2l. 15s. and in winter for 2l. 10s.

Sir M. Chapman will keep a cow for any of his herds for 4l. a year (ordinary price 7l.), and Mr Ramage's herds can have a cow kept for them at 2s. a week.

Conacre.

70. Conacre is let by farmers at 2l. for an Irish rood of good land, that is 8l. an Irish acre (over 1½ statute).

Small farmers.

71. It was stated at the inquiry, as in the other districts I visited in Ireland and England, that the men on very small holdings have to work much longer hours and far harder than labourers. Mr. Michael Mulligan, a farmer at Delvin, referring to this subject says:—"A man on 10 or 15 acres is a much harder worked man than the labourer and has more anxieties and risks."

Mr. Jack, steward to the Earl of Longford, says:—"To make a decent living here, a man cannot have less "than 50 acres. The small farmers on 15 acres keep "one horse and have to borrow another from a "neighbour."

Labourers' pigs.

72. A good many pigs appear to be kept in the country districts by labourers. One of the advantages of the estate cottages is that there is space enough to keep them and also poultry.†

* Mr. Jack, steward to the Earl of Longford, writes: "The men on the "Pakenham Hall estate are kept in regular [illegible] [illegible] in [illegible] "[illegible] [illegible] [illegible] [illegible] [illegible] [illegible] "[illegible] [illegible] [illegible] [illegible] [illegible] "[illegible] [illegible] [illegible] [illegible] [illegible] "[illegible]."

† At Crookedwood, M. Leach, a labourer, said "Nearly all the

In the towns and villages of Castle Pollard, Delvin, and Ballymore, where a good many cottages have either no garden or only small ones, it is, of course, impossible to keep live stock.

On the properties I have already mentioned, where land is provided with the cottages, and also styes and sheds, and the grass of a cow is let at a cheap rate, or given free, cows, pigs, and fowls are generally kept. (For number of live stock in county, see Appendix A. [illegible])

VII.—Benefit Societies and Trade Unions.

73. There are no benefit societies of any sort existing.

On the Earl of Longford's Pakenham Hall estate clubs exist for the benefit of the workmen, and they have advantages which no labourers on any other estates I visited in Ireland enjoy. Mr Cochrane, agent to the Earl of Longford, sends me the following notes, which I print in full, to show that upon this estate work and wages are not the only ties between employer and employed.

"Our workmen during sickness are paid full or half time according to circumstances, such as the size of the family, the amount the rest of them are earning, &c. As the men become old and infirm, they are put to light or almost nominal work, and when unfit for any work they are pensioned. At present there are three getting full pay as pensioners, and 11 others getting from 5s. to 10s. in quarterly payments.

"There is a clothing club, towards which they pay 3d. a week. At the end of the year a sum equal to the amount subscribed is added. Clothes selected by the workmen and their wives are then bought for them on the best terms possible, and the workmen get them at cost price. For a great number of years tea has been bought in large quantities, and retailed to the workmen at cost price, but, since the general fall in the price, this is not so great an advantage as formerly.

"During the winter months there is a night school, free to all. Lord Longford pays the schoolmaster, and provides the room, fire, lights, &c. A room is also provided where the men can eat their dinners, and the following papers are supplied, 'Irish Times,' 'Daily Express,' 'Westmeath Guardian,' and 'Farmers' Gazette.'

"There have been two serious outbreaks of influenza here during the last two or three years. On each occasion a trained nurse was got from Dublin, who went from house to house attending to the sick, and everything necessary in the way of refreshments was supplied from the castle. In some cases every member of a family was ill."

74. There are no Trade Unions among the labourers or herds, and I could hear of no cases of strikes at the present, or any other time.

VIII.—General Relations between Employers and Employed.

75. The relations between the masters and men are good. Many of the farmers say that the men of the present day do not do as good a day's work as those of former times (paragraph [illegible]), and some assert that the men are more independent in their manner, but there do not appear [illegible] which promote discord.

Mr Peter Cully, Vice-chairman of the Board of Guardians, is of opinion that the masters and men get on better than formerly, as the wages are now higher, and cottage accommodation is better.

As regards the men, a very common expression to hear them make is that "We get on all right with our employers except on the question of wages." Without any doubt a man, even though he is in regular employment, on a wage in summer of 9s. a week and in winter of 7s. 6d., out of which, perhaps, he has to pay a rent, must have a great struggle to support himself and his family, and it is, perhaps, only natural that he should feel some resentment towards the man who pays this wage, no matter what the circumstances may be which regulate the rate of wages in the district.

As I have already shown in this Report, the labourers on the estates are as a rule better off than those employed on the farms, as they have better cottages, more land, and more perquisites and privileges, besides more regular and certain work and, in some cases, rather higher wages, though I am far from saying that in the [illegible] the farmers do not treat their men with consideration in wet weather and in the winter time. As far as I have been able to ascertain they are in consequence more contented on the large estates than on the farms.

IX.—General Condition of the Agricultural Labourer.

76. The general condition of the agricultural labourer in this district has been improving of late years, though but slowly. For the past 20 years a gradual rise in wages (Appendix B. [illegible]) and gradual decrease in the prices of the necessaries of life has enabled the labourer to feed and clothe himself and his family better. Again, being now possessed of more education, and consequently enlarged views, he demands for himself a better house, which both landlords and ratepayers in their turn, recognising the degree which the modern standard of living requires on them, are giving him with no lack of generosity.

Further the labourer's work has been considerably lightened, not only because his working hours have been reduced to definite and more reasonable limits, but because machinery and a better class of tools have relieved him of much ordinary exertion.

Still, men with families, even in regular employment, must have a hard struggle to live with any degree of comfort.

Even on the Earl of Longford's property, where employment is regular, wages rather above the average, and good cottages provided with gardens and land, and every facility given for the keeping of cows, pigs, and fowl, a ploughman said to me:—"I have a wife and eight children, one of my boys is employed by Lord Longford. We have 15s. 6d. a week to support ourselves, last year we did not make both ends meet, and if it had not been for our cow, pigs, and hens, we could not have done."

If this man finds it difficult to make both ends meet, how great must be the difficulties of a man on 9s. in the summer and 7s. 6d. in the winter and with no land on which to keep a cow, pigs, or hens, and with no turf provided.

In this union, as in all others I visited, I heard that the food now eaten by the labourers and small farmers, though more according to their taste, is not so good for them as the plain diet of milk, oatmeal, and potatoes which formerly was their staple food. It is said, as in the other districts both in Ireland and in England, that taking tea and white bread, instead of milk and oatmeal, is having a harmful effect on the stamina of the people, and that in consequence their bodily strength is less. (Appendix B, [illegible])

The ploughman in the service of the Earl of Longford, to whom I have just alluded, gave the following account of the daily food of himself and his family:—

Breakfast - -	Tea, white bread and stirabout.
Dinner - -	Fried eggs, potatoes, bread, tea and fried bacon and cabbage about twice a week
Supper - -	Stirabout and milk

The following is the food provided by a farmer living near Collinstown for his hired men:—

Breakfast - -	Stirabout, milk, bread, butter, tea.
Dinner - -	Beef or mutton,* or bacon, always potatoes.
Tea - -	Tea, bread, butter
Supper - -	Stirabout and milk

No doubt, the high prices obtained in recent years for cattle and sheep have been prejudicial to small holders and labourers who keep stock, though fortunately this year pigs have fetched higher prices than for 10 years past. Notwithstanding a decrease in the population, the number of horses and cattle have increased in the county, which points to a general increase in prosperity, though of course the increase of stock may partly be accounted for by the conversion of arable land into grass.

There does not appear to be much drinking among the rural population, but Dr Cochrane, medical officer of health, and several other witnesses, state that

* Meat is not so often given for dinner in [illegible] [illegible]. The food provided, of course, depends on the [illegible] of the [illegible].

† Mr [illegible], steward to the Earl of Longford, says that the price of [illegible] is lower by [illegible] than in the last [illegible] years.

[illegible] in the number of livestock and poultry in the county of Westmeath between 1881 and 1891.

	1881	1891	Increase.
Horses	[illegible]	[illegible]	[illegible]
Mules and Asses	[illegible]	[illegible]	[illegible]
Cattle	[illegible]	[illegible]	[illegible]
Sheep	[illegible]	[illegible]	[illegible]
Poultry	[illegible]	[illegible]	[illegible]

whisky drinking is on the increase in the towns and villages.

No doubt a good deal of money is remitted to the people in this district from their relations and friends in America. Several labourers told me that "many "people really could not get on without the American "money."

I have, &c.
(Signed) ARTHUR WILSON FOX,
Assistant Commissioner.

APPENDIX A.

TABLE OF CONTENTS.

A. 1.

AREA, INHABITED HOUSES, AND POPULATION.

Electoral Division.	Area in Statute Acres.			Inhabited Houses 1891.	Population, 1881.	Population, 1891.
	Acres.	Roods.	Poles.			
Ballinlough	2,149	2	32	64	386	344
[illegible]	2,849	[illegible]	30	48	[illegible]	321
Ballyhealy	2,873	1	14	67	[illegible]	[illegible]
Bracklin	1,460	3	21	63	[illegible]	293
Ballymanbough	2,896	[illegible]	13	[illegible]	457	[illegible]
Clonarney	4,287	[illegible]	37	123	720	[illegible]
Collinstown	2,284	[illegible]	1	[illegible]	540	[illegible]
Copperalley	2,728	[illegible]	30	67	311	[illegible]
Delvin	2,516	[illegible]	1	116	727	[illegible]
Faughalstown	2,808	[illegible]	30	75	487	[illegible]
Fore East	4,190	[illegible]	[illegible]	123	[illegible]	636
Fore West	4,684	1	27	145	[illegible]	766
Killallon	3,137	12	—	130	433	[illegible]
Kilcumny	2,848	1	31	91	445	[illegible]
Killua	4,885	[illegible]	37	160	[illegible]	717
Killulagh	3,380	[illegible]	78	[illegible]	430	497
Kilpatrick	4,338	[illegible]	24	74	[illegible]	534
Coole	2,867	[illegible]	5	277	1,178	1,075
Riverdale	5,085	[illegible]	16	91	543	[illegible]
19	74,220	2	17	1,887	10,719	9,885

Wages paid to Men regularly employed on certain estates and farms.

Employer.	Estates.	Summer Wages.	Winter Wages.	Perquisites.
The Earl of Longford	Pakenham Hall	9s. to 10s.	8s. to 10s.	For two hours' overtime in hay and harvest each man is paid 1s. 6d. They seldom work overtime on other occasions, but if they do they are paid at the same rate. Many of Lord Longford's men have excellent cottages, with garden and allotment at a cheap rate. They can also have the grass of a cow for a year at 2l. 10s. The ordinary charge for this would be 4l. (see Appendix A 4). They have a turf bank free, which they have to cut and save themselves.
Mr. Battersby-Kenough	Rathowen	9s.	7s. 6d.	Most have houses rent free.
Sir M. Chapman	Killua Castle, Clonmellon	9s. from April 1 to Oct. 1.	7s. from Oct. 1 to April 1.	Fuing given at times.
Mr. Pollard Urquhart	Kinturk Castle, Castlepollard	10s. from March 1 to Nov. 1.	9s. from Nov. 1 to March 1.	If they work overtime they are given porter. Each man has two pints of porter a day at hay harvest.
Mr. M. Halligan (farmer)	Delvin	7s.	7s.	Breakfast and dinner.
Mr. Edward Murray (farmer, 340 acres)	Ballymanbough	8s. to 9s.	7s. to 8s.	—
Mr. James Reilly (farmer and publican)	Raharney	8s.	7s.	—
Mr. L. Ramage, J.P. (farmer)	Crookedwood	8s.	7s.	—
Mr. King (farmer) 350 acres	Thomastown	9s. April 1 to Nov. 1	8s. to 9s.	—

A. 3.

Herds' Wages.

Perquisites and Allowances.	[illegible]	[illegible]	[illegible]	[illegible]	[illegible]	[illegible]	[illegible]	[illegible]
House-rent	[illegible]	[illegible]	[illegible]	[illegible]	—	[illegible]	[illegible]	—
Keep of [illegible]	—	[illegible]	—	—	—	—	[illegible]	—
Fuel	[illegible]	[illegible]			[illegible]	—	—	—
Milk and [illegible]	[illegible]	—	—	—	—	—	—	—
Cash	[illegible]	[illegible]	[illegible]	[illegible]	[illegible]	[illegible]	[illegible]	[illegible]
Total [illegible]	[illegible]	[illegible]	[illegible]	[illegible]	[illegible]	[illegible]	[illegible]	[illegible]
Remarks	[illegible]	[illegible]	—	—	[illegible]	[illegible]	[illegible]	[illegible]

A. 4.

Particulars of Weekly Wages, Annual Earnings [illegible] and Cottage Rents on Lord [illegible] [illegible] Hall Estate.

Name.	[illegible]	Age.	[illegible]	[illegible]	[illegible]	[illegible]	House.	[illegible]	[illegible]	[illegible]	Remarks.
[illegible]							[illegible]	[illegible]			[illegible]
[illegible]	[illegible]	[illegible]	[illegible]	[illegible]	—	[illegible]	[illegible]	[illegible]	[illegible]	[illegible]	
[illegible]	[illegible]	[illegible]	[illegible]	—	—	[illegible]	—	—	—	—	[illegible]

Particulars as to Earnings of two individual Families

Name	Length of service	Age	Rate per Week	No. of days	No. of days	Total earnings	Rates	Cottage	Value	Charge	Remarks
James Smith	[illegible]	[illegible]	[illegible]	[illegible]	—	[illegible]	[illegible]	[illegible]	[illegible]	[illegible]	
Arthur Smith	—	[illegible]	[illegible]	[illegible]	—	[illegible]	—	—	—	—	
William Smith	—	[illegible]	[illegible]	[illegible]	—	[illegible]	—	—	—	—	
Thomas Smith	—	[illegible]	[illegible]	—	—	[illegible]	—	—	—	—	
						[illegible]					
James Walsh	[illegible]	[illegible]	[illegible]	[illegible]	—	[illegible]	[illegible]	[illegible]	[illegible]	[illegible]	
Patrick Walsh	—	[illegible]	[illegible]	[illegible]	—	[illegible]	—	—	—	—	
Robert Walsh	—	[illegible]	[illegible]	—	[illegible]	[illegible]	—	—	—	—	
						[illegible]					

A. 5.

Table showing Total Amount spent on Wages of Labourers, and Current Rate of Wages paid for 20 years on the Earl of Longford's Pakenham Hall Estate, West Meath

Year	Amount spent	Employees		Wages (Weekly)			
		1 Jan.	1 July	[illegible]	[illegible]	[illegible]	[illegible]
[illegible]	[illegible]	[illegible]	[illegible]	[illegible]	[illegible]	[illegible]	[illegible]

Note.—[illegible]

A. 6.

Prices of certain Articles supplied to the Board of Guardians by Contract, March 18[illegible].

Articles		Price
Tea, by half chest [illegible]		[illegible]
Sugar, [illegible]	per cwt.	[illegible]
" refined	per lb	[illegible]
Rice	"	[illegible]
Soap, white, [illegible]	per cwt.	[illegible]
" [illegible]	"	[illegible]
Salt, [illegible]	"	[illegible]
Starch	per cwt.	[illegible]
Blue	per lb.	[illegible]

Articles		Price
Candles, paraffin, 6 to lb.	per lb	[illegible]
Washing Powder	per doz	[illegible]
Tape, White	per yard	[illegible]
Calico, 27-inch	"	[illegible]
" 36-inch	"	[illegible]
Twilled Calico, [illegible]-inch unglazed	"	[illegible]
Linen, 27-inch	"	[illegible]
" [illegible], 33-inch	"	[illegible]
Check Linen, 36-inch ([illegible])	"	[illegible]
" [illegible]	"	[illegible]
Frieze, 54-inch (Irish manufacture)	"	[illegible]
Corduroy, 27-inch	"	[illegible]
Tweed, 27-inch	"	[illegible]
Felt Linsey, brown, 36-inch	"	[illegible]
Coarse Linsey, 36-inch	"	[illegible]
[illegible], 27-inch	"	[illegible]
Ticken, 30-inch, heavy	"	[illegible]
Worsted	per lb	[illegible]
Thread, sewing	"	[illegible]
Spools	per doz	[illegible]
Tape, broad	"	[illegible]
[illegible]	"	[illegible]
Tape, narrow	per doz	[illegible]
Braids	per gross	[illegible]
Braces, Men's	per pair	[illegible]
" Boys'	"	[illegible]
Caps, Men's	each	[illegible]
" Boys'	"	[illegible]
Slippers	per pair	[illegible]
Brushes, Sweeping	each	[illegible]
" Cloth	"	[illegible]
" Whitewash	"	[illegible]
" Laundry	"	[illegible]
" Scouring	"	[illegible]
" Shoe	"	[illegible]
" [illegible]	"	[illegible]
Kettles, metal, 4 quarts	"	[illegible]
Coal Scuttles	"	[illegible]
Metal Saucepans	per quart	[illegible]
Nails, [illegible]	per 100	[illegible]
Tins, quarts	per doz.	[illegible]
" pints	"	[illegible]
Spoons, iron	"	[illegible]
Pins	per [illegible]	[illegible]
Needles, Tailors', &c.	per 100	[illegible]
Spades and Shovels, with handles	each	[illegible]
[illegible]	per lb.	[illegible]
Twine	"	[illegible]
Cotton	"	[illegible]
Whiting	per lb.	[illegible]
Combs, large	per doz	[illegible]
" small	"	[illegible]
Shoes, Men's, to do	"	[illegible]
" Women's, to do	"	[illegible]
" Children's, below 12 years of age	"	[illegible]
Whiskey, 11 O. P.	per gall	[illegible]
Hennessy's Brandy (one star)	"	[illegible]
Port Wine	per doz	[illegible]
Sherry Wine	"	[illegible]

A. 7.

Persons engaged in Agriculture in Delvin Union, 1891.

(This Table, and also A. 8, A. 9, A. 10, and A. 11, is taken from the Agricultural Statistics (Ireland) for 1891.)

Description	Male	Female
Farmers, Graziers	411	117
Farmer's, Grazier's, Son, &c. } Gardener, Drainer, Hedger }	481	—
Farm Bailiff	79	—
Agricultural Labourer, Cottager	497	[illegible]
Shepherd, Shepherdess	[illegible]	—
Farm Servant (indoor)	164	5
General Labourer*	187	—

* Probably some of these are agricultural labourers.

A. 8.

Extent of Land under Crops in statute acres and estimated produce in 1891.

Crops.	Extent.	Estimated Produce.
	Acres.	
Wheat	27	371 cwts. of 112 lbs.
Oats	2,870	62,139 ,,
Barley	4	97 ,,
Rye	25	371 ,,
Potatoes	1,534	4,877 tons.
Turnips	918	12,789 ,,
Mangel Wurzel and Beet-root.	146	5,401 ,,
Carrots and parsnips	8	141 ,,
Cabbage	125	1,681 ,,
Vetches	1	8 ,,
Rape	12	118 ,,
Other green crops	1	—
Clover, sainfoin, and grass under rotation.	3,574	5,689 ,,
Permanent pasture	7,[illegible]	14,[illegible] ,,
	13,[illegible]	

A. 9.

Poor Law Union.	Number of Holdings and their Size in Statute Acres not exceeding									
	1 Acre.	5 Acres.	15 Acres.	30 Acres.	50 Acres.	100 Acres.	200 Acres.	500 Acres.	Over 500 Acres.	Total Number of Holdings.
Delvin	319	[illegible]	[illegible]	330	312	167	80	64	11	1,[illegible]

A. 10.

Cultivation of Delvin Union in 1891, and proportion per cent. under Crops, Grass, Woods, Mosses, &c.

Crops, including Meadow and Clover.	Grass.	Fallow.	Woods and Plantations.	Turf Bog.	Marsh.	Barren Mountain Land.	Water, Roads, Fences, &c.	Total.
Acres.	Acres.	Acres.	Acres.	Acres.	Acres.	Acres.	Acres.	Acres.
16,[illegible]	47,[illegible]	16	1,941	6,107	770	[illegible]	3,[illegible]	74,[illegible]

Proportion per cent.

20·6	63·3	—	2·6	8·0	1·1	0·0	4·2	—

A. 13.

PARTICULARS of certain COTTAGES in the [illegible] UNION.

COTTAGES IN [illegible] TOWN.

Name.	Number in Family.	Living Rooms, &c. on Ground Floor.	Bedrooms.	Rent.	Land.	Remarks.
[illegible]	[illegible]	[illegible]	[illegible]	[illegible]	[illegible]	[illegible]
[illegible]	[illegible]	[illegible]	[illegible]	[illegible]	[illegible]	[illegible]

COTTAGES [illegible]

Name.	Number in Family.	Living Rooms, &c. on Ground Floor.	Bedrooms.	Rent.	Land.	Remarks.
[illegible]	[illegible]	[illegible]	[illegible]	[illegible]	[illegible]	[illegible]
[illegible]	[illegible]	[illegible]	[illegible]	[illegible]	[illegible]	[illegible]

COTTAGES IN [illegible] VILLAGE.

Name.	Number in Family.	Living Rooms, &c. on Ground Floor.	Bedrooms.	Rent.	Land.	Remarks.
[illegible]	[illegible]	[illegible]	[illegible]	[illegible]	[illegible]	[illegible]
[illegible]	[illegible]	[illegible]	[illegible]	[illegible]	[illegible]	[illegible]

COTTAGES IN [illegible] VILLAGE.

Name.	Number in Family.	Living Rooms, &c. on Ground Floor.	Bedrooms.	Rent.	Land.	Remarks.
[illegible]	[illegible]	[illegible]	[illegible]	[illegible]	[illegible]	[illegible]
[illegible]	[illegible]	[illegible]	[illegible]	[illegible]	[illegible]	[illegible]
[illegible]	[illegible]	[illegible]	[illegible]	[illegible]	[illegible]	[illegible]

Name.	Members of Family.	Weekly Earnings, and Estimated Value.	Perquisites.	Rent.	Land.	Remarks.
		COTTAGES IN CASTLE POLLARD TOWN.				
[illegible]	[illegible]	[illegible]	[illegible]	[illegible]	[illegible]	[illegible]
		EARL OF LONGFORD'S COTTAGES, PAKENHAM ESTATE.				
[illegible]	[illegible]	[illegible]	[illegible]	[illegible]	[illegible]	[illegible]
[illegible]	[illegible]	[illegible]	[illegible]	[illegible]	[illegible]	[illegible]

APPENDIX B.

TABLE OF CONTENTS.

B. 1.

The efficiency of men's work as compared with the past.

Name.	District.	Evidence.
[illegible]	[illegible]	[illegible]
[illegible]	[illegible]	[illegible]
[illegible]	[illegible]	[illegible]

Name.	District.	Evidence.
[illegible]	[illegible]	[illegible]
[illegible]	[illegible]	[illegible]

Name.	District.	Evidence.
[illegible]	[illegible]	[illegible]

E. 2.

EFFICIENCY OF MEN'S WORK AS COMPARED WITH OTHER DISTRICTS.

Name.	District.	Evidence.
[illegible]	[illegible]	[illegible]

E. 3.

RELATIONS BETWEEN EMPLOYERS AND EMPLOYED.

Evidence of Employers.

Name.	District.	Evidence.
[illegible]	[illegible]	[illegible]

Name.	District.	Evidence.
[illegible]	[illegible]	[illegible]
[illegible]	[illegible]	[illegible]
[illegible]	[illegible]	[illegible]
[illegible]	[illegible]	[illegible]
[illegible]	[illegible]	[illegible]

Evidence of Employed.

Name.	District.	Evidence.
[illegible]	[illegible]	[illegible]
[illegible]	[illegible]	[illegible]
[illegible]	[illegible]	[illegible]
[illegible]	[illegible]	[illegible]
[illegible]	[illegible]	[illegible]
[illegible]	[illegible]	[illegible]
[illegible]	[illegible]	[illegible]
[illegible]	[illegible]	[illegible]
[illegible]	[illegible]	[illegible]
[illegible]	[illegible]	[illegible]
[illegible]	[illegible]	[illegible]
[illegible]	[illegible]	[illegible]
[illegible]	[illegible]	[illegible]
[illegible]	[illegible]	[illegible]

B. 4

THE EXTENT OF MODERN DIET AS COMPARED WITH THAT OF THE PAST.

Name.	District.	Evidence.
[illegible]	[illegible]	[illegible]
[illegible]	[illegible]	[illegible]
[illegible]	[illegible]	[illegible]
[illegible]	[illegible]	[illegible]
[illegible]	[illegible]	[illegible]
[illegible]	[illegible]	[illegible]
[illegible]	[illegible]	[illegible]
[illegible]	[illegible]	[illegible]

Name.	District.	Evidence.	Name.	District.	Evidence.
[illegible]	[illegible]	[illegible]	[illegible]	[illegible]	[illegible]

G 4.

General Condition of the Agricultural Labourer.

Employers' Evidence.

Name.	District.	Evidence.
[illegible]	[illegible]	[illegible]

Evidence of Employed.

[illegible]	[illegible]	[illegible]

[illegible]	[illegible]	[illegible]	[illegible]	[illegible]
	[illegible]	[illegible]		[illegible]
	[illegible]	[illegible]	[illegible]	[illegible]
[illegible]	[illegible]			
	[illegible]	[illegible]	[illegible]	[illegible]
[illegible]	[illegible]			
[illegible]	[illegible]	[illegible]	[illegible]	[illegible]
[illegible]	[illegible]	[illegible]	[illegible]	[illegible]

www.ingramcontent.com/pod-product-compliance
Lightning Source LLC
Chambersburg PA
CBHW022130160426
43197CB00009B/1226